THE CYRENAICS

THE CYRENAICS

Ugo Zilioli

ACUMEN

First published in 2012 by Acumen
First published in paperback, 2013

Acumen Publishing Limited
4 Saddler Street
Durham
DH1 3NP

ISD, 70 Enterprise Drive
Bristol, CT 06010, USA

www.acumenpublishing.com

ISBN: 978-1-84465-290-7 (hardcover)
ISBN: 978-1-84465-763-6 (paperback)

British Library Cataloguing-in-Publication Data
A catalogue record for this book is available
from the British Library.

Typeset in Minion Pro.
Printed in the UK by 4edge Ltd, Essex.

CONTENTS

ACKNOWLEDGEMENTS

This book is the main outcome of a fellowship offered by the Irish Research Council for the Humanities and Social Sciences (IRCHSS) during the academic years 2008–9 and 2009–10, at the Department of Philosophy/Plato Centre of Trinity College, Dublin. I thank the board warmly for having supported my research with generosity. During the last stages of the project, I have also been helped financially by the Department of Classics of the University of Pisa, which I am here happy to thank.

People in Dublin have given feedback on my work and discussed it in various ways: John Dillon, Harold Tarrant, the late John Cleary and all the people at the Plato centre. I have had fruitful discussions with Alberto Artosi (Bologna), Mauro Tulli (Pisa) and George Boys-Stones (Durham) that helped me shape the full philosophical and historical implications of my own understanding of the Cyrenaics.

Steven Gerrard at Acumen has been a patient and supportive editor. He has tolerated my delays and encouraged me to carry on just before the final revision of the manuscript, which has been more demanding than expected. Two anonymous referees for Acumen have provided useful comments. In particular, one referee was so critical towards the overall interpretation of Cyrenaic philosophy I provided that I hope to have argued for it in a more persuasive way in light of the criticism. Lastly, I thank

Kate Williams warmly for her copy-editing and help in the final stages of the process.

The approach I adopt in the book is thoroughly revisionary, in so far as I attempt to modify fairly widespread assumptions about the Cyrenaics. If at times I advance interpretations that may strike the reader as excessively novel or radical, I hope I shall be forgiven: "To get a bent iron straight, we have to bend it from the opposite side" (Lenin).

This book is dedicated to my wife Cristiana, with whom I have discussed the core ideas of this study and who is beside me every single minute of my life, with her love and concern for my well-being; to our two children, Zoe and Delio, so full of life and of curiosity; to the memory of my beloved parents, Alberta and Attilio, too soon departed and much missed; to Christopher Rowe and Christopher Gill, who have taught me with their example the importance of philosophy in everyday life and whose friendship I am glad to cherish.

PREFACE

This book aims to fill in a lacuna for the English-speaking reader by providing an introduction to the Cyrenaic school. It is intended both for undergraduates of philosophy, ancient philosophy and classics approaching the Cyrenaics for the first time and for more skilled postgraduates and scholars, who lack a general account of Cyrenaic philosophy at the moment. The book can be read at two different levels, corresponding to the two different readerships I have in mind. Informative parts will alternate with more philosophically sophisticated parts. These latter will be useful also to readers with little philosophical expertise but they are specifically targeted for a more skilled readership. Those readers, especially undergraduates, wishing to delve immediately into the philosophy of the Cyrenaics can begin with Part II. Part I intermixes philosophical questions with more historical matters and is more scholarly tuned.

The overall interpretation of the Cyrenaics I recommend in the course of the book is that of a school with a complete philosophical agenda, spanning ethics, epistemology, metaphysics and philosophy of language. More unconventionally, I also defend the claim that, together with other ancient philosophers such as Protagoras and Pyrrho, the Cyrenaics can be inscribed into a line of metaphysical enquiry that is centred on indeterminacy; namely, the view that things in the perceptual world do not have any intrinsic ontological essence. This claim is doubly radical, in its own right and in relation to the Cyrenaics. It will also be one of the main scholarly gains of this book. In promoting such a positively integrated account of Cyrenaic philosophy, I contrast most of the interpretations that are currently available. The ultimate aim of the book is to add further justification for Grote's idea that "in the history of the Greek mind, these two last mentioned philosophers [Antisthenes and Aristippus] are not less important than Plato and Aristotle" (1865: III, 555).

The book is divided into eight chapters in three parts. In Chapter 1, "Schools and Scholarship", I explain why the Cyrenaics are a Socratic school and I briefly review the scholarship on them with particular reference to the past fifty years. I also offer a brief genealogy of the school, beginning with Aristippus the Elder and ending with the later sects and epigoni of the Cyrenaic school.

In Chapter 2, "Aristippus", I reconstruct the life and doctrine of Aristippus by relying on the biographical account of Diogenes Laertius. The main problem I am faced with is whether Aristippus could ever be considered the real founder of the school. On the basis of Diogenes' testimony, I argue that Aristippus was a proper philosopher and that he originally formulated the key ideas of Cyrenaic philosophy.

In Chapter 3, "The *Theaetetus*", I argue against the view that Aristippus could not have been the real founder of the Cyrenaic school and thus that Plato's testimony is to be regarded as unfaithful. On the contrary, I argue that those subtler thinkers (*hoi kompsoteroi*) that are named in the *Theaetetus* (156a3) are Aristippus and the early Cyrenaics. I do so by providing textual and conceptual linkage with other important sources on Cyrenaic thinking, such as the anonymous commentator of Plato's *Theaetetus*, Sextus and Plutarch.

In Chapter 4, "Indeterminacy", I explore the Cyrenaic commitment to the metaphysical view that things in the world are indeterminate, that is, to the view that objects in the world do not have a unitary and stable essence. Once I rule out the possibility that they are idealists, I review those ancient sources suggesting that the Cyrenaics may be understood as committed to indeterminacy in metaphysics.

In Chapter 5, "Persons, Objects and Knowledge", I focus on the main doctrine of Cyrenaic epistemology: that affections alone can be known. On the basis of this doctrine I can say that, to use their neologism, I am "being whitened", that is, that I see an object as white but I cannot say that the object itself is white. I show that the Cyrenaics appear also to have allowed extra-affective judgements, which can be interpreted as subjective appearances. Last, I relate Cyrenaic subjectivism with other cognate epistemologies, such as Protagoras' relativism.

In Chapter 6, "Language and Meaning", I show that, in striking contrast with the semantic realism dominating ancient philosophy of language, the Cyrenaics appear to have adopted a behavioural theory of meaning. On the basis of this theory, we learn the meaning of words not by relating them to their referents in the world, but by reacting to linguistic stimuli and by seeing how other people do so.

In Chapter 7, "Pleasure and Happiness", I illustrate the meaning of the Cyrenaic view that pleasure is the end. I explore the relationship, in Cyrenaic ethics, between pleasure and happiness. In so doing, I discuss the two alternatives mostly debated in current literature: namely that the Cyrenaics are just concerned about present pleasures with no interest for happiness; and, alternatively, since happiness can be considered the sum of one's enjoyed pleasures, the Cyrenaics are concerned about happiness as well. I defend the latter alternative on the basis of some textual evidence.

In Chapter 8, "Cyrenaic Philosophy and its Later Epigoni", I present a brief overview of the later sects of the Cyrenaic school, namely the Annicerians, the Hegesians and the Theodorians. I conclude by showing that the Cyrenaics can be best interpreted not as a minor philosophical school centred exclusively on ethics, but as a group of philosophers who formulated innovative doctrines in epistemology, metaphysics and the philosophy of language.

The Appendix provides translations of all the main sources on the Cyrenaics.

ABBREVIATIONS AND TRANSLATIONS

I usually follow the abbreviations, for both authors and works, of the *Greek–English Lexicon* (*LSJ*; Liddell & Scott 1996). For Latin authors and works, I refer to the *Oxford Latin Dictionary* (Glare 1993).

In references to *Socratis et Socraticorum Reliquiae* (Giannantoni 1991), still the standard work on the Socratic schools, I use the following conventions: Giannantoni (1991: vol. IV, n. 17, 171) refers to the fourth volume (note 17, page 171), the volume where Giannantoni examines all the scholarship on the Socratic schools; *SSR* IV A 121 means chapter IV (on Aristippus), section A, source 121.

Aristocles' *On Philosophy* (with Eusebius' indices) will be quoted on the basis of the text established by Chiesara (2001): F5 Chiesara refers to fragment 5 in Chiesara's edition of *On Philosophy*.

For Plato's *Theaetetus*, I adopt Levett's translation in Burnyeat (1990) while for *Philebus* I follow Dorothea Frede's translation (1993). For Aristotle, I usually follow the standard translations edited by J. Barnes, *The Complete Works of Aristotle* (1984).

Throughout, whenever I quote a passage on the Cyrenaics that is particularly relevant, I indicate the corresponding testimony in the Appendix. For example, T 1 refers to the first testimony given in translation in the Appendix.

Joy and balm of my life: the memory of the hours
when I found and held into pleasure as I wished.
Joy and balm of my life: for me who spurned
every delight of routine amours.   —Cavafy

I
HISTORY

1

SCHOOLS AND SCHOLARSHIP

This book is an introduction to the main figures and to the philosophical thought of the Cyrenaic school, one of the three (minor) schools that – together with the Cynics and the Megarics (or Dialecticians) – goes under the traditional label "Socratic schools". On these terms, the Cyrenaic school is a Socratic school: why is it Socratic and why a school?

THE CYRENAICS AS A SOCRATIC SCHOOL

On a minimalist interpretation, the Cyrenaics are Socratic thinkers because the supposed founder of the school, Aristippus of Cyrene, was a close associate of Socrates. On a more committed interpretation, the Cyrenaics are Socratic thinkers because they developed further both the kind of personal commitment to knowledge that is already fully present in Socrates' theoretical activity and his lifelong concern for ethics. In particular, the Cyrenaics had a major interest in Socrates' idea – dealt with in the last part of the *Protagoras* – that pleasure and good are closely related, if not fully identifiable.[1] On the basis of this more committed interpretation, the Cynics were instead exclusively concerned with the ethical aspect of Socrates' philosophy, which, again, was developed by them in ways that were

3

different from Socrates' original ethics. On the other hand, the Megarics were interested in the logical side of the Socratic activity, but they also shared, like all the other Socratics (and this is the overall common feature of the three schools), a certain interest in ethics.[2]

Although there is some truth in it, the more committed interpretation is, like its minimalist counterpart, too schematic and reductive. It seems to answer more to a scholarly demand (namely, to find a unified account for the Socratic schools) than to a real interest for what is philosophically peculiar and characteristic of each Socratic school. In addition, such a resolute interpretation does not say much that may be, from a hermeneutical point of view, helpful or illuminating: Plato himself is Socratic, since most of his philosophy, especially his earlier philosophy, can be interpreted as a development of Socratic themes. Even the Stoics can be seen, on certain grounds, to be fully Socratic for the kinds of solution they advance to certain philosophical (ethical) problems. This is only to cite some examples: most Greek philosophy after Socrates is Socratic in spirit and there is little point in labelling a certain school as Socratic on the ground that its philosophy resembles and develops that of Socrates.

It seems more reasonable to accept the first, minimalist, interpretation of the reason why the Cyrenaics are a Socratic school: they are such because the supposed founder of the school was Aristippus, an intimate of Socrates. But also this explanation seems to be too general in so far as it apparently reduces the Socratic origins of the Cyrenaics either to the fortunate outcome of a biographical fact, or, indeed, to the result of a mere historical coincidence. Yet, the minimalist view is such only at a first sight. To maintain that the Cyrenaics are Socratics because the supposed founder of the school was Socrates' intimate carries with it a huge historical (as well as philosophical) commitment, since it credits Aristippus with the actual foundation of a school and with the paternity of a clearly identifiable philosophical outlook.

The view that Aristippus was the actual founder of the Cyrenaic school has been rejected by most recent scholars, although with different emphasis and for different reasons. In particular, as far as the appreciation of the Socratic schools is concerned, Gabriele Giannantoni is the scholar to whom we owe most, since he edited and commented on all the sources on Socrates and the Socratic thinkers (Giannantoni 1991). He has argued for the doubly negative thesis that Aristippus cannot be credited with the foundation of a real philosophical school. Giannantoni's highly negative view implies the complete discharge of Plato's testimony. On his view, all the places in Plato's dialogues where one could profitably detect a reference to Aristippus or to doctrines held by him have no real historical value. In those places there is no certainty that Plato is actually referring to Aristippus.

In line with the glorious tradition of George Grote and Eduard Zeller, and with the more recent attempt of Klaus Döring, and at the risk of putting the clock back, in this book I shall accept the minimalist sense of the label "Socratic" attached to the Cyrenaics and endorse the view that Aristippus was the actual founder of the school. In doing so, I shall make positive use of Plato's crucial testimony, especially the *Theaetetus* and *Philebus*. Accordingly, I shall defend the controversial view that Aristippus the Elder was responsible for the initial formulation of the main philosophical claims of the Cyrenaic school, which later, in the second half of the fourth century BCE, his grandson Aristippus the Younger, the son of his daughter Arete, may have systematized into a coherent picture. This may be enough to show how I interpret the adjective "Socratic" in the locution "Socratic schools" (in general and with reference to the particular case of the Cyrenaics). In Chapter 5, I shall become more explicit with regard to the meaning of "Socratic" when referred to the Cyrenaics. A clarification of the term "school" in the locution "Socratic schools" is, however, needed now.

SCHOOLS IN THE CLASSICAL WORLD

There has been much debate with regard to what a philosophical school was in classical antiquity, especially in Greek society. At the time of Socrates, there was no proper philosophical school. Socrates himself performed his philosophical activity by talking to people and by challenging them to assess whether their beliefs were coherent and rationally grounded. The sophists were coeval with Socrates. They were itinerant philosophers who had different teaching agendas, but whose varied teaching was all based on the sharing of certain common philosophical views. The best term to capture the features of the sophists as a group of philosophers involved in itinerant teaching and endorsing common doctrinal views is "movement".[3]

In the ancient world the birth of philosophical schools in the usual meaning we attach to the word "school" relates to philosophy after Socrates. We know enough about Plato's Academy, Aristotle's Peripatos and Epicurus' Garden. A classical theory about philosophical schools in the ancient world is that of Ulrich von Wilamowitz-Moellendorff (1881). According to the view of the great German philologist, philosophical schools in Greek society were religious societies (*thiasoi*), dedicated to worshipping the Muses. Wilamowitz believed that Athenian law recognized such religious societies as legal bodies. Philosophical schools had the exterior and official aspect of religious societies, so could be granted lawful recognition, but in the interior they were structured as universities with (i) research activities, (ii) teaching divided in (exoteric) public lectures and private (esoteric) seminars, and (iii) a clear division between senior and junior teachers. Moreover, each school had a leading scholarch (the head of school in modern parlance) who, given the legal status granted to the school, was also the legal owner of the property.

Wilamowitz's effort to understand the real scope and nature of a philosophical school in the classical world has been seminal. It has also been very helpful in providing a systematic reading of a complex phenomenon that seemed resistant to an overall explanation. Criticisms of Wilamowitz were made soon after he made his views public in print. Theodor Gomperz (1899) observed that the features Wilamowitz recognized as typical of religious societies were also shared by other kinds of schools, such as children' schools, and gymnasia. Those features could not, therefore, be taken as constitutively belonging to philosophical schools as such. More recently, Hans Gottschalk (1972: 320) has been highly critical of the idea that scholarchs were the legal owners of the schools. More forcefully, it has been argued that philosophical schools in antiquity had no legal recognition, and are best seen as institutions with private funding (hence not depending at all on the state's authorization) whose aim was the propagation of philosophical knowledge over time (Wehrli 1976: 129–30).

Despite its evident imperfection, we still rely today mainly on Wilamowitz's account (Dorandi 1999b: 55–6). A fresher analysis of the features and organization of philosophical schools in the ancient world is lacking, perhaps because it is hard to subsume the empirical evidence about those schools under a unique concept (Isnardi Parente: 1974: esp. footnotes, 1986). Philosophical schools in antiquity were each very different. Plato's Academy has often been understood as the paradigmatic case with regard to which all the others have to conform or diverge. Aristotle's Peripatos was modelled – it is traditionally believed – on the Academy, but both schools display important differences with the Garden of Epicurus. While the former schools are often likened to modern universities with a well-focused commitment to scientific research, the Garden was based more on such principles as commemoration, imitation and the sharing of life. As Seneca remarks in this respect, in the Garden a shared life (*contubernium*) is like that of an organism with many members but with one, unique body (*Ep.* 33.4). Other relevant differences among these schools were the acceptance of women (the Academy and the Garden allowed women to join the school,

7

while the Peripatos did not) or, for example, the way in which scholarchs were chosen, either by election or by direct mandate from the preceding scholarch.

In antiquity philosophical schools also underwent substantial modification over time, the case of Plato's Academy being the most significant of all. It is therefore difficult to give a precise account of what a philosophical school was in antiquity. Despite the lack of further historical information, we know that the differences among schools were many. A school with a clear organization and structure in one period could become, in another period, something close to a restricted circle of people, sharing some common philosophical interests. I suggest caution when dealing with the notion of a philosophical school in antiquity because there is a consolidated interpretative pattern in the scholarship on the basis of which the philosophical schools of Plato, Aristotle and Epicurus are contrasted with the less structured entities we label "Socratic schools". While the former can rightly be regarded as proper schools, the traditional argument goes, the latter ones are so on a more modest scale. Together with Pyrrhonism, Dorandi (1999b: esp. 61) calls them "pseudo-schools" or "philosophical tendencies" (here translating the Greek terms *agōgai* or *haireseis*, as the Socratic schools are often referred to in ancient sources).

My argument here is that there are certainly differences between the structured schools of Plato, Aristotle and Epicurus and the less structured schools of the Cyrenaics, the Megarics and the Cynics (and even of Pyrrho). Because a philosophical school in the ancient world is an elusive concept, it is arbitrary to contrast major and minor schools in the way this is often done. It may be safer to recognize that, after Socrates' death, ancient philosophy witnessed the birth of various groups that, by meeting and discussing in Socratic fashion Socrates' ideas, represented a kind of school in the wider sense of the term. This remark applies both to the Socratic schools as well as to Plato's Academy and Aristotle's Peripatos. These schools also had doctrinal commitments, in so far as they developed doctrines that were already considered as peculiarly belonging to this or that school by ancient sources. Since philosophy in the ancient world was primarily a way of life, as Pierre Hadot (1995, 2004) has shown, the members of ancient philosophical schools tried to translate the doctrinal commitments originating from their philosophical discussions into a visible way of life. Again, every school after Socrates shares these features, be it the Cyrenaic school, the Academy or even the Garden.

Philosophical schools in antiquity had different fortunes, some of them becoming more structured, influential and lasting through great modifications over the centuries, others being more flexible, peripheral and extinguished over two or three centuries. The reasons for such different fortunes can be many, the locations of the schools and their adherents being perhaps the most obvious. The Academy, the Peripatos and the Garden were all in Athens, the centre of the Greek world, whereas the Cyrenaic school was in Cyrene, in the north of Africa, and the Megaric was in Megara, in both cases cities that were much less important and central. Someone may add that the schools that flourished and stayed alive over centuries were those whose philosophical views were more wide-ranging and appealing. This, however, does not mean that the schools that lasted for a shorter time had no influential or original doctrines to propound and defend. On the contrary, the so-called minor Socratic schools had, I claim, a clear doctrinal agenda, and in this book I hope to show the impact Cyrenaic epistemology, ethics, metaphysics and philosophy of language had on ancient thought and, for that matter, even on us today.

It seems safer, therefore, to accept that the Socratic schools and the more structured schools of Plato, Aristotle and Epicurus were all schools in a wider sense of the term. In all those schools the discussion of doctrines was not an empty exercise of the mind but an exercise ideally leading their members to transform those doctrines into a peculiar way of life. That the ancients did not see a great difference between the Academy of Plato and the Socratic schools is clear from a remark by Diogenes the Cynic, when he observes that the term "school" is better applied to the visitors of Euclides the Megaric than to those of Plato (Diogenes Laertius [DL] VI 24). The Cyrenaic school is no exception to the general rule: its members met in Cyrene to discuss their philosophical views and to make those views the backbone of their practical conduct. They were labelled Socratics, because the founder of the school was an intimate of Socrates.[4]

ARISTIPPUS AND CYRENAIC PEOPLE

The Cyrenaic school takes its name from the city where Aristippus was born and where the school is supposed to have been located, although we do not know anything about the structure and organization of the school itself. What we do know, however, is that Aristippus had a daughter, Arete, who was herself a philosopher (one of the very few cases of women philosophers in classical antiquity).[5] Arete had a son, Aristippus the Younger, who was trained in philosophy by his mother (hence the nickname "Mother-taught", or "Metrodidactus", the appellative with which he is often referred to in antiquity). Aristippus the Younger is said, with good reason, to have systematized the doctrines elaborated more or less completely by his grandfather (and mother perhaps) into a coherent whole as a kind of reaction to the challenges the Epicureans and Pyrrho posed to Cyrenaic doctrines. After Aristippus the Younger, the Cyrenaic school underwent a period of great modification. We usually recognize three subgroups of the school in the later period: the Annicerians, the Hegesians and the Thedorians, named after, respectively, Anniceris, Hegesias (the "death-persuader") and Theodorus (the "godless", or self-proclaimed "god").

Doctrinally the last branches of the school differed among themselves and also from the original body of Cyrenaic doctrines. In this connection, it may be noted that throughout this book when I speak of Cyrenaic doctrines, I always refer to the main doctrinal body of the school as initially elaborated by Aristippus the Elder and later further shaped by Aristippus the Younger. In Chapter 8 we shall be confronted with the later sects of the Cyrenaic school. We shall see in more detail what kind of philosophical views they formulated and why, in spite of relevant differences, they can be still regarded as Cyrenaic philosophers. Since Aristippus was a contemporary of Socrates (late fifth/fourth century BCE) and Theodorus died around 250 BCE (while Hegesias is ideally placed around 290 BCE), the life of the Cyrenaic school extends over the space of approximately two centuries.

The school appears to have had a privileged field of enquiry into ethics. The Cyrenaics also had an extended interest in epistemology and, on the interpretation I defend in this book, they also endorsed a peculiar metaphysics of indeterminacy. For the completeness of their philosophical interests, the longevity of the school and the peculiar views they developed (they are usually praised for being the first and only group of ancient philosophers who were aware of the concept of subjectivity), the Cyrenaics and their thought are well worth investigating.

SCHOLARSHIP, WITH PARTICULAR REFERENCE
TO THE PAST FIFTY YEARS

In the course of this book I defend the position that Aristippus is the actual founder of the Cyrenaic school and the one who formulated its first doctrinal views. At the same time, I shall make a strong case for using Plato as a reliable source for Cyrenaic philosophy. In so doing, I shall engage with the more recent literature on the Cyrenaics, where the dominant trend is to negate any foundation to Aristippus and to minimize the importance of Plato's testimony. In the context of a wider temporal perspective, however, things have not always been so negative. Great historians of ancient philosophy of the calibre of Friedrich Schleiermacher

(1804–28: II 1, 183ff.), Grote (1865: III, 542–61) and Zeller (1923: 287–331) all believed in the reliability of Plato's testimony and in the active role of Aristippus as responsible for the elaboration of the doctrinal views upon which the school built up its reputation and influence. In the wake of these scholars, many others of that time argued for similar positions (Dümmler 1901: 59–65; Natorp 1890: 347ff.; 1895: colls 902–6; Joel 1921).

The first systematic attempt to understand the figure and the philosophy of Aristippus was, however, that provided by von Stein in his 1855 Göttingen dissertation, *De philosophia cyrenaica*, which shares with the briefer accounts provided by the scholars just mentioned a positive understanding of Aristippus and his philosophy.[6] The first critical contribution that questioned the legitimacy of Aristippus as the founder of the school and as the original formulator of the doctrinal views of the Cyrenaics is again a Göttingen dissertation by Antoniades in 1916. It offered for the first time a conceptually sophisticated understanding of the philosophical content of those doctrines the Cyrenaics were renowned for in antiquity. Since it was an unpublished dissertation and had very limited circulation, the study of Antoniades did not break the scholarly unanimity on Aristippus until Giannantoni wrote his voluminous book on the Cyrenaics, *I Cirenaici* (1958).

Giannantoni's study is even today the most serious scholarly attempt to offer a detailed account of the sources on – and doctrines of – the Cyrenaics. It also offers a reconstruction and a philosophical assessment of the doctrines thus identified. Most of the material Giannantoni collected for his 1958 study was later edited for his monumental edition on Socrates and the Socratic schools, *Socratis et Socraticorum Reliquiae* (*SSR*; 1991). This edition is still the standard work of reference for Socrates and the Socratic schools.[7] Because of this, the influence of Giannantoni's views has been and still is very high. Although he has in some important points edulcorated his opinions on Aristippus in his 1991 study, Giannantoni's overall interpretation of the Cyrenaics is highly reductive. Aristippus cannot be regarded as the founder of any school and cannot be seriously credited with the formulation of any doctrinal view that may be considered as authentically Cyrenaic. Since Aristippus was not the original philosopher some scholars believed him to be, Plato's testimony has to be fully discharged. There is no evidence whatsoever that in his dialogues Plato is actually referring either to Aristippus or to doctrines he may have elaborated.[8]

The appearance of Giannantoni's 1958 study witnessed the resurgence of a certain scholarly interest in the Socratic schools, most notably the Cyrenaics and the Megarics. Although the pioneering effort of Giannantoni was widely recognized, his study met fierce criticism, especially in Italy, then the country with the leading expertise in the field of the study of the Socratic schools. An exchange of reviews and notes between Giannantoni and Alberto Grilli is the best witness to this scholarly climate.[9] Grilli concludes his first review of *I Cirenaici* by listing a long series of serious mistakes in translation that Giannantoni made in the lengthy collection of the sources he provided in his 1958 study. In his 1960 reply, Giannantoni provides a list of corrections for those mistakes. Rather surprisingly, Giannantoni accepts most of Grilli's suggestions, without even attempting to defend his previous translations.

The exchange between the two scholars about translations can be interpreted as too harsh an academic confrontation, but Grilli's observations make a serious point, not only as regards faults in translations, but also from an interpretative point of view. In his overall interpretation of the Cyrenaic school, Giannantoni endorses the idea that Aristippus was neither the founder of the school nor the elaborator of its doctrinal views. He does so by suggesting that the tradition of sources that make Aristippus the founder of a school is in effect a tradition that invented that philosophical genealogy – from Aristippus down to the later sects into which the school divided – for reasons of internal and historical coherence. Giannantoni (1958: 27; 1981) refers to the literature of the *Successions* as the ideal-type of ancient literature purportedly aimed at reconstructing such *ad hoc* genealogy.[10] If this were true, however, how would Giannantoni explain the extraordinary abundance of ancient sources on Aristippus and his doctrines? In his 1958 study, Giannantoni provides a collection of those sources that is more than 165 pages long. Does it make sense to say that all those sources rely on the literature of the *Successions* and that the figure of Aristippus as a real philosopher (as described by most of such sources) is an invention?

In this respect, as Grilli (1959: 344) correctly observes, the great problem left unsolved by Giannantoni's interpretation of the Cyrenaics is that there is no *pars construens* in his interpretation. After having (more or less successfully) demolished most of the preceding interpretations in the *pars destruens* of his study, Giannantoni seems unable to account for a convincing explanation of the wide presence of Aristippus as an important figure in the sources and, for that matter, in the context of ancient thought. Is Aristippus a myth? Is he just a name? Even if Aristippus had been the symbol of a way of life, he would have had reasons for choosing that way of life. How could we make sense of his choice philosophically? Giannantoni comes back to these objections in his 1960 reply to Grilli. He says that there is no way to offer a *pars construens* for the figure of Aristippus because "le fonti nulla ci dicono" (the sources don't say anything on this; Giannantoni 1960: 64). But this statement is plainly false: it seems more an aprioristic belief than the result of a scholarly enquiry. Giannantoni's other counter-reply to Grilli does not seem to score better: Aristippus' way of life is just the expression of a peculiar personal inclination and does not need any philosophical justification (*ibid.*). Again, why did ancient sources make Aristippus attached to a way of life on the basis of philosophical reasons? To invoke the literature of the *Successions* is not enough, I believe, and the burden to offer a reasonable explanation is on those – like Giannantoni – who have too simplistic an interpretation of the scope and importance of the ancient tradition on Aristippus.

Despite these critical remarks, Giannantoni's 1958 study is to be praised for its groundbreaking interest in the Cyrenaics as a philosophical movement worthy of considerable attention. Giannantoni's highly critical approach is partially counterbalanced by another important work on the Cyrenaics that appeared shortly after Giannantoni's: Erich Mannebach's *Aristippi et Cyrenaicorum Fragmenta* (The fragments of Aristippus and the Cyrenaics; 1961). The work is a revised edition of a 1948 Bonn dissertation. It is much more selective than Giannantoni in the collection of sources and rightly so. Erich Mannebach is very much against Giannantoni's view that Aristippus was neither a philosopher nor the founder of any school. On the contrary, he believes that Aristippus was the actual founder of the Cyrenaic school and that he also elaborated the nucleus of those *placita* that were later fully developed by the other Cyrenaics, in particular by Aristippus the Younger. Mannebach restricts the doctrinal paternity of Aristippus to ethics, while he argues that Cyrenaic epistemology cannot be properly individuated in Plato's dialogues or in the influence Protagoras had on Aristippus, since the epistemology of the school was elaborated only by Aristippus the Younger, who was influenced by Pyrrho.

Although counterbalancing Giannantoni's interpretation, Mannebach's effort was not enough to make full sense of a man who I believe is a key philosophical figure of the Socratic tradition. Much in the more positive direction I recommend has been attempted by Döring, who wrote a short book that had restricted circulation, even among specialists: *Der Sokratesschüler Aristipp und die Kyrenaiker* (1988). Döring had already published a collection of the sources on the Megarics and their thinking in 1972. With the publication of his monograph on the Cyrenaics, he went further in fostering a fresher philosophical appreciation of the Socratic schools and their importance in the context of Greek philosophy. In his appreciation of the Cyrenaic school, Döring recognizes the central role of the figure of Aristippus, granting him with the first elaboration of both the ethical and epistemological views that were characteristic of the school. In so doing, he also re-evaluates Plato's testimony as fully reliable. (Another salient feature of Döring's study is the positive evaluation of Anniceris. Döring sees him as ultimately responsible for important innovations in the doctrinal body of the Cyrenaic school.)[11]

As far as the English-speaking world is concerned, a recent book has been very influential in promoting a more ambitious understanding of the Cyrenaics: Voula Tsouna's *The Epistemology of the Cyrenaic School* (1998). Although it does not take issue on the more historical side – or does so only tangentially[12] – Tsouna's book is important in so far as it focuses on one aspect of the school, namely its epistemology, which was often considered only secondary. Contrary to the standard assumption, Tsouna shows how Cyrenaic epistemology is deeply rooted in the ethics of the school and how such epistemology is the first, and to some extent the only, philosophical doctrine of antiquity that is close to what we today know as epistemological subjectivism. In so doing, Tsouna explains how the Cyrenaics are best understood as a Socratic school with a philosophical spectrum that goes well beyond their ethical commitment to pleasure.

2

ARISTIPPUS

Omnis Aristippum decuit color et status et res, temptantem
maiora, fere praesentibus aequum.   (Horace)[1]

TEXTUAL EVIDENCE: DIOGENES LAERTIUS

Diogenes Laertius gives us by far the most extended treatment
of the Cyrenaic school and its genealogy, in terms of the persons
involved in that school and of the doctrinal views endorsed by its
members. Diogenes' life of Aristippus is contained in *The Lives of
Eminent Philosophers*, book II, sections 65–104: rather a lengthy
exposition. Before entering into the details on Aristippus' life and
doctrine that Diogenes offers us, I shall give a brief outline of
the whole section.[2] Diogenes' account opens (DL II 65) with a
brief biographical note on Aristippus; a long section on anecdotes
about him follows, where many of his apothegms are reported
(II 66–83). A short section (II 83) on the homonyms is then
followed by the catalogue of Aristippus' writings (II 83–5). At the
end of this section, there is a much-debated sentence reporting
the attribution of an important doctrinal view to Aristippus.
According to Diogenes, "he declared that the end [*telos*] is
the smooth motion [*leian kinēsin*] resulting in perception [*eis
aisthēsin anadidomenēn*]". After this sentence, there is the proper

17

doxological section (II 85–104), reporting, in a detailed way, the main philosophical views to be attributed to the Cyrenaics. This section itself can be subdivided as follows: there is a brief section on the genealogy of the school (II 85), which is followed by a section where the views of those whom Diogenes considers the initial and proper followers of Aristippus are reported (II 86–93). At this point, too, there is another sentence whose interpretation is crucially important. Diogenes says, "those who adhered to the way of life [agōgē] of Aristippus and were known as Cyrenaics held the following beliefs" (II 86, end). Does this sentence imply that Diogenes is here suggesting that Aristippus was the propounder of a mere way of life, with no explicit philosophical commitment? Is Diogenes telling us that Aristippus did not properly found a school? More problematically, is Diogenes suggesting that the doctrinal views he is about to expound are ascribable to the followers of Aristippus and not directly to him? The last three parts of Diogenes' account are on the doctrinal views of the last sects of the Cyrenaic school, namely the Hegesians (II 93–6), the Annicerians (II 96–7) and, eventually, the Thedorians (97–104). This last part can be more precisely subdivided into two subparts: the first part (II 97) on the followers of Theodorus; the second (II 98–104) a proper Life of Theodorus, ending with a list of the homonyms.[3]

The biographical section on Aristippus is not abundant in detail. It merely says that he was a citizen of Cyrene and that he went to Athens, drawn there by the fame of Socrates. To get more information on Aristippus we have to try to integrate the meagre biographical account Diogenes offers us with others, but the overall image of the life of Aristippus is, in any case, not enthusiastically rich.[4] That Aristippus was actually born in Cyrene is not in doubt. The city at that time was one of the richest in the Greek world because of its excellent location and the fertility of its soil.[5] On the basis of the flourishing state of Cyrene, Zeller (1923: 337 n.3) thought that Aristippus was of an affluent family, but this may be disputable.

We know few chronological details of the life of Aristippus. According to Diodorus (*Bibl. Hist.* XV 76, 4=*SSR* IV A 1), Aristippus was still alive in the third year of the 103rd Olympiad (336 BCE). Plutarch (*Life of Dio* 19=*SSR* IV A 27, 28) places the narration of anecdotes about Plato and Aristippus at Syracuse to the time of the third visit of Plato to that city, namely 361 BCE. On the basis of this information, we may think that Aristippus' birth date was around 430 BCE, Zeller believing that the exact date was 427 BCE and other historians that it was 435 BCE. Scholars are inclined to make Aristippus arrive at Athens to meet Socrates around 416 BCE, when Socrates' reputation was already high. Aristippus left Athens after Socrates' death and travelled widely, like many other Socratics, Plato included. We have information on his visits to Corinth (DL II 71) and to Megara (II 62), where he met another Socratic, Aeschines of Sphetto. Aristippus is said (*SSR* IV A 107; see also DL II 74) to have spent part of the year in Aegina with Lais, a sort of courtesan. He is likely to have gone also to Scillus, where Xenophon seems to have read his *Memorabilia* to him and Phaedo (*SSR* IV A 21).[6] He also went to Asia Minor, where he was taken prisoner by the satrap Artaphernes (DL II 79). We know that he eventually travelled to and stayed in Syracuse, where he met Plato. The extent of his travelling has been interpreted by some as an indicaton of his being a sophist (Zeller 1923: 339 n. 1; Natorp 1895: col. 903; *contra* Giannantoni 1991: vol. IV, n. 13, 140).

At DL II 62 it is said that Aeschines of Sphetto did not dare teach philosophy in Athens when he returned in 356 BCE because at that time Aristippus and Plato were too successfully active there. Some scholars have taken this information as clear evidence about the real existence of the school of Aristippus and of his role as a proper philosopher.[7] Zeller (1923: 340 n. 1) has, however, argued that Diogenes' text needs to be amended and the name of Aristippus replaced with that of Speusippus. In the most recent edition of Diogenes' *Lives*, the long-awaited Teubner edition edited by Miroslav Marcovich (1999), the editor does not raise any doubt about the name of Aristippus in the text. This may be the first sign that Aristippus was active as a teacher, even in Athens, and that his fame was at that time similar to Plato's, the founder of the Academy and Socrates' most famous student.

As far as Aristippus' death is concerned, nothing is known for sure.[8] It may be guessed that Aristippus spent the last part of his life in Cyrene, where he may have been engaged in the proper organization of his school: almost all the disciples of Aristippus listed by Diogenes at II 85 were from Cyrene and all were much younger than him (*contra* Giannantoni 1958: 69).

ARISTIPPUS THE SOPHIST?

Since Cyrene was a rich city, the sophists may have targeted it as an interesting place to go and have pupils to teach. One may thus conjecture an influence of Sophistic thinking on Aristippus, but this is hard to prove historically. There are, however, hints making us speculate about a linkage between Aristippus and Protagoras. We have already mentioned Aristippus' wide travelling in the Greek world, from Asia Minor to Sicily, and we know that the sophists were famous for their itinerant teaching, so here is the first similarity. The famous mathematician of Cyrene, Theodorus, was an intimate of Protagoras, as Plato's *Theaetetus* tells us. This can make one guess that Protagoras went to Cyrene on some occasions and that Aristippus may have profited from his visit. The philosophical affinity between Protagoras' and Aristippus' doctrines may strengthen the idea that there was an exchange between the two thinkers. Since Aristippus and Protagoras did not live in the contemporary world, where mutual influence can be exercised by conversing over the telephone or over the internet, there may be good reasons for thinking that they met.

On the contrary, Giannantoni argues that the attribution of the epithet of "sophist" to Aristippus by ancient sources is not appropriate. Those sources make that attribution on unjustified grounds, Giannantoni claims, only because Aristippus was the first follower of Socrates who, like the sophists, asked for money for his teaching. Giannantoni adds that, although there are some reasons for postulating the possible influence of Protagoras on Aristippus, there is no concrete evidence of a direct meeting between the two thinkers, or of any doctrinal impact of the former upon the latter (Giannantoni 1958: 18–38).

Aristippus is named "sophist" in two very early sources: Aristotle and the peripatetic Phanias of Eresus (reported by Diogenes). As far as the latter passage is concerned, Diogenes informs us, on the authority of Phanias, that Aristippus was a sophist and that he was the first among the Socratics to ask for money for his teaching (DL II 66). The first source ever to mention Aristippus as a sophist, however, is Aristotle, who says, "some of the sophists, e.g. Aristippus, ridiculed mathematics; for in the arts, even in handicrafts, e.g. carpentry and cobbling, the reason always given is 'because it is better or worse', while mathematics takes no account of good and bad" (*Metaph.* B 2 996a32–b1). In this passage there is no reference to a linkage between Aristippus being named "sophist" and his being remunerated for teaching. In addition, Aristotle's passage provides a kind of doctrinal linkage with Protagoras, who adopted a critical approach towards the legitimacy of mathematics and geometry in light of the empiricism that his relativism seems to have endorsed. One of Protagoras' few authentic fragments goes thus:

Astronomy cannot be dealing with perceptible magnitude nor with this heaven above us. For neither are perceptible lines such lines as the geometer speaks of (for no perceptible thing is straight or curved in this way; for a hoop touches a straight edge not at a point, but as Protagoras said it did, in his refutation of the geometers).
(Arist. *Metaph.* B 2 997b32–998a3=DK80B7)[9]

It may be worth noting that this view of Protagoras is referred to by Aristotle just after the passage of the *Metaphysics* where Aristippus' position towards mathematics is briefly formulated, as if Aristotle was effectively dealing with the same, or very similar, doctrinal view.

The reference to the explanation of the kind "because it is better or worse" to be found in the first of Aristotle's quotations also sounds Protagorean. In the *Theaetetus* the sophist is made to defend the perceptual incorrigibility on which his own relativism is centred by maintaining, on the one hand, that all perceptions are true for those who have them and, on the other, that some perceptions are better or worse than others. The proper task of the wise man is actually to transform bad perceptions into better ones, as Socrates, on Protagoras' behalf, says:

> when a man's soul is in a pernicious state, he judges things akin to it, but giving him a sound state of the soul causes him to think different things, things that are good. In the latter event, the things which appear to him are what some people, who are still inexperienced, call "true"; my position is that the one kind are better than the others, but in no way truer. (Pl. *Tht.* 167b1–4)[10]

In addition, when he comments on the passage of the *Metaphysics* where Aristippus is named (Arist. *Metaph.* B 2 996a32–b1), Alexander of Aphrodisias, the most important of Aristotle's ancient commentators, clearly establishes a conceptual linkage between the sophists and Aristippus. He says:

> having said that in mathematical entities there is no final cause, that is, the good, in that connection Aristotle refers to the beliefs of the Sophists and mentions Aristippus, who – like the other sophists – considered mathematics inferior to the most perfect techniques.
> (Alex.Aphr. *in Metaph.* 182, 30–38; see also 739, 21–4)

In conclusion, Aristotle is the first to label Aristippus a sophist and does not make any connection between Aristippus being called a sophist and his being paid for teaching. The reference to two doctrinal views Aristippus seems to have shared with Protagoras (namely, the rejection of mathematics and the better–worse explanation) is enough, at least for Aristotle, to grant the former the same epithet of sophist for which the latter was famous in antiquity. To explain that epithet when referred to Aristippus as evidence that he asked for money for his teaching appears to be misguided. When they call him a sophist, ancient sources establish a conceptual linkage between Aristippus and the sophists, in particular between Aristippus and the main exponent of that movement, namely Protagoras. The conceptual affinity between Protagoras' relativism and Cyrenaic subjectivism will be supplied in Chapter 5, as indication of further linkage between the two philosophies.

ARISTIPPUS' SAYINGS

Diogenes Laertius is more generous on the sayings and apothegms of Aristippus. I here report and comment on a few of them, namely on those that are more famous and relevant for a possible reconstruction of Aristippus' *ethos*.[11] Diogenes reports that Aristippus "was capable of adapting himself to place, time and person, and of playing his part appropriately in whatever circumstances" (DL II 66). This capacity for adapting himself to varying circumstances is seen also as a capacity to dominate his desires and not to indulge in them. Diogenes reports the following episode. Dionysius gave Aristippus the choice of three courtesans, asking him to choose one out of three. Aristippus replied to Dionysius' request by saying, "Paris paid dearly for giving the preference to one out of the three" (II 67). He is said, however, to have brought the three courtesans as far as the porch and to have let them go. Diogenes comments on the episode in the following way: "to such lengths did he go both in choosing and in disdaining" (*ibid.*). Because of his superior behaviour in such circumstances, Strato or Plato, Diogenes remarks, observed, "you alone are endowed with the gift to flaunt in robes or go in rags" (II 67; see also II 78).

It seems that Aristippus' contempt derived from his awareness that philosophy (more narrowly) and education (in general) are crucially essential in human life. On the basis of what Diogenes says, Aristippus appears to have thought that education and philosophy could really inform one's life and drastically change it by making that life lift from the lower level of basic instincts to the highs of a reasoned control on them. Two anecdotes to which Diogenes refers are illuminating. Questioned about the advantage he gained in cultivating philosophy, Aristippus replied, "The ability to feel at ease with anybody" (II 68), and added, "should all laws be eliminated, we shall go on living as we do now" (*ibid.*). Philosophers are thus seen by Aristippus as those who are able to manage the business of life and to act appropriately in every circumstance. Philosophers do not need any abiding law, since they are able to dominate themselves by surmounting the restricted limits their individuality imposes on them.

Questioned again on the meaning of education, he replied by pointing out that the difference between the educated and the uneducated is the same one as that between horses that have been trained and those that have not (II 69). At the same time, he was against cultural versatility and encyclopaedic erudition (II 71, 79). One reason for this opposition is that Aristippus seemed to take education and philosophy as means of controlling the excess of desire and our mere animality. Another episode told by Diogenes is illuminating. Aristippus "enjoyed the favours of Lais" (II 74), the courtesan with whom he is supposed to have spent a certain amount of time each year in Aegina. To those who censured him for his behaviour, he replied in the following fashion: "I have Lais, not she me: and it is not abstinence from pleasures that is the best thing, but mastery over them without being worsted" (II 75). This apothegm has been so famous and believed to be so typical of Aristippus' way of life as to be translated into the Latin motto *habere, non haberi*, which was much used by dandies of every sort and age.

The overall meaning of this Lais episode is not that Aristippus was a man devoted to pleasures but, on the contrary, that unlike other thinkers he did not refuse human passions, but suggested their reasoned mastery. Diogenes provides us with information about how Aristippus educated his daughter: "[Aristippus] gave his daughter Arete the very best advice, training her up to despise any excess" (II 71). Asked by someone how his son would be better if educated by him, Aristippus replied, "If nothing more than this, at all events, when in the theatre he will not sit down like a stone upon stone" (II 72). The suggestion in these cases is that the role of education is not the mortification of any passions, but the evocation of their proper role in human life, in the context of a wider rejection of any instinctual excess. We are not stone because we feel and sense, but our feelings and sensations have to be confined within a certain limit and to be subjected to our reasoned control.

The main feature of Diogenes' account of Aristippus is that of a man philosophically interested in human passions and in those affections that are central to the psychology and practical conduct of every human being. Aristippus seems to have been fully conscious of how passions needed to be channelled into a larger construction – be it philosophy or education – that could lead human beings to live a good life. In advocating such views, he is indeed fully Socratic. I do not find any extravagance in Diogenes' account that could make Aristippus extraneous to the Socratic spirit. Some scholars, however, and some ancient sources have depicted Aristippus as the main advocate of pleasure in classical antiquity.[12] Of course, the name of Aristippus, like that of Epicurus, is associated with the doctrine of hedonism in the mind of the philosophically educated. We all need symbols, and these two thinkers are justly regarded as advocates of pleasure.

But the different hedonism they advocate is deeply rooted in their philosophy, which is also a way of life. That way of life is such exactly in so far as it is not shaped as a mere pattern of practical conduct, but because it is grounded on (the sharing of) doctrinal views elaborated as aimed at the gaining of truth.

"PLEASURE AS A SMOOTH MOVEMENT": DIOGENES LAERTIUS II 85

Diogenes' portrait of Aristippus is, therefore, that of a philosopher endorsing a way of life that has doctrinal reasons behind it. More particularly, Diogenes ascribes to Aristippus the fundamental doctrine of Cyrenaic ethics: "He [Aristippus] proclaimed as the end the smooth motion resulting in perception" (II 85=T 18). This sentence provides us with the fundamental idea of Cyrenaic ethics: that the goal of human life is smooth motion, which is pleasure. Much has been said on this sentence and on the place it has in the context of Diogenes' report. Mannebach (1961: fr. 193, 104–6) is inclined to expunge it from the text because it may be a later addition. His reasons are not textual, or related to different readings in the codices, but exclusively philosophical. An essential source for the reconstruction of the philosophy of the Cyrenaics is a passage from the work of Aristocles of Messene, a peripatetic philosopher of the second century CE, entitled *On Philosophy* (the work is partially preserved by Eusebius of Caesarea in *The Preparation for the Gospel*). In the passage that concerns us most now (F5 Chiesara=*SSR* IV A 173 and B 5), Aristocles appears to be saying that Aristippus the Younger was responsible for the definition that the end of life is pleasure. Aristocles also adds that Aristippus the Younger catalogued human affections (*pathē*) into three kinds:

> one, in which we are in pain, is like a storm at sea; another, in which we experience pleasure and which can be compared

to a gentle wave, for pleasure is a gentle movement, similar to a fair wind; and the third is an intermediate condition, in which we experience neither pain nor pleasure, which is like a calm. He said we have perception of these affections alone. (T 4)[13]

Aristocle's passage clearly ascribes to Aristippus the Younger the distinction between three kinds of affections. On the ground of this ascription, some scholars attribute to Aristippus the Younger the actual organization of the whole conceptual body of Cyrenaic doctrines. They thus suggest that Aristippus the Elder cannot have properly formulated any philosophical view that was later recognized by ancient sources, and even by us, as properly Cyrenaic. On my account, however, Aristocles' passage does not imply the exclusion of Aristippus the Elder as the initial elaborator of Cyrenaic doctrines. What Aristocles says in the passage under scrutiny is that Aristippus the Younger was responsible for the tripartition of human affections. But the definition of pleasure as a gentle movement is not, even in Aristocles' passage, ascribed exclusively to Aristippus the Younger. In formulating the tripartition of human affections, Aristippus the Younger may well, in fact, be reusing a definition of pleasure that was circulating before him and that, in principle, can be attributed to his grandfather.

The context of Aristocles' passage allows this interpretation, which will appear even more probable if one looks at the preceding section of Aristocles' text. There, Aristocles says:

[Aristippus the Elder] did not clearly speak of the end [telos] in public. However, he said that the essence of happiness lies in particular pleasures. And, by always speaking about pleasure, he led his followers to think that he affirmed that living pleasurably is the goal of life. (F5 Chiesara=T 3)

Aristippus the Elder, thus, did not offer an explicit definition of pleasure as the end of life, but he implicitly made pleasure the

27

essence of happiness. He kept talking so frequently of pleasure that his followers thought that pleasure was the end of life for him. One may well imagine that Aristippus the Elder could have originally formulated the view that pleasure is the end. He could have also given the definition of pleasure as a gentle movement that Aristippus the Younger later rephrased and systematized into a more coherent doctrinal picture. In this connection, it may be worth noting that in Aristocles' passage there is a clear recognition that Aristippus the Elder was the founder of the Cyrenaic *agōgē*. At the beginning of Aristocles' passage in Eusebius there is the following sentence: "Aristippus was a friend of Socrates, and was the founder of the so-called Cyrenaic *agōgē*" (*Praep. evang.* 14.18.31). Now, *agōgē* is not easily translatable. In § "The foundation of the Cyrenaic school II: the meaning of *agōgē*", below, I shall argue that *agōgē* may indicate a philosophical school. If Aristippus the Elder kept talking about pleasure and were, even on the basis of Aristocles' passage, the founder of the Cyrenaic school, there would be room for claiming that he had already elaborated some doctrinal views central to Cyrenaic thinking, even before Aristippus the Younger completed the job.

There are other sources openly ascribing to Aristippus the Elder the doctrine of pleasure as the end. A passage by the pseudo-Plutarch goes like this: "Aristippus from Cyrene maintains that the end of good things is pleasure, of bad things pain; he rejects all the other sciences of nature, saying that the only useful thing to do is to look for what is good and bad" (Euseb. *Praep. evang.* 1.8.9=T 2). Another source attributing to Aristippus the Elder the view that pleasure is the end is Athenaeus: "The Cyrenaic school began with Aristippus the Socratic; having approved of the affection of pleasure, he claimed that pleasure is the end of life, and that happiness is based on it" (*Deiphnosophists* XII 544a=T 8). Cicero too often attributes to Aristippus the Elder the view that pleasure is the end. In one passage Cicero says, "Others declare that pleasure is the end [*finem*]: among these, the most important is Aristippus, who followed Socrates and from whom the Cyrenaics all derived" (*Acad. Pr.* II 42, 131=T 12). In another passage, Cicero remarks, "When Epicurus said that pleasure is the highest good [*summum bonum*], on the one hand he did not fully understand that idea; on the other, that idea is not his own: before him and in a better way, that idea was of Aristippus" (*Fin.* I 8, 26=T 13; see also *Fin.* II 6, 20=*SSR* IV A 183). Other important sources attribute to Aristippus the Elder the view that pleasure is the end (August. *De civ. D.* VIII 3=*SSR* I H 13; Lactant. *Instit. Epit.* 28, 3=*SSR* IV A 195; Epiph. *Adv. haeres.* III 2, 9=*SSR* IV A 177).

It is not convincing to say, as Giannantoni does (1958: 101–2), that these sources aim to discuss hedonism and, in so doing, they just wish to identify a target, Aristippus being the perfect choice. The authors just mentioned clearly attribute to Aristippus the Elder the view that pleasure is the end. Diogenes makes the same attribution (DL II 85). The argument for expunging the sentence on Aristippus and the end from Diogenes' text, therefore, is not philological, but philosophical, based on a comparison with Aristocles' passage. This passage, however, cannot be interpreted as excluding the idea that Aristippus the Elder was responsible for the initial formulation of the doctrine of pleasure as the end that his grandson was later able to give, on the basis of Aristocles' authority, new philosophical strength.

ARISTIPPUS' PHENOMENALISM: DIOGENES LAERTIUS II 66

In his detailed account of Aristippus, Diogenes provides evidence of Aristippus being a philosopher. He does so also by attributing to him the Cyrenaic doctrine that the end is pleasure. There is another passage in Diogenes' life of Aristippus that may be relevant for our purposes here. I refer to a satiric fragment from the *Silloi* of Timon of Phlius, the enthusiast follower of Pyrrho: an earlier (third-century BCE)[14] source for us on Aristippus. Diogenes Laertius quotes the fragment in question at II 66, reporting Timon's mockery of Aristippus for his luxurious life: "Such was the delicate nature of Aristippus, who groped error by touch [*hoia t'Aristippou truphere phusis amphaphoontos pseude*]" (T 37).

Timon's *Silloi* is a satirical poem in hexameters, a lampoon of the most prominent philosophical figures of classical Greek philosophy. Aristippus is put among these figures by Timon and satirized for his delicate nature (*truphere phusis*). Of course, by using the adjective *trupheros* (delicate, dainty), Timon aims to suggest that the nature of Aristippus was not only delicate (as that of infants), but that he also had a voluptuous nature (i.e. a derived meaning of *trupheros*; see *LSJ*). The key expressions in the fragment are not only "delicate nature" (*truphere phusis*), but also the syntagm "*amphaphoontos pseude*", which is used to refer to Aristippus and which literally means "[Aristippus] touching lies". Timon's expression is satirical and in need of further interpretation. The idea that Aristippus touches lies suggests, at least on the basis of one interpretation, that Timon is here lampooning Aristippus' phenomenalism, namely the view attributed more generally to Cyrenaic epistemology that only our (perceptual) affections are knowable to us (see Ch. 5, § "Cyrenaic knowledge"). On the ground of this interpretation, Timon appears to be suggesting that Aristippus makes truth wholly dependent (i) on the senses and (ii) on the perceptions we derive *from* them and *through* them. In particular, Timon identifies touch as the main sense organ for Aristippus. The reference to touch is not at all an out-of-place suggestion on Timon's part. There are, in fact, two passages from Cicero attributing to the Cyrenaics a doctrine of internal touch (*tactus intumus* or *interior*), to be interpreted as a kind of epistemological criterion of truth.[15]

Even if it is satirical, Timon's hexameter on Aristippus may contain trustworthy philosophical information, even in the very compressed form that is typical of the satirizing pictures of philosophers that Pyrrho's pupil draws in the *Silloi*. Timon's fragment has been interpreted as alluding to the epistemological predominance of the senses that is central in Cyrenaic epistemology by other scholars. Diogenes' fifteenth-century translator Ambrosius (Ambrogio Traversari) first commented on it by saying that "*quae [nature] potuit tactu a falso discernere verum*" (that nature – of Aristippus – could differentiate truth from falsehood by means of touch). Diogenes' main editors and translators, such as Apelt (in German), Hicks (in English) and Gigante (in Italian), share the epistemological reading of the fragment.[16] If this is the case, Diogenes' account of Aristippus will contain two references to Cyrenaic doctrines. First, there is the ethical position that the smooth motion resulting in sensation is the end (DL II 85). Second, there is an allusive reference, contained in the satirical fragment from Timon (II 66), to Aristippus' phenomenalism and to the epistemological doctrine that truth can be achieved only by means of the affections generated by the senses.

DID ARISTIPPUS WRITE ANYTHING AT ALL?

Diogenes' life of Aristippus not only contains the attribution of some important philosophical mottos to the supposed founder of the Cyrenaic school, but also grants him two doctrinal views, on pleasure and knowledge, that later will be seen as constituting the kernel of Cyrenaic philosophy. Diogenes' picture of Aristippus as a proper philosopher is strengthened by a further element: the list of the writings attributed to Aristippus. In his hypercritical appreciation of the role of Aristippus, Giannantoni remarks that two questions – about the actual writings of Aristippus and about the actual foundation by him of the Cyreanic school – are strictly interrelated. If Aristippus were the original formulator of the doctrinal views of the Cyrenaic school, the probability would be higher that he had actually written books or treatises where he had originally expounded those views. After a careful evaluation, Giannantoni (1958: 55, 67) concludes that, since the question

31

about Aristippus' writings is confused in a rather dense fog, we had better conclude that he is unlikely to have written anything, or at least anything philosophically significant. The chances that he has actually founded the Cyrenaic school are, therefore, very low, if not null.

Giannantoni's remark that the problem of Aristippus' writings and the foundation of the Cyrenaic school are closely related is true. What we have to assess, however, is whether he may be right in thinking that Aristippus is likely to have written nothing or, indeed, nothing philosophically relevant. Giannantoni later understood how badly founded his idea about Aristippus' writings was and, above all, how such an idea rested on a biased interpretation of Diogenes' testimony. The first evidence that Giannantoni has a biased view on Aristippus' writings in his 1958 study is his attempt to emend Diogenes' text in I 16, where Diogenes lists all the philosophers who did not write anything, by adding Aristippus' name to the list (Giannantoni 1991: vol. IV, n. 16, 156–9). Diogenes' list includes Socrates, Stilpon, Pyrrho and Theodorus, the Godless. In II 64 Diogenes informs us that – as far as Socratic dialogues are concerned – Panetius observes that only those written by Plato, Xenophon, Antisthenes and Aeschines are genuine. Before reporting the second catalogue of Aristippus' writings at II 85, Diogenes says that Sosicrates of Rhodes affirmed that Aristippus did not write a book of essays. On the basis of this information, Giannantoni (1958: 55–8) argues that Aristippus is likely not to have written anything. He thus suggests amending the text of I 16, where Diogenes does not include Aristippus among those philosophers who wrote nothing.

That Aristippus wrote something is not in doubt. Two ancient sources mention Aristippus' writings. The first is the historian Theopompus, who says that Plato was a plagiarist, since he copied most of his dialogues from those of Aristippus, Antisthenes and Brison (*SSR* IV A 146). The second is a fragment from Epicurus' letters, to be found in the work of Philodemus against the sophists (*SSR* IV A 147), where Epicurus asked to be sent Aristippus' books of essays, which dealt with some of Plato's dialogues. Diogenes' testimony on Aristippus' writings is also not as deluding as Giannantoni initially thought. There is, in fact, no need to suggest any emendation to Diogenes' text (at I 16). When he informs us that those Socratics who wrote genuine (*alētheis*) Socratic dialogues do not include Aristippus, Panetius obviously does not mean that Aristippus did not write anything, much less that Aristippus did not write any dialogue or, for that matter, any Socratic dialogue. The adjective *alētheis*, referring to the kind of Socratic dialogues Panetius speaks of, may mean "authentic", but also "trustworthy". Panetius' remark is not meant to exclude other Socratics writing dialogues where Socrates is not the main protagonist, or where he is just a character represented with no historical accuracy. Even the comment by Sosicrates of Rhodes, reported by Diogenes, that Aristippus did not write anything refers only to the books of essays that are mentioned in the preceding sentence, and is not to be taken absolutely.[17]

Giannantoni has argued for a strict linkage between the fact that Aristippus wrote something and the fact that he had actually founded the Cyrenaic school. I share with Giannantoni the legitimacy of the linkage just established, on the ground that, if Aristippus is likely to have written some philosophical works, one can reasonably postulate that he, at least in principle, elaborated some doctrinal views that are at the root of Cyrenaic philosophy and were at the basis of the foundation of the school. The views in question may well be that on pleasure (as the end) and on knowledge (as wholly centred on perceptual affections), which we saw hinted at in Diogenes' account of Aristippus. Since he did write something (and quite a lot, if we trust the list of works Diogenes reports), the chances that Aristippus was something more than a transitory presence on the scene of Greek philosophy and something more than just a symbol of a sybaritic way of life are far higher than first expected.

ARISTIPPUS' WRITINGS

Diogenes gives us two lists of Aristippus' works; he does not tell us the paternity of the first list, and the second is provided on the basis of the authority of Sotion and Panetius. The first catalogue includes the letter to Arete among the dialogues of Aristippus. This makes us inclined to think that it is not a very ancient catalogue. It is also much less philosophical than the second one, which is a more reliable list. Diogenes tells us (DL II 83) that Aristippus wrote a work in three volumes on the history of Libya (the country to which the city of Cyrene belonged), dedicated to Dionysius. Aristippus is also said to have written another work, containing twenty-five dialogues, some written in Attic and others in Doric. Diogenes gives a full list of the titles of the dialogues: this is the first catalogue of Aristippus' work. Some of the titles listed in the first catalogue are given also in the second. Before providing us with the second catalogue of Aristippus' writings – on the basis of Sotion and Panetius – Diogenes observes that some say that Aristippus also wrote six books of essays. The second catalogue of Aristippus' works lists: *On Education*; *On Virtue*; *Introduction to Philosophy*; *Artabazus*; *The Ship-Wrecked*; *The Exiles*; six *Books of Essays*; three *Books of Maxims*; *To Lais*; *To Porus*; *To Socrates*; and *On Fortune*.

Mannebach (1961: 80–84) provides a detailed analysis of these titles (and of those of the first catalogue), trying to reconstruct, at least in their very general lines, the topic and content of Aristippus' works (see also Giannantoni 1991: vol. IV, n. 16). The reconstruction he provides, although helpful, is based on scanty evidence and is very hypothetical. What can be guessed at a first glance, however, is that some of Aristippus' works that Diogenes lists in the second catalogue have somewhat philosophical titles, while others seem to have historical content. In the latter group, one may include those works that seem to deal with historical characters, such as *To Artabazus*, *To Prorus*, *To Lais* and even *To Socrates*. Of the last two people, we know enough: the former was Aristippus' partner, the latter his master. Prorus could have been the runner who won an Olympiad. Artabazus could have been the satrap Aristippus may have met on his trip to Asia. For our own purposes here we focus on the philosophical titles.

We know that virtue (*arēte*) was a much discussed topic in Socrates' circle: Plato's *Protagoras* is, for instance, one of the classic examples of the interest Socrates and the Socratics had in virtue. It would be no surprise that Aristippus wrote something on the topic. Although we don't know the content of Aristippus' work on virtue, the very fact that he did write something on the topic witnesses how much he was privy to the philosophical discussions that animated Socrates' circle. Another striking title is *On Education*. We saw earlier that Aristippus had a great interest in education and in how education could shape the practical conduct of human beings by distancing them from their mere animality. I see no obstacle in believing that – given his interest in education – Aristippus could have written a book on education.[18] The title that is more significant for us is *Introduction to Philosophy* (*Protreptikos*). The title itself reveals that Aristippus wanted to instruct people in philosophy and that he wrote something for that purpose. In so doing, he appears to be responding to the main task Socrates is traditionally believed to have assigned to his dialogical activity: to make people revise their beliefs and ways of life by means of an education centred on philosophy. Socrates is the philosopher *protreptikos par excellence*. On the basis of the evidence that Aristippus wrote an *Introduction to Philosophy*, it has been argued, I believe with good reason, that Aristippus, together with another Socratic, Antisthenes, introduced the genre of the *protreptikos* into philosophy (Hartlich 1888: 228–9; see also Giannantoni 1991: vol. IV, n. 16, 163).

There is another testimony that may prove Aristippus' seminal introduction of the genre of the *protreptikos* into philosophy. This is a passage from the work "On Elocution" by Demetrius Phalereus. The passage goes like this: "'Men leave their richness to

their sons, but at the same time they do not give them the knowledge to be used for what they have left'; this kind of discourse [*to
eidos tou logou*] is called Aristeppean" (*Eloc.* 296=*SSR* IV A 148).
After mentioning the Aristippean kind of discourse, Demetrius
refers to two other kinds: that of Xenophon, and one more
prominently Socratic, to be attributed to Aeschines and Plato.
In two other passages (*Discourses* III 23, 33; III 21, 19), Epitectus
distinguishes three types of philosophical discourse: *protreptikos*
(introductive), *elenkitikos* (aimed at refuting) and *didaskalikos*
(illustrative). Antonio Carlini (1968) has provided a comparison
between the division of philosophical discourses suggested by
Epitectus and Demetrius. He suggests that the Aristippean *logos*
is similar, if not equivalent, to the introductive or to the illustrative. Given the fact that Aristippus wrote an *Introduction to
Philosophy*, I am inclined to believe that Demetrius' Aristippean
logos corresponds to Epitectus' introductive one. Aristippus
can therefore be seen as an inventor of a philosophical kind of
discourse, more precisely the one that is aimed at introducing
people to the study of philosophy. This is another element in
Diogenes' account that can be seen as reinforcing the picture of
Aristippus as a real philosopher.

THE FOUNDATION OF THE CYRENAIC SCHOOL I: MANNEBACH'S ARGUMENT

What is still disputable, however, is whether Aristippus was actually the founder of the Cyrenaic school. On this problem, we will
not be offered a certain answer, and shall have to proceed with
caution. If we can grant Aristippus with having written some
philosophical works, the possibility that he actually founded
the school will be higher. Such a possibility would be much
higher if we could attribute to Aristippus the initial formulation of some doctrinal views that were later openly interpreted
by ancient sources and by us today as 'Cyrenaic' views. On

my interpretation, there is nothing preventing us from taking Diogenes as openly attributing to Aristippus the view that pleasure is the end. Moreover, the hexameter of Timon, reported by Diogenes himself, suggests that Aristippus could have already highlighted the epistemological importance of the senses in the cognitive process that is central to Cyrenaic epistemology. If there are grounds for attributing to Aristippus the initial formulation of these doctrinal views, which are at the centre of Cyrenaic philosophy, we will be offered a good argument for maintaining that Aristippus was the actual founder of the Cyrenaic school.

Diogenes' account, however, seems to offer counter-arguments too to those who maintain that Aristippus was not responsible for the foundation of the Cyrenaic school. These counter-arguments are, however, not at all conclusive. The first counter-argument is based on the use the adjective "Cyrenaic" (*kurēnaikos*), as referred to Aristippus. Before listing the titles of his works, Diogenes labels Aristippus as the "Cyrenaic" (*kurēnaikos*) philosopher (II 83). Followed by Marcello Gigante (1983: 482 n. 231), Mannebach (1961: fr. 121, 76–9) proposes to amend the text by replacing "Cyrenaic" (*kurēnaikos*) with "from Cyrene" (*kurēnaios*), on the basis that in many doxographical sources Aristippus is always said to be from Cyrene (*kurēnaios*), while the term "Cyrenaics" (*kurēnaikoi*) is very rarely mentioned in connection with Aristippus (see Classen 1958: 185). Mannebach (1961: 86–90) observes that there are also two expressions for mentioning the members of the Cyrenaic school: *hoi kurēnaikoi*, "the Cyrenaics", is the most frequent. Sextus also uses the expression *apo tēs Kurēnēs*, "from Cyrene". Mannebach believes that the latter expression has to be referred to the later sects of the Cyrenaic school, while the former expression refers to Aristippus the Younger and his immediate followers (see also Giannantoni 1991: vol. IV, n. 17, 170).

Mannebach is, I believe, wrong on both points. It is true that Sextus uses the expressions "the Cyrenaics" and "from Cyrene" when he refers to the members of the Cyrenaic school. There is too much emphasis, however, on distinguishing the referents of the two expressions on the ground that the expression "the Cyrenaics" is meant to indicate Aristippus the Younger and his followers, while "from Cyrene" designates the later sects of the Cyrenaic school. Sextus uses the expression "from Cyrene" in two passages, where he reports that the Cyrenaics rejected two of the traditional branches of philosophy, namely logic and physics, to concentrate only on ethics (*Math*. VII 11, 15=*SSR* IV A 168). In reporting the division of philosophy they adopted, Sextus refers to the Cyrenaics with the expression "from Cyrene", but he does not seem to confine that division only to the later sects of the Cyrenaic school. There is nothing in Sextus' text that may allow one to think so. Moreover, the stress upon ethics is rather typical of the whole school, especially of its main core exponents, as part of the Socratic inheritance and legacy. On the other hand, when he offers one of the most extended pieces of information on Cyrenaic epistemology and language, Sextus always speaks of "the Cyrenaics" (see *Math*. VII 191–200). Even in this case, there is no element in Sextus' text to make us think that he may be referring to the thought and doctrines of Aristippus the Younger and his followers only. A further element that may be highlighted in this connection is that in his report at 191–200, Sextus identifies some epistemological and linguistic views that represent the kernel of Cyrenaic doctrine. Nothing prevents us from thinking (at least in Sextus' account) that those views were initially argued for by Aristippus the Elder and later refined by Aristippus the Younger. In short, in Sextus' account there is nothing that could make us think that the views he reports were developed by the later sects of the Cyrenaic school.

With this remark we come to the first point Mannebach raises, namely about the emendation in Diogenes' text of "Cyrenaic" (*kurēnaikos*) with "from Cyrene" (*kurēnaios*), as referred to Aristippus (DL II 83). Mannebach (1961: 87) proposes that emendation on the basis of the argument that Aristippus is rarely referred to as "Cyrenaic" in ancient sources. Where he is, it is done to draw attention to his city of provenance, and not to him being a Cyrenaic philosopher (i.e. someone endorsing doctrinal views that are typical of the Cyrenaic school). In short, Mannebach believes that if Diogenes is correct in labelling Aristippus a "Cyrenaic philosopher"', there will be good reasons to think that Diogenes did so on some legitimate grounds. Aristippus was not only a philosopher from Cyrene, but a Cyrenaic philosopher: someone who had already – even if not fully or organically – elaborated doctrinal views. On the basis of this argument and by relying on the analysis of the other few occurrences where Aristippus is called "Cyrenaic", Mannebach proposes the emendation of "Cyrenaic" to "from Cyrene", an expression containing no philosophical commitment.

The reasons for Mannebach's emendation are, once again, mainly philosophical, based on the assumption that Aristippus could not be correctly regarded as the proper founder of the Cyrenaic school. The assumption is misplaced for several reasons. First, Diogenes' account of Aristippus is consistently philosophical: Aristippus is pictured as someone not only with philosophical concerns, but also with some doctrinal views on pleasure and ethics to propound. There is, therefore, no surprise to see Aristippus called a "Cyrenaic philosopher" (*Kurēnaikos philosophos*) by Diogenes. Second, as suggested by Grilli (1960: 417–18), it would be pleonastic to call Aristippus "Cyrenaic" in the same way that it would be absurd to call Epicurus "Epicurean". On the ground that Aristippus is rarely termed Cyrenaic in ancient sources, it is arbitrary to propose the emendation in Diogenes' text Mannebach suggests.

Third, and more forcibly, Diogenes knows pretty well when to call Aristippus "Cyrenaic" or "from Cyrene". When he deals with the philosophical schools of antiquity in the proem of the *Lives*, Diogenes says that the head of the Cyrenaic school was Aristippus from Cyrene (*kurēnaios*) (DL I 19), because he has just explained the name of the philosophical schools, including the Cyrenaic one, with reference to the city where the school originated (I 17). If in II 83 Diogenes calls Aristippus "Cyrenaic philosopher", there is no reason to believe that he does so wrongly. He may do so exactly because he wishes to convey to the readers the impression that Aristippus was in effect the actual founder of the school, and not only a philosopher from Cyrene. That Mannebach's decision to emend Diogenes' text goes beyond a textual necessity, and owes more to a philosophical assumption, is confirmed by the new edition of *The Lives of Eminent Philosophers* (Marcovich 1999). Marcovich adopts the original *kurēnaikos* (Cyrenaic) with reference to Aristippus the philosopher at II 83.

THE FOUNDATION OF THE CYRENAIC SCHOOL II: THE MEANING OF *AGŌGĒ*

The second counter-argument aimed at showing that Aristippus was not responsible for the foundation of the Cyrenaic school is, once again, based on an interpretation of a crucial passage of Diogenes' text. After listing all the disciples who "derived from him" (DL II 85, end), Diogenes observes, "Those who adhered to the way of life of Aristippus and were known as Cyrenaics held the following opinions [*hoi men oun tēs agōgēs tēs Aristippou meinantes kai Kurēnaikoi prosagoreuthentes doxais echrōnto toiautais*]" (II 86; Hicks trans.). The opinions Diogenes refers to are given in details in a doxological section, from II 86 to II 93.

Since Diogenes offers us his survey into Cyrenaic philosophy after having dealt with the figure of Aristippus, some scholars maintain that Aristippus cannot be credited with the philosophical views Diogenes reports in the doxological section. The sentence I have just quoted (II 86, end) is the textual hinge between the strictly Aristippean section and the doxological one. In that sentence it is said that those who share the "way of life" of Aristippus held the beliefs about pleasure and knowledge that Diogenes is about to expound on. One possible interpretation of this sentence may be that the Cyrenaics proper held those views while Aristippus himself did not. The Cyrenaics Diogenes refers to in the doxological section are, in fact, said to share Aristippus' way of life (*agōgē*). On the basis of this argument, Aristippus developed only a way of life, whereas those who followed him not only adopted a way of life (*agōgē*), but, most crucially, also defended a complete set of doctrines (*hairesis*) that gave definitive form to what we know as the Cyrenaic school.[19]

I do not find this argument convincing. First, it is true that the doxological part of Diogenes' account refers explicitly to the followers of Aristippus, but there is nothing in the text implying Diogenes to be suggesting that Aristippus did not himself, in a nutshell, elaborate any of those doctrinal views. More naturally I interpret the hinging sentence in question (II 86) as Diogenes' warning that he is passing from the part of his account that is exclusively centred on Aristippus to the doxological part concerning the doctrinal views of the whole school, Aristippus the Elder included. In Diogenes' overall account there is no discrepancy, either conceptual or textual, between the part on Aristippus and that on Cyrenaic doxology. Diogenes has labelled Aristippus himself as the "Cyrenaic philosopher" at II 83. In another passage, Diogenes seems to be proposing a strict derivation between Aristippus and his followers. In the sentence following the one where Diogenes ascribes to Aristippus the doctrinal view that the end of life is the smooth movement coming forth to perception (II 85), Diogenes says, "after having described his life, let me know to pass in review the Cyrenaics who derived from him" (II 85, end).

How are we to interpret this derivation, if not philosophically? What would be the linkage between the part of Diogenes' account that is strictly and solely on Aristippus (II 66–85) and the other part that is doxological (II 86–93), if Aristippus were only a historical figure with no theoretical commitment? By accepting the interpretation on the basis of which the part on Aristippus (II 66–85) has no particular philosophical relevance and is instead followed by the part (II 86–93) that has a real philo-sophical connotation, Diogenes' account would become totally unbalanced. If it were so, we would lose the conceptual connec-tion between the mere biographical part and the more relevant conceptual one. I therefore claim that we should interpret the derivation of the Cyrenaics from Aristippus that Diogenes speaks of in a philosophical way. The views Diogenes ascribes to the Cyrenaics are a philosophical derivation of the doctrinal views he has earlier attributed to Aristippus, in so far as the former may constitute a conceptual elaboration of the latter.

Let us go back to the hinging sentence (II 86). There is no particular need to take this sentence as meaning that Aristippus proposed only a way of life, with no further theoretical commit-ment. R. D. Hicks translates the sentence in question in this way: "those who adhered to the way of life of Aristippus and were known as Cyrenaics held the following opinions". Although correct, this translation is, to some extent, misleading. A more textual translation would be: "those who remained faithful [mein-antes] to the way of life and doctrines [agōgē] of Aristippus …". The idea I take Diogenes to be conveying in the sentence is that the followers of Aristippus, by remaining *faithful* to his teaching and doctrines, held those philosophical beliefs Diogenes is about to report.

Agōgē is a term that does not exclusively indicate a way of life, but also refers to a system of doctrines, generally philosophical doctrines, which are taken to support that way of life from a more doctrinal point of view (see *LSJ*). This is evident in many places in Sextus' text, where *agōgē* is clearly meant to indicate a philosophical school (in one case, referring precisely to the school of Aristippus).[20] In addition, if we have to suggest a term in Diogenes that is contrasted with *hairesis*, namely with the term that more explicitly is meant to indicate a philosophical school and the doctrines the school advances, it will be *enstasis biou* (literally, "way of life"), not *agōgē*. When he speaks of the Cynics, Diogenes remarks, "Such are the lives of each of the Cynics. But we will go on to deal with the doctrines they held in common – if, that is, we believe that Cynicism is really a philosophy [*philosophian*] and not, as some maintain, just a way of life [*enstasin biou*]" (DL VI 103).

More crucially, Diogenes himself does not contrast *hairesis* with *agōgē*. When he gives an overall systematization of the philosophical schools in the proem of the *Lives*, Diogenes says that in antiquity there were nine schools and ways of life (*hairesis* and *agōgē*), including the schools of Plato, Aristotle, Epicurus and the Stoics, and, rather surprisingly, three schools and ways of life that are Cyrenaic: the Cyrenaics proper, the Annicerians and the Thedorians (I 19=*SSR* I H 6). With this remark we return to the concept of school in classical antiquity, which we briefly remarked on in Chapter 1. In the context of the classical world there is something artificial in distinguishing a school and a way of life, since all the philosophical schools of antiquity, from the most structured and enduring schools of Plato and Aristotle to the less organized schools of Aristippus and the other Socratics, were schools (in a broad sense of the term) based on a common way of life. Conversely, a certain way of life was such because it was based on doctrinal views that gave that way of life the theoretical support it needed, to be viewed paradigmatically as "a way of life". On the basis of this understanding, we had better follow Diogenes in not strictly distinguishing a "way of life" (*agōgē*) from a school with a proper set of doctrines (*hairesis*).

Not only does Diogenes take *hairesis* and *agōgē* to be almost equivalent to each other, but in the proem of the *Lives* he clearly ascribes to Aristippus the Elder at least the historical paternity of the Cyrenaic school. After having divided philosophy into three canonical branches – physics (about the world and the things therein contained), ethics (on the lives and customs of human beings) and dialectics (which is about the arguments and reasons of both physics and ethics) – Diogenes says that ancient ethics gave birth to ten schools (*haireseis*), one of which is the Cyrenaic school (DL I 18). In addition, he clearly recognizes

Aristippus as the leader of the school, in the sense of both its initial philosophical guidance and its historical foundation: "the founders of these school were: of the Old Academy, Plato; of the Middle Academy, Arcesilaus ...; of the Cyrenaic, Aristippus of Cyrene" (I 19).

In conclusion, there is no need to read Diogenes' remark about those who adhered to Aristippus' *agōgē* (i.e. the hinging sentence at II 86) as suggesting that Aristippus did not found any proper school or that he really had no doctrinal views to elaborate. On the contrary, there is much in Diogenes to argue that he viewed Aristippus as the original founder of the Cyrenaic school and as the philosopher who elaborated the kernel of Cyrenaic philosophy. In this connection, it may be noted at last that Galen offers us a valuable testimony on Aristippus and his school. He says:

> Some philosophical schools are defined by the name of their founder, by the city [of foundation], by the doctrines [it elaborated]; on the basis of this, that school who derived from Aristippus is termed "Aristippean" by the name of its founder, "Cyrenaic" by the city to which he belonged, "hedonistic" by the ultimate end of its philosophy.
>
> (*Phil.Hist.* 4=*SSR* I H 18)

I take this to be a perfect summary of the kind of understanding of the figure of Aristippus (and of his role in the context of the foundation of the Cyrenaic school) that I have recommended throughout this chapter.

CYRENAIC GENEALOGY

After listing the titles of Aristippus' works, Diogenes offers us a genealogy of the school by sketching a biographical map of the Cyrenaics:

The disciples of Aristippus were his daughter Arete, Aethiops of Ptolemais, and Antipater of Cyrene. The pupil of Arete was Aristippus, who went by the name of mother-taught [*mētrodidaktos*], and his pupil was Theodorus, known as the Godless, subsequently as "god". Antipater's pupil was Epitimides of Cyrene, his was Paraebates, and he had as pupils Hegesias, the advocate of suicide, and Anniceris.

(II 86)

The genealogy of the Cyrenaic school can thus be represented as follows:

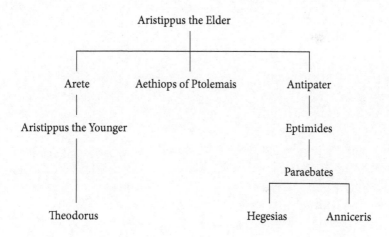

The main genealogical line is that of Arete and Aristippus the Younger. On Arete there is very little information, if any. We can only conjecture that she must have been very active philosophically since she, a woman, was in charge of educating her son, Aristippus the Younger, or Metrodidactus. On Metrodidactus, too, there is very little information, but we are lucky to have the rather detailed piece of evidence by Aristocles of Messene in Eusebius that we saw earlier.[21]

The later sects of the Cyrenaic school are named after their leaders: Hegesias, Anniceris and Theodorus the Godless. The main source of information for all these sects is Diogenes Laertius (II 93–104). The evidence for them is, however, scanty, with the exception of Theodorus. I shall deal with these later exponents of the Cyrenaic school in Chapter 8.

3

THE *THEAETETUS*

Together with Aristippus, Plato was a follower of Socrates. Plato and Aristippus were contemporaries and, both being philosophers, could have met and had discussions on many occasions. More importantly, Plato could have had first-hand knowledge of Aristippus' philosophy and doctrine. If this is so, Plato is likely to have confronted Aristippus' views in some of his dialogues. So if there is evidence that Plato discusses Cyrenaic views in some of his dialogues, we shall be in an excellent position to have vital information on Aristippus and his school. In short, we will be in a better position to argue for the foundation by Aristippus of the Cyrenaic school. It is plain that if Plato refers in his dialogues to some philosophical views that we can, with good reason, ascribe to Aristippus, this will show that Aristippus was a real philosopher whose views Plato wished to discuss for their doctrinal relevance. If Plato held Aristippus to be a philosopher, the probability that he founded a Socratic school would be much higher. That is why detractors of Aristippus aim to disregard Plato's testimony. They wish to prove that, since there is no real evidence that Plato refers to Aristippus in his dialogues, that is a clear sign that Aristippus did not elaborate any of the views that are characteristic of the Cyrenaic school (see Giannantoni 1958: 117–69; 1991: vol. I, 1H Appendix). Plato's testimony will thus become a crucial element in providing a correct assessment of the Cyrenaic school (and of the role played by Aristippus in the foundation of that school).

PLATO AND ARISTIPPUS

A related problem faced by scholars when dealing with Plato as a source for other thinkers is how much we may rely on him as a trustworthy witness. Plato is not only a great philosopher, but also an excellent writer, one of the finest of all times. When he wrote his dialogues, he was very much concerned about the overall effect on readers that his literal artefacts might produce. It may be the case that historical truthfulness was not the main ingredient Plato had in mind when he produced his master-pieces. The characters of Plato dialogues are, however, historical characters in so far as they represent rhetoricians, sophists, philosophers and politicians of Socrates' and Plato's time. In representing historical characters at work, Plato's dialogues combine a sort of historical setting and climate with a larger philosophical project: Plato's. Recently, it has been persuasively argued that the overall aim of Plato's dialogues is exactly to persuade readers of different cultural provenance (namely those rhetoricians, sophists and so on who are populating his dialogues) (see Rowe 2007: 1–54).

With that aim in mind, in his dialogues Plato has to confront, discuss and show to be incoherent the ideas of those rhetoricians, sophists and so on. For these reasons, surely, there is a historical record in the dialogues, and Plato himself is, to some extent, respectful of historical setting and characters. Obviously enough, Plato elaborates history to produce philosophical arguments. This elaboration does not prevent one from attempting to use Plato as a source of information on the doctrines of other philosophers. Interpreting the views Plato discusses in some of his dialogues as views ascribable to one philosopher or another is an exercise that needs to be done with extreme caution, but it is not an impossible task. Elsewhere (see Zilioli 2007), I have attempted this task with reference to Protagoras.[1]

Scholars have found possible traces of Cyrenaic thinking in many of Plato's dialogues (see Giannantoni 1958: 116–69, with further bibliography). I think here of the *Greater Hippias* (especially with reference to Socrates' first definition of the beautiful), the *Protagoras* (especially with reference to the final section of the dialogue, where Socrates seems to be equating pleasure with the good), the *Gorgias* (with reference to the views on happiness endorsed by the sophist Callicles), the *Cratylus* (where, in some interpretations, Aristippus' views on language are represented by the conventionalism defended by Hermogenes) and the *Republic* (especially with reference to the discussion between Socrates and Glaucon on the good in book VI and even with reference to the myth of the cave), the *Theaetetus* and the *Philebus*. The probable ubiquity of Aristippus throughout the whole of the Platonic corpus is further evidence that Plato is likely to have been well acquainted with Aristippus and his views.

This is not the right place to offer a detailed overview of the possible presence of Aristippus in Plato's dialogues, since that would require at least a book in itself. As far as this book is concerned, one of Plato's dialogues is outstandingly important: the *Theaetetus* (the *Philebus* being important, too, but not essential in the same way that the *Theaetetus* is). In the *Theaetetus* Plato famously deals with the question of knowledge, while in the *Philebus* he has to do with the role of knowledge and pleasure in the good life. In this chapter we shall deal exclusively with the *Theaetetus* (the *Philebus* will be briefly dealt with at the end of Chapter 7).

THE *THEAETETUS* AS A PEIRASTIC DIALOGUE

The *Theaetetus* is the dialogue on which scholars wishing to assess the presence of Aristippus in Plato's works have always focused.

This is because Plato develops a phenomenalist doctrine in the *Theaetetus*, reinforced by a peculiar kind of metaphysical theory, which Socrates is made to attribute to some subtler thinkers (*hoi kompsoteroi*) (*Tht.* 156a3–160c).[2] The doctrine the subtler thinkers are made to endorse is a fascinating perceptual theory, paired with a metaphysics of processes, which represents one of the finest speculations about perception in the whole of Greek philosophy. Scholars wonder about the actual identity of those subtler thinkers. The best candidates have always been Aristippus and the early Cyrenaics, who, on the ground of their epistemology as reconstructed through the use of other ancient sources, are the thinkers closest to the kind of phenomenalism endorsed by those subtler thinkers.

The identity of the subtler thinkers has, however, often been disputed, and there is no unquestionable evidence that *hoi kompsoteroi* of *Tht.* 156a3 are some clearly identified thinkers. I believe that there are good reasons for maintaining that the subtler thinkers in question are likely to be Aristippus and the early Cyrenaics. In particular, I claim that the reasons for believing that *hoi komposteroi* are Aristippus and the early Cyrenaics are stronger than the reasons for thinking they are not. My claim is shared by the overall majority of scholars who have dealt with the problem, but not by the majority of the scholars who have dealt with the problem *more recently*. Scholars such as Schleiermacher (1804: II 1, 183ff.) and Paul Natorp (1890: 347) defended the view that the subtler thinkers are likely to be Aristippus and his first followers. Once again, Giannantoni (1958: 142–3) disagrees, maintaining that there are no conclusive arguments for identifying the subtler thinkers with the Cyrenaics. In particular, he has claimed that other sources, especially Sextus, offer an account of Cyrenaic thinking that is incompatible with the philosophical views endorsed by *hoi kompsoteroi*. For different reasons, Mannebach (1961: 114–16) too has rejected the identification between the subtler thinkers and Aristippus and the early Cyrenaics. More challenging for us, Tsouna (1998: 124–37) has argued that the

subtler thinkers cannot be the Cyrenaics because the former philosophers hold a non-identity thesis, namely the non-persistence
over time of individuals and objects, which is in striking contrast
with the epistemological and metaphysical views of the Cyrenaics,
as these are reconstructed by means of other sources.

I am now about to construct the best case I can to identify the
subtler thinkers of the *Theaetetus* with Aristippus and the early
Cyrenaics by showing, among other things, that Giannantoni
is wrong when he claims that the doctrinal views endorsed by
the subtler thinkers in the *Theaetetus* are in contrast with those
doctrines Sextus attributes to the Cyrenaics in *Math.* VII 191–200.
In addition, Tsouna, too, is on the wrong path when she claims
that a non-identity thesis cannot be attributed to the Cyrenaics.
Although I shall explore this issue more fully in Chapter 4, I shall
also make clear in this chapter that the Cyrenaics may have well
adopted a metaphysics of indeterminacy, on whose basis objects
in the world are ontologically indeterminate. I begin my strategy
by sketching a general interpretation of the *Theaetetus* that will
set up the argument supporting the kind of identification I am
proposing.

On the interpretation I shall be recommending throughout,
the *Theaetetus* is a dialogue *ad homines*. What I believe Plato
does in the dialogue is give answers to the question "What is
knowledge?" by melding ingredients that are, for the most part,
neither Socratic nor Platonic. Let me put it this way: the answers
provided in the *Theaetetus* to the question of what knowledge
is are the products of Plato's (and, perhaps, even Socrates') own
confrontation with the theories of knowledge that were dominant at their time. I think here of Protagoras' relativism and of
the various epistemologies elaborated, more or less completely,
by Aristippus, Euclides and Antisthenes (the last two being the
supposed founders of the Socratic schools of the Megarics and
the Cynics).[3] I take it that, obviously enough, Plato's aim in the
Theaetetus is not purely exegetical: he believes that those views
were worth investigating in themselves for their widespread

currency and theoretical appeal. In particular, Plato's Socrates criticizes those views because they propose accounts of knowledge as exclusively perception based.

On the basis of this interpretation, in the *Theaetetus* Plato's Socrates is arguing *ad homines*; namely, against the theory of those thinkers who maintained perception-based accounts of knowledge. This explains why the dialogue is aporetic: it ends with no answer to the question of what knowledge is because its main aim is confutative.[4] This reading of the dialogue is as old as the history of Platonism and surfaces now and then in Platonic scholarship. The *Theaetetus* was understood in antiquity as a peirastic dialogue (and not as a maieutic one, according to the classification reported by Diogenes Laertius [III 49–51]); namely, as a dialogue explicitly written to refute someone's theories.[5] In his commentary on the *Parmenides*, Proclus indirectly suggests a view that the whole dialogue is designed to refute Protagoras' doctrines (*in Prm.* 657, 5–10; 654, 15–26). In the third book of the *First Principles*, Damascius alludes to an interpretation of Socrates' Dream – the philosophical core of the third part of the *Theaetetus* – that understands it as a Protagorean dream, ideally extending Protagoras' critique until the final section of the dialogue.

Alcinous' *Didaskalikos* 4 offers insight into a different interpretation of the dialogue, on the basis of which the *Theaetetus* shows what knowledge is not, since the dialogue addresses the epistemology of the sensible world (while the *Sophist* is concerned about the knowledge of what is not sensible, namely the Forms). Although this interpretation is different from the sceptical one endorsed by the Academics (on whose basis the dialogue aims to show that knowledge is unattainable), they both insist on the confutative character of the dialogue and both allow for the serious confrontation between perception-based theories of perception and Socrates/Plato that I see at play in the *Theaetetus*. Closer to us in time, another interpreter of the *Theaetetus* who takes it as a battlefield of contrasting ideas about knowledge is Lewis Campbell (1883: xxviii–xli). In addition to Protagoras, in his commentary on the *Theaetetus* he carefully detects traces of Megaric, Cyrenaic and Cynic thinking throughout the whole dialogue.[6] On the same lines, more recently there is Julia Annas's (1994) contribution on "Plato the Sceptic"; Timothy Chappell's (2005) running commentary on the *Theaetetus* defends the view that Plato is actually arguing in the dialogue against empiricist theories of knowledge of his own time.

If the *Theaetetus* is best understood as a peirastic dialogue, where Plato seriously confronts his rivals' views about perception and knowledge, it will make sense to try to locate in the dialogue his references to the philosophers whose views he is examining. It is in this context that I place my attempt to give reasons for identifying the subtler philosophers of *Theaetetus* 156a3 with Aristippus and the early Cyrenaics.[7]

THE SUBTLER THINKERS

After having dealt with the first exposition of Protagoras' relativism at *Theaetetus* 151eff., Socrates suggests that Protagoras taught a Secret Doctrine to some of his disciples (152c10). The content of Protagoras' Secret Doctrine is briefly enunciated at 152d2–e1, later expanded at 153d8–154b8 and eventually fully dealt with at 156a2–157c3, the passage that interests us most. Contrasted with some unidentified materialists, the subtler thinkers have their own mysteries that Socrates is just about to reveal. In accordance with Protagoras' Secret Doctrine, these thinkers maintain that everything is in movement (*kinēsis*); there is nothing beyond movement (156a5). They believe that there are two kinds (*eidē*) of movement, each infinite in extension, one with an active power (*to poiein*), and the other with a passive one (*to paschein*) (156a6–7). From the intercourse of these two kinds of movement, "there come to be offspring, infinite in number, but always twins: one is the perceived thing, the other is the corresponding perception, which is on every occasion generated and brought to birth together with the perceived thing" (156a7–b2). These perceptions have such names as "seeings", "hearings" and so on (i.e. sensorial perceptions) and "pleasure, pains" and so on (i.e. emotions) (156b3–4).

A few lines later, Socrates explains how things, in the context of this theory of perception, stop being ontologically indeterminate and become determinate (e.g. coloured) for a perceiver: a stone does not possess the whiteness in itself but it becomes white once the perceiver and the perceived thing have come across each other so that the perception eventually arises (156c6–157a5). It is clear that in this picture there is no room at all for perceptual error: the perceiver is unmistakably aware that the stone is white for her. As Socrates has put it earlier when commenting on Protagoras' relativism, "perception is always of what is, and free from falsehood, and it is knowledge" (152c5–6). This is a reason why the subtler thinkers may have been the disciples of Protagoras: they restate the kind of incorrigibility his relativism attaches to the perceptions of the individual.

For the subtler thinkers, things are ontologically indeterminate prior to perception. By suggesting a linkage with the initial formulation of Protagoras' Secret Doctrine, Socrates highlights that indeterminacy – on the basis of which "nothing is one thing just by itself, but things are always coming to be for someone" (157a8–157b1) – is an essential philosophical element in the subtler thinkers' theory of perception. In light of this, the verb "to be" has to be abolished, as "those wise people say" (157b3–4). A whole range of new expressions need to be coined. Such new expressions include: "coming to be", "undergoing production", "ceasing to be", "altering", in place of "something", "someone's", "my", "this" (157b4–7). Even the relation of simple denotation is at risk. "Stone" or "man" is a convention we stipulate for the words to be meaningful, but there is nothing out there in the world, such as a man or a stone. We had better describe things in the world as simply aggregates or collections (*hathroisma*) of parts (157b9–c2).[8]

The whole point about the need for a new language is that, in place of a metaphysics of objects, in the theory of perception endorsed by the subtler thinkers there is a metaphysics of processes. This kind of metaphysics is the only one that is able to make good sense of the kind of indeterminacy that is at the root of the subtler thinkers' theory. The only way things can display a certain onto-logical feature (i.e. being white) and come out from their intrinsic indeterminacy is by coming into contact with a perceiver at a certain time. But this interaction can only be momentary, since it does not last. It is also private to both the perceived thing and the perceiver (154a2).[9] Since perceivers are many, many are also the ways in which things are perceived. The best way to account for such a vast array of conflicting perceptions is to replace objects with processes. This, however, forces the subtle thinkers endorsing such a replacement to call for a new language. In place of an object-centred language, there has to be a language shaped around processes, where names such as "stone" or "man" are empty terms. They do not really indicate any ontologically stable and determi-nate object out there. Still, we keep those names as a kind of useful convention in the context of a new language centred on processes.

The key ideas in the theory of perception endorsed by the subtle thinkers are, therefore, as follows: (i) everything is (in) movement; (ii) perceptions are incorrigible and private to the single perceiver; and (iii) there is a need for a new language (required by the fact that things are indeterminate). Let us now see whether these key ideas are also present in one of the richest sources on the thought of the Cyrenaics: Sextus Empiricus, *Against the Mathematicians* VII, 191–200.

SEXTUS ON THE CYRENAICS

Sextus' report is placed in the context of his survey into the criterion of truth of the dogmatic philosophers. With regard to the Cyrenaics, Sextus says:

(191) The Cyrenaics hold that affections [*pathē*] are the criteria [of truth] and that they alone are apprehended and are infallible. None of the things that have caused the affections is, on the contrary, apprehensible or infallible. They say that it is possible to state infallibly and truly and firmly and incorrigibly that we are being whitened [*leukainometha*] or sweetened [*glukazometha*]. It is not possible however to say that the thing productive of our affection is white or sweet (192), because one may be disposed whitely even by something that is not-white or may be sweetened by something that is not-sweet.　(*Math.* VII 191–2=T 32)

Several lines later, he adds:

(194) We must therefore say either that the affections are the *phainomena* or that the things productive of the affections are the *phainomena*. If we say that the affections are the *phainomena*, we will have to maintain that all *phainomena* are true and apprehensible. If, on the contrary, we say that the things productive of the affections are the *phainomena*, all *phainomena* will be false and not apprehensible. The affection occurring in us tells us nothing more than itself. If one has to speak but the truth, the affection alone is therefore actually a *phainomenon* for us. What is external [*to d'ektos*] and productive of the affection perhaps is a being, but it is not a *phainomenon* for us. (195) We all are infallible as far as our own affection is concerned; we all are in error about what is out there [*to ektos hupokeimenon*].

(*Math.* VII 194–5=T 33)

Two of the three ideas earlier identified in the theory of perception ascribed to the subtler thinkers of the *Theaetetus* are immediately present in Sextus' account. I refer to (ii) the privacy and incorrigibility of one's own perceptions and (iii) the use of another kind of language, more in accordance with how the world actually is. On (ii), Sextus insists that, for the Cyrenaics, each perception is infallible and incorrigible. Indeed, every affection – *pathos* in canonical Cyrenaic terminology –is incorrigibly private for the perceiver undergoing the affection. Again, as in the *Theaetetus*, the first example Sextus reports is of an affection of white. The expression the Cyrenaics were reported to use is "to be whitened".

With the expression "I am being whitened", the Cyrenaics invented a neologism for capturing the philosophical innovation that was already present in the theory of perception ascribed by Plato to the subtler thinkers in the *Theaetetus*. In the latter theory much emphasis is put both on the movement that makes every perceptual act so momentary and on the dissolution of reality into an indeterminate substratum, where processes replace objects. The tense of the expression "I am being whitened" may refer to the instantaneousness of the perceptual act: every perception (by using the term employed in the *Theaetetus*), or affection (to use the canonical term referred to by Sextus) is limited to the very moment when it occurs. Second, and most crucially, the expression "I am being whitened" avoids any reference to the (reality of the) objects causing the perception or affection. Despite the fact that Sextus often uses sceptical terms to characterize Cyrenaic views, he also describes the objects as "causing" the affections. In short, I believe that he is just plainly expounding the doctrines of the Cyrenaics by adopting the distinction between appearance and reality. The Cyrenaics may have indeed adopted the same distinction (which was central throughout Greek philosophy), but they ended up with a quite new approach to reality. If it is true – as the subtler thinkers tell us – that the world is utterly indeterminate and that we are equipped exclusively with a metaphysics of processes, not of objects, the best way to explain this philosophically would be by using an expression that avoids any reference to objects.[10]

The need to avoid any reference to objects appears to be lurking behind the Cyrenaic view about the conventionality of language, which Sextus briefly reports. Since we all are infallible in our affections, but we all make mistakes about the real nature of the object causing the affections, the Cyrenaics say that:

> No criterion is common to human beings, common names are assigned to objects [onomata de koina tithesthai tois chrēmasin]. (196) All in common in fact call something white or sweet [leukon men gar ti kai gluku kalousi koinōs pantes], but they do not have something common that is white or sweet [koinon de ti leukon ē gluku ouk echousin]. Each human being is aware of his own private affection. One cannot say, however, whether this affection occurs in oneself and in one's neighbour from a white object.
>
> (Math. 195–6=T 34)

According to Cyrenaic epistemology, we are incorrigibly aware of our own affections, but we can never know whether the object we perceive as white is white in itself. Nor can we know whether another person perceives the object as white. We do not have any common affection or a common world of objects from which our affections arise. If we had that one world, our affections could still be private to us, but we could compare them with those of others on the basis of an objectively shared element. Since we do not share any common world or have common affections to be felt at the same time and under the same circumstances, we have to revert to common names, to be assigned to those qualities, such as white or sweet, which we all, as human beings, experience, although with reference to different objects and in different circumstances.

Other important analogies can again be drawn, in this respect, with the *Theaetetus*. Socrates says there with reference to the theory of the subtler thinkers that "nothing is one thing just by itself, but things are always coming to be for someone" (*Tht.* 157a8–157b1). Socrates also remarks that, according to this theory, we had better not speak of things, such as stones or men. There is really nothing in the world out there as such (what we term "man" or "stone" are aggregates of parts emerging, so to speak, from perceptual processes) (157b9–c2). On the same lines, in his report Sextus points out that, in the Cyrenaic view, "what is external and productive of the affection perhaps is a being, but it is not a *phainomenon* for us" (*Math.* VII 194). On the basis of this, the Cyrenaics may have maintained that there is something out there, but that this is not a being and is no more than an indeterminate *hupokeimenon*. This *substratum*, however, is not, on this view, either discrete or made up of objects perfectly identifiable by their essence (in the strong sense intended by, for instance, Aristotle). There is no essence there to be grasped. That is why it makes no sense to say "I perceive the stone as white". It makes much better sense to say "I am being whitened", when I happen to see what we – rather conventionally – call a stone. In the *Theaetetus*, the subtler thinkers are still referring to objects, although their theory implies that there are none, and although they are also made to invoke the invention of a new language, which replaces the language of being with that of becoming and which avoids direct reference to objects as determinate entities. Despite the way Sextus presents the position, the later Cyrenaics, and not Aristippus and his early followers, are likely to have been responsible for the invention of a new language, expressing both the indeterminacy of things and the privacy of the individual's affections. Both views, however, were already at the kernel of the Cyrenaic thinking of the origins.

THE ANONYMOUS COMMENTATOR

Further evidence that the Cyrenaics are likely to have grounded their epistemological subjectivism on the metaphysical view that reality is indeterminate is provided by an important source on Cyrenaic doctrines (and on Plato's *Theaetetus*): the anonymous commentary on the *Theaetetus*. The anonymous commentator glosses the text of the *Theaetetus* line by line. In doing so, he comments on the doctrines that are being discussed by Plato, thus drawing conceptual connections between those doctrines and the views of other philosophers he reports. For our own purposes here, let us concentrate on the comment at col. LXV, 19–35, where the commentator scrutinizes *Theaetetus* 152b5–6. These are the lines where Socrates, to express the real significance of the relativism endorsed by Protagoras' maxim, makes the example of the blowing wind (152b1–3, col. LXIV, 21; LXV, 14): if the same wind is blowing, will one feel it as cold, the other as not-cold? Or, will one of us feel it intensively cold, the other just a little? Socrates goes on by asking whether "the wind in itself is said to be cold or not-cold" (152b5–6). Here is the commentary on this line:

> Something is the agent [*to poiēsan*], something else is the patient [*to paschon*]. But, if people undergo affections that are opposed to the thing in itself, they will agree that the intrinsic feature of the agent is not defined [*mē einai hōrismenēn tēn tou poiēsantos idiotēta*]; if it were so, the same thing at the same time will not produce different affections. Because of this, the Cyrenaics say that only affections are apprehensible, while external things are not. That I am being burnt – they say – I apprehend; that the fire is such as to burn is obscure. If it were such, all things will be burnt by it. (col. LXV, 19–35=T 1)

The commentary is interesting for two reasons. First, it explicitly connects the initial discussion of Protagoras' relativism with the theory of perception endorsed by the subtler thinkers and, more crucially, with the Cyrenaics. The linkage between Protagoras' relativism and the theory of the subtler thinkers is provided by the terms used in commenting on the ontological status of the perceived wind. The anonymous commentator says that the agent (the active element; *to poiesan*) and the patient (the passive element; *to paschon*) are different. These two terms are the key words in the theory of perception of the subtler thinkers, as illustrated at length at *Theaetetus* 156a–157c. The basic ingredients of such a theory, in fact, are the passive and active elements that, in the perennial change and flux in which they are immerged, interact one with the other, thus producing both the whiteness and the corresponding (and symmetrical) sensation of white in the perceiver.[11] On the other hand, the linkage between Protagoras' relativism/the theory of perception of the subtler thinkers and the Cyrenaics is openly established in the commentary on *Theaetetus* 152b5–6, where the anonymous commentator explicitly compares, using the example of the burning fire, the epistemology and the metaphysics that are endorsed by Protagoras and by the theory of the subtler thinkers with those endorsed by the Cyrenaics. By providing these linkages, the commentator therefore recognizes that there is a close conceptual affinity between the perceptual theory of the subtler thinkers and the Cyrenaics.

A second reason why the commentary is important is that it clearly explains the Cyrenaic view about knowledge with reference to the metaphysical view that objects in the world are ontologically indeterminate. When he comments on *Theaetetus* 152b5–6 by suggesting a linkage with the active and passive elements that are so central in the subtler thinkers' theory of perception at *Theaetetus* 156a–157c, the anonymous commentator remarks that, by being affected by the same object in different ways, it has to follow that "the intrinsic feature of the agent is not defined". Objects are not ontologically determinate in their structures, since the object (i.e. the wind in Socrates' example at *Tht.* 152b1–7) may appear cold to someone and not-cold to someone else. The wind in itself is neither cold nor not-cold. It is simply neutral, that is, it does not possess any ontological feature of its own. "Because of this, the Cyrenaics say that only affections are apprehensible, while external things are not. That I am being burnt – they say – I apprehend; that the fire is such as to burn is obscure. If it were

61

such, all things will be burnt by it." According to this explanation, the Cyrenaic view that affections alone are apprehensible relies on external objects in the world being inapprehensible because of their ontological indeterminacy. The fire in itself is not caustic because, if it were so, everybody would be burnt by it. The anonymous commentary on which we have been focusing so far thus confirms the commitment to indeterminacy that seems to be lurking behind Cyrenaic epistemology as depicted by Sextus' passages and as already noted in Plato's *Theaetetus*.

The last element present in the theory of the subtler thinkers worth investigating is (i) the idea that everything is (in) movement. From the intercourse of the two kinds of movement, active and passive, there come to be twin offspring: the perceptions and the corresponding perceived objects. These perceptions have such names as hearings, seeings, pleasures and pains (*Tht.* 156b4–6). Perceptions are seen as the results of movement and as movement themselves, being they themselves subject – as any other thing is – to the law that everything is movement. The reference to pleasures and pains is, in this context, particularly illuminating. Before the subtler thinkers' theory in the *Theaetetus*, there had been no reference at all to pleasures and pains as kinds of perception. Why does Plato now present pleasure and pains, quite naturally, as perceptions? The answer may be that, by including pleasures and pains in the category of perceptions, he is here signalling (albeit indirectly) his reference to the Cyrenaics.

One of the fundamental tenets of the Cyrenaic philosophy is that there are two main ethical affections: pleasure and pain. These affections are best interpreted as movements. As Diogenes puts it, "The philosophers who followed the teaching of Aristippus and were called Cyrenaics had the following beliefs. There are two affections [*pathē*], pain and pleasure, pleasure being a smooth motion [*leia kinēsis*] and pain a rough motion [*tracheia kinēsis*]" (DL II 86). If this is the case, we will find a striking resemblance between the concepts of pleasure and pain as defined by the Cyrenaics and what the subtler thinkers of the *Theaetetus* hold about perceptions, including those – such as pleasure and pain – that are not mentioned in that dialogue until the subtler thinkers' theory of perception. In both cases, pleasure and pain (and all other perceptions) are best understood as (the results of) movements. The analogies between the ideas around which the subtler thinkers' theory in the *Theaetetus* is constructed and the ideas we recognize as authentically Cyrenaic are so many that it may hardly be a case of superficial coincidence.

THE WOODEN HORSE

A serious case has now been made to identify the subtler thinkers of *Theaetetus* 156a3 with Aristippus and the early Cyrenaics. In the *Theaetetus* Plato cannot name the Cyrenaics directly as the more sophisticated propounders of the philosophical theory of perception originally set out by Protagoras because, at the time the dialogue is ideally imagined to be set (399 BCE), Aristippus and his early followers had not already elaborated their doctrines. Yet, the identification between the subtler thinkers and the early Cyrenaics does not only help us to understand the philosophical content and implications of the theory of perception ascribed to the former in the *Theaetetus* by highlighting conceptual affinities with later reports on Cyrenaic epistemology, such as that by Sextus. This identification is, I believe, crucial for understanding Plato's final critique of the thesis that perception is knowledge (*Tht.* 184b–186e). I claim that the critique is directed against the theory of perception endorsed by the subtler thinkers. If my hypothesis about the identity of the subtler thinkers is correct, that critique will be profitably read against a theory of perception of Cyrenaic inspiration.

Almost at the end of his lengthy treatment of Protagoras, Heraclitus and the subtler thinkers, after having dealt with the refutation of the view that all is movement (179d–183b), Socrates puts forward his final argument against the identification of knowledge with perception (184b–186e). Very briefly, the argument goes like this. We perceive a thing as white by means of our sense organs. By means of these sense organs we are, however, unable to say whether the object we see as white is identical to something else, whether it is really something, or whether it is similar to something else. In short, by means of the sense organs, we are unable even to conceive of "being and not being, likeness and unlikeness, the same and different" (185c9–10). As Theaetetus puts it, "the mind itself [*autē psuchē*], by means of itself [*di'hautēs*], considers the things which apply in common to everything" (185e1–2). There is a clear distinction, Socrates adds, between, on the one hand, perceptions and, on the other, the cognitive operations the mind makes by itself. Truth and being can be grasped by the mind and not by the senses (186c1–10). Since the operations the mind makes by itself in its search for truth and being cannot be performed by simple perceptions, the latter has no share in the grasping of being and, hence, it has no share in the grasping of truth either. It therefore cannot be knowledge.

What is at the root of this epistemological picture is the organizing activity the mind has to perform to account for those properties that are not perceptible, such as identity and similarity. More crucially for us, the mind itself is responsible, on Plato's account, for organizing the various pieces of information that perception, through our sense organs, provide us with. For these purposes, perceptions have to be conceptualized. He eloquently condenses his view in the metaphor of the wooden horse:

It would be surely strange if we had several perceptions sitting inside us [*ei pollai tines en hēmin aisthēseis enkathēntai*], as if in wooden horses [*hōsper en doureiois hippois*], and it wasn't the case that all those perceptions converged on some one kind of thing, a mind or whatever one ought to call it: something with which we perceive the perceptible things by means of the senses, as if by means of instruments. (184d1–5)

As the scholiast witnesses, in this passage Plato refers to the well-known wooden horse of Troy; no Greek would have misunderstood the reference.[12] It is clear that by employing this metaphor Plato is not only putting forward his view about the relationship between perceptions and the mind, but is also indirectly criticizing the alternative view that does not properly recognize the fundamental activity of the mind in the cognitive process. If we do not recognize the organizing activity of the mind, we would conceive of ourselves as kinds of wooden horses, with a plurality of perceptions sitting inside us, with no organizing centre. Plato suggests that in this case these perceptions would be deceiving perceptions, as the wooden horse of Troy was deceiving for the Trojans. Perceptions' being deceitful does not consist in their being false perceptions, but in their being uni-sensorial perceptions, namely isolated perceptions that simply register an affection of the body, without being able to interact epistemologically with other similar perceptions. On this view, perception is simply a unidimensional affection of the body, through the solicitation of the appropriate sense organ. On the basis of this picture it can hardly be denied that the affection someone undergoes is true. Yet, on Plato's view, an affection is deceiving in so far as it partially focuses on just one perceptual property of the object. We can see a stone as white; we can sense a stone as hard, but there is no way, according to this theory, to put these two isolated affections into the same epistemological picture (see *Tht.* 185a1–6).

In two other passages Socrates highlights again the epistemological gap between mind and perceptions. "There are some things that both men and animals are able to perceive by nature from the moment they are born: namely all those affections [*pathēmata*] that, by means of the body, converge on the mind" (186b12–c1). A few lines later he goes back to the point: "Knowledge is located not in our affections [*en tois pathēmasin*], but in our reasoning upon these" (186d2–5). In these passages, the term Plato uses to refer to the simple alteration of the body in the perceptual process is, strikingly enough, *pathos* (affection), and not the more common *aisthēsis*, with which he has so far indicated the sensations throughout the *Theaetetus*. In two other passages of the *Theaetetus* Plato uses *pathos* when he refers to perceptions and memory. The first occurrence is at 179c3, where Socrates says, "if we focus on the momentary affection each of us has [*peri de to paron hekastoi pathos*], from which there come to be his perceptions and the judgements which conform to them – well, it is harder to refute these latter as not being true" (179c2–4).

In another passage Protagoras is made to ask whether it is possible that "a man's present memory of an affection [*pathos*] which he has experienced in the past but is no longer experiencing is the same sort of affection as he then had" (166b2–4). In the latter passage, the point Socrates raises forms part of an argument designed to show how teaching will not be possible if one is incorrigibly correct in one's affections (this is seen as one of the main upshots of the subtler thinkers' theory of perception; see 161b–162a). The relationship between the affection and its memory is the kernel of the passage. Socrates denies the possibility that the *memory* of the affection is the *same* affection as was earlier experienced. This point sounds undoubtedly Cyrenaic: Aristippus famously denied any value to the memory of past pleasures on the basis of the argument that what counts is the pleasurable affection of the moment (however long this may be) and that we cannot recreate the affection of past pleasures as this was originally experienced (see Ath. *Deipnosophists* XII 544a–b [=*SSR* IV A 174]).

The analogies between some of the views presented and criticized at *Theaetetus* 184b–186e and other sources on Cyrenaic thinking, together with the use of the key term *pathos* in the wooden horse section (in place of the more common *aisthēsis*), may once again point us towards the identification between the subtler thinkers and the early Cyrenaics that I have been defending so far. In his critique of the thesis that perception is knowledge, Plato is, on my interpretation, in effect arguing specifically against a position stated and defended earlier in the dialogue (at 156a1–157c3), namely, the full-scale identification of perception and knowledge. This section is, without doubt, the one where the subtler thinkers, namely the frontrunners of perceptual subjectivism and relativism in Plato's time, propose their theory of perception. In showing the unavoidable role of the mind in cognitive processes (including perceptual processes) at *Theaetetus* 184b–186e, Plato is at the same time showing the main fault in the account of perception he has so far been confronting.

On this account, namely that defended by the subtler thinkers at 156a–157c3, a perception is simply an affection. We can grant to such affections (to use the term recurring in 184b–186e) or perceptions (to use the term Plato employs at 156b–157c) their incorrigibility and we cannot properly say that they are false. Yet, these affections and perceptions are unable to tell us anything about those properties (such as identity, similarity, being etc.) that only the mind is able to grasp. Even worse, on the basis of Plato's argument, affections and perceptions, so Cyrenaically conceived, are uni-sensorial events, with no residual capacity to be elaborated into a perceptual picture that pulls together the unidimensional information provided by the different sense organs into a coherent whole.

THE SIEGE

I now move on to the final argument to show that there are good chances that the subtler thinkers of the *Theaetetus* are Aristippus and the early Cyrenaics. That Plato's main target in the wooden horse section of the *Theaetetus* is the Cyrenaic account of affection – ascribed to the subtler thinkers earlier in the dialogue (156b1–157c3) – is clear also from two other main sources on Cyrenaic thought: Aristocles, *On Philosophy*, and Colotes' account of Cyrenaic epistemology, as preserved by Plutarch *Adv. Col.* 1120d–1121e.

67

In his critique of Cyrenaic epistemology, Aristocles first takes aim against the idea, which forms part of the subtler thinkers' theory of perception, that subjects and objects of perception do not exist independently of each other, by remarking in Aristotelian fashion:

> Three things must necessarily exist at the same time: the affection itself [*to te pathos auto*], what causes it [*to poioun*], and what undergoes it [*to paschon*]. The person who apprehends the affection must necessarily perceive also what undergoes it. It cannot be the case that, if someone is for example warm, one will know that one is being warmed without knowing whether it is himself or a neighbour, now or last year, in Athens or Egypt, someone alive or dead, a man or a stone.
>
> (F5 Chiesara=Euseb. *Praep evang.* 14.19.3–4=T 6)[13]

Second, he adduces an argument about the self-consciousness of affections that is very close to Plato's argument in the wooden horse metaphor. Aristocles asks:

> How will the man undergoing the affection be able to tell that this is pleasure and that pain? Or that one is affected, when one is tasting or seeing, or hearing? Or that one is tasting with his tongue, seeing with his eyes and hearing with his ears?
>
> (F5 Chiesara=Euseb. *Praep evang.* 14.19.5=T 7)

With such questions, Aristocles suggests that simple (Cyrenaic) affections are impossible to have without a proper organ that is ultimately responsible for organizing the data provided by the sense organs.[14] This is Plato's main point in the critique he advances in the wooden horse section of the *Theaetetus* against the thesis that knowledge is perception. In short, in the passages just quoted Aristocles formulates two arguments: the first is about the absolutely symmetrical existence of the perceived object and the percipient subject, while the second is about the proper role of the organizing mind in the perceptual process. In providing two counter-arguments readable as directed against two arguments developed at *Theaetetus* 156b–157c and 184b–e, Aristocles appears to be confirming the philosophical linkage between those passage of the dialogue, passages on which we have been concentrating and which, even on Aristocles' reading, expound Cyrenaic views.

A last passage strengthening the suggestion that in *Theaetetus* 184b–186e Plato is, among other things, elaborating his critique of a Cyrenaic theory of perception comes from the earliest source on the thought of the Cyrenaics, namely the account of the Epicurean Colotes, as preserved by Plutarch. Plutarch reports Colotes' view on the epistemology of the Cyrenaics:

> [The Cyrenaics], placing all affections and all sense-impressions in themselves, believed that the evidence coming from them was not enough, as far as assertions on external objects are concerned. Distancing themselves from external objects, they shut themselves up within their affections as in a siege [*en poliorkiai*]. In doing so, they adopted the locution "it appears" but refused to say in addition that "it is" with regard to external objects.
>
> (*Adv. Col.* 1120d=T 16)

Colotes is here made to report the kernel of Cyrenaic epistemology: only affections are knowable, and incorrigibly true. What is striking, however, is how he describes such an epistemological view. The Cyrenaics are said to "shut themselves up within their affections as in a siege". This undoubtedly reminds us of Plato's wooden horse, which, in turn, would have reminded any Greek, including Colotes, of the siege *par excellence* in Greek legend: that of Troy. I suspect that what is at the back of Colotes' image of the siege is, in fact, Plato's wooden horse metaphor.

In that metaphor, Plato speaks of a plurality of perceptions sitting inside us as if in wooden horses. In using this metaphor, I have claimed, he implies that perceptions are deceitful in so far as they are partial and need to be further elaborated by the mind. These deceiving perceptions are the same kind of affections Colotes speaks of in the passage just reported. By exclusively accepting the evidence provided by the affections of the individual and by refusing to make any statement about how the world out there really is, the Cyrenaics, Colotes argues, are deceived by themselves in so far as they believe as incorrigibly true what they sense. These affections are deceitful, since they do not say anything about the real objects (and their actual properties) causing the affections. The best image able to capture this state is that of a siege. The metaphor of the siege is as evocative as the wooden horse image. Colotes' metaphor draws inspiration from Plato's metaphor and points in the same direction. In both cases, ultimate responsibility for the deceit lies in the perceiving subject adopting a Cyrenaic epistemology. This is plainly evident in the passage by Colotes and in the *Theaetetus* passage (184d1–5). By comparing individuals to Trojan wooden horses, Plato makes clear that the siege for the (Cyrenaic) individual is brought by the individual himself.

If the metaphor of the siege takes its inspiration from the metaphor of the wooden horse, it is also reasonable to say that the earliest source on Cyrenaic doctrines, namely Colotes, understands the critique Plato elaborates at *Theaetetus* 184b–186e as directed against the Cyrenaics. If this is so, we shall be in a better position than earlier to understand more fully the thread of critical arguments Plato advances against perception at *Theaetetus* 184b–186e. More particularly, we shall be in a better position to grasp how these arguments are targeted against a model of perceptual knowledge that Plato has depicted vividly in a preceding section of the dialogue, namely at 156a–157e, where the subtler thinkers make their appearance on the scene.

In this chapter I have constructed the best possible case to show that the subtler thinkers of the *Theaetetus* are likely to be Aristippus and the early Cyrenaics. I have done so by sketching an interpretation of Plato's *Theaetetus* that may be congenial for the identification provided between *hoi kompsoteroi* and the Cyrenaics. In providing reasons for showing that the subtler thinkers are likely to be Aristippus and the early Cyrenaics, I have likened the doctrinal views, around which *hoi kompsoteroi* construct their perceptual theory, with other important sources on Cyrenaic thinking (i.e. Sextus, the anonymous commentator, Colotes in Plutarch's account and Aristocles). The comparison has produced striking similarities between the philosophical doctrines attributed to the Cyrenaics in those sources and the doctrines ascribed to the subtler thinkers in Plato's *Theaetetus*. The reasons for believing that the subtler thinkers are Aristippus and the early Cyrenaics are now stronger than the antithetic reasons for believing that they are not. I am sure some scholars are left unconvinced by my attempt, but, for the time being and while awaiting further reasons against the identification I have proposed, the picture of Aristippus as the founder and the leading figure of the Cyrenaic school has been reinforced by Plato's testimony.

II
PHILOSOPHY

4

INDETERMINACY

In this chapter, we start off by focusing on Cyrenaic metaphysics: a quite unfashionable topic to address because the general view among scholars is that the Cyrenaics had no real interest in metaphysics. The Cyrenaics are traditionally believed to concentrate only on ethics, leaving aside, if not rejecting, the other branches of philosophy. This view rests on a misunderstanding of two passages by Sextus and Seneca (Sext. Emp. *Math.* VII 11 and 15 [=*SSR* IV A 168=T 31]; Sen. *Ep. ad Lucilium* XIV 1, 12 [=*SSR* IV A 165]). In those passages Sextus and Seneca explain that the Cyrenaics only *apparently* adopted a moral approach to philosophy. They effectively reintroduced those branches of philosophy (such as logic, the study of nature and of the causes [=metaphysics], and the study of affections [=epistemology]) that they seem to have rejected by dividing their moral philosophy into these sub-branches.

One may add that Aristotle is historically responsible for the invention of metaphysics as a proper branch of philosophy in the middle of the fourth century BCE, that is, at the time when the Cyrenaics were flourishing. The focus on metaphysics as a proper branch of philosophy is something that only Hellenistic philosophers could have witnessed. It would be inappropriate to say that Plato, Protagoras, Democritus and the Socratic schools had no interest in metaphysics and did not elaborate any metaphysical views. It is safer to recognize that Greek philosophers before and coeval with Aristotle had a wide interest in metaphysics, some of them, like Plato, displaying a powerful ontology, and others being less incisive than Plato but with an ongoing interest in metaphysics. The Cyrenaics are no exception to that. I do not mean to say that the Cyrenaics spent most of their philosophical activity in dealing with metaphysical issues. What I claim is that Cyrenaic philosophy is compatible with a metaphysics of indeterminacy. If it were so, the Cyrenaics would belong to a line of metaphysical thought that, beginning with Protagoras (and Democritus), goes all the way down to Pyrrho, and even later.

A correct reconstruction of Cyrenaic metaphysics will help us to understand the proper meaning of the subjectivist theory of knowledge and language endorsed by the Cyrenaics by rooting it into a peculiar kind of metaphysics. That is why we begin our enquiry into Cyrenaic philosophy by asking what kind of metaphysics the Cyrenaics are likely to have adopted.

IDEALISM

We have already briefly referred to the main tenet of Cyrenaic epistemology: only our affections are knowable to us. This view can be found in many classical sources on Cyrenaic epistemology: Sextus, Cicero, Aristocles, Diogenes Laertius, Colotes in Plutarch and the anonymous commentator of the *Theaetetus*. In Diogenes, it is said, "they [the Cyrenaics] say that affections are apprehensible, not the things from which they originate [*ta pathē katalēpta: elegon oun auta, ouk aph'hōn ginetai*]" (DL II 92); Sextus rephrases the same view when he says, "only affections are apprehended [*mona ta pathē katalambanesthai*]" (*Math.* VII 191). The anonymous commentator on the *Theaetetus* expounds the same doctrine when he says, "only affections are apprehensible [*mona ta pathē katalēpta*]" (col. LXV, 30). A slightly different version of the same doctrine is attested by Aristocles: "we have

76

INDETERMINACY

perception of our affections alone [*tōn patōn monōn hēmas tēn aisthēsin echein*]" (F5 Chiesara=Euseb. *Praep. evang.* 14.18.32). In the Cyrenaic world, human beings are directly aware of their affections, which, in turn, are the only and infallible source of knowledge. What is, however, the relation between affections and the world? Are these affections totally independent of the world, so that we may postulate that the Cyrenaics are the first idealists in the history of philosophy? One possible interpretation of Cyrenaic epistemology could be that, since we know only our internal states, these are ultimately responsible for the ways we conceive of the world. In short, is the Cyrenaic world a construction of the mind, as idealists of all times and ages have maintained? Myles Burnyeat has claimed that idealism is the only philosophical thesis foreign to Greek thought. He writes:

All these philosophers [Protagoras, Democritus, the Cyrenaics], however radical their scrutiny of ordinary belief, leave untouched – indeed they rely upon – the notion that we are deceived or ignorant about something. There is a reality of some sort confronting us; we are in touch with something, even if this something, reality, is not at all what we think it to be. (1982: 32)

Is Burnyeat right in maintaining that idealism is foreign to Greek philosophy as a whole and that the Cyrenaics are no exception to that? My answer is twofold. The ultimate answer to this question is, I believe, yes: idealism as such is foreign to Greek philosophy. But the counter-evidence for the opposite thesis, at least as far as the Cyrenaics are concerned, has not been studied with the accuracy it deserves. There are ancient sources that appear to be effectively hinting at the Cyrenaics as actually putting in serious doubt the existence of the world out there.

More importantly, there is a distinction between idealism and indeterminacy that has not been seriously observed, even in the latest attempts to deal with the problem of Cyrenaic subjectivity.[1]

Idealism is, roughly, the view that, in an essential sense, reality is our mental construction. Indeterminacy, by converse, is a metaphysical view, not at all idealist, on whose basis reality is not a construction of the human mind, since there is actually and really something out there, independent of us for its own existence. But – the argument of indeterminacy goes – although there is a real world out there independent of us, reality is inextricably indeterminate in so far as it does not possess any ontological feature of its own. The advocate of indeterminacy is not an idealist, but she is someone who seriously jeopardizes the common-sense view of world and reality by challenging the metaphysical foundations of that view. What I ultimately wish to suggest is that the Cyrenaics, together with other important Greek thinkers historically close to them such as Protagoras and Pyrrho, are not idealist but adherents of indeterminacy.

Some sources are susceptible to being interpreted as suggesting that either the Cyrenaics really put the existence of the material world under serious threat or that they conceived of that world as the product of our mental construction. On the other hand, other sources may well allow the interpretation that the Cyrenaics did not really question the existence of the material world, but that they conceived of it as an indeterminate substratum, made up of no discrete and distinct objects. In this latter case, no idealism is presupposed. If the world is an indeterminate substratum, we shall be still confronted with "something" that, despite its indeterminacy, is independent of us and of our mental constructions. On the basis of this view, the world is really out there but it is ontologically indistinct and indeterminate. Let us now review the sources dealing with Cyrenaic metaphysics by starting with those that seem to allow the Cyrenaics to be endorsing a form of idealism.

THE CYRENAICS AS IDEALISTS

Three sources are important for someone wishing to make the case for the Cyrenaics being idealists: two passages from Sextus (*Math.* VII 193–4; VI 53) and one from Augustine (*C. acad.* III 11.26). Sextus' first passage goes like this: "If one has to speak but the truth, the affection alone is therefore actually a *phainomenon* for us. What is external and productive of the affection perhaps is a being, but it is not a *phainomenon* for us" (*Math.* VII 194=T 33). At first sight, this passage may indeed be understood as questioning the actual existence of the material world. What is real for us is the affection we have, but what produces the affection (namely the objects in the world) perhaps is there and exists but it could not be real for us. What produces the affection is not real for us in so far as its existence derives from our grasping it and thinking of it in the way we actually do. In this case, the world would really be existent in so far as we conceive of it: and this is surely idealism. Looking more closely, however, one may wonder whether Sextus is not just making a sort of dialectical concession in the context of his argument about Cyrenaic epistemology when he says that what is external is perhaps a being.

Initially Sextus states the kernel of the theory of knowledge endorsed by the Cyrenaics when he says:

> They say that it is possible to state infallibly and truly and firmly and incorrigibly that we are being whitened or sweetened. It is not possible however to say that the thing productive of our affection is white or sweet, because one may be disposed whitely even by something that is not-white or may be sweetened by something that is not-sweet.
>
> (*Math.* VII 191–2=T 32)

To corroborate the Cyrenaic argument about the incorrigibility of one's affections, Sextus puts forward the argument about madness and altered perceptions that Plato himself has used in the section of the *Theaetetus* where the subtler thinkers are the protagonists (*Tht.* 158a–e).[2] The argument in Sextus' version is as follows. Just as the sufferer from vertigo or jaundice is stirred by everything yellowly and the one suffering from ophthalmia by everything redly and the madman sees Thebes as if it were double, "in all these cases, it is true that people undergo a particular affection, for instance that they are being yellowed or reddened or doubled, but it is false that the thing which stirred them is itself yellow, or red or double" (*Math.* VII 192–3).

Sextus concludes this argument by pointing out that "it is very plausible for us to assume that one can grasp nothing but one's own affections". If one must speak only the truth, Sextus says, "the affection alone is therefore actually a *phainomenon* for us. What is external and productive of the affection perhaps is a being, but it is not a *phainomenon* for us" (VII 194). After making the examples of the madman and of those undergoing altered perceptions, Sextus makes the dialectical concession, for the sake of argument, that in those cases one may indeed wonder whether what is external and productive of the affection is really existent. "Perhaps it will be not", Sextus rhetorically answers, if one considers the cases just listed, where it is hard to deny the incorrigibility of the altered affections undergone by the sufferer from jaundice or opthalmia. On the contrary, what one can deny is that what has caused those affections of yellow or of red is really yellow or red. In those cases, one may be allowed to wonder whether what has caused the affection of yellow in the sufferer from jaundice really exists.

Sextus' first passage does not appear to offer, therefore, a valid argument for attributing to the Cyrenaics the idealist view that the existence of the external world is dependent on its being perceived by us. Let us see whether the passage by Augustine scores any better for those arguing that the Cyrenaics are idealists. The passage is usually taken, on a standard interpretation, to anticipate Descartes' suspicion about the existence of anything external to the mind.[3] The passage goes like this:

Someone when he is tasting something, can swear with good faith that he knows through his own palate that what he is tasting is sweet, or the contrary. He cannot be brought away from that knowledge by any Greek trickery. Who could in fact be so shameless as to ask when I am licking something with delight: "Maybe you are not tasting, but this is a dream"? Do I resist? That will delight me even if I happen to be asleep. No likeness of false things can confuse what I said to know. An Epicurean philosopher or the Cyrenaics may perhaps say many other things in favour of the senses, against which I have remarked that nothing was said by the Academics.   (*C. acad.* III 11.26 [=*SSR* IV A 210]=T 9)

This passage does not really put forward any view that sounds Cartesian at its core. Even less does the passage suggest that the Cyrenaics were doubtful about the real existence of the external world. As far as I can understand it, Augustine's passage tells us that, even when I am sleep, I am infallible in my affections (in the case Augustine reports, we would feel an affection of delight even if we were asleep). It is exactly this view about infallible affections that Augustine appears to be ascribing to the Cyrenaics. Since one's affections are infallible even when one is asleep, and since one expresses those affections with I-sentences – namely sentences reporting one's affection, like the Cyrenaic "I am whitened" – this is enough for Augustine to express the infallibility and incorrigibility of I-sentences reporting I-affections. Accordingly we do not need any further argument by Epicurus and the Cyrenaics in favour of perceptual infallibility and incorrigibility. In short, on my interpretation, the core of Augustine's argument in the passage reported here is another version of the argument about altered affections Sextus puts forward at *Math.* VII 192–3. Whereas in Sextus we are faced with sufferers of jaundice, ophthalmia and madmen, in Augustine we are confronted with the case of someone who is asleep.

The third passage that may point towards a possible idealist commitment of the Cyrenaics is again a passage by Sextus. The passage in question is as follows:

> Cyrenaic philosophers hold that affections alone exist and nothing else. Since it is not an affection but rather it is something capable of producing an affection, sound is not one of the things that exist [mē gignesthai tōn huparktōn]. By denying the existence of every sensory object [aisthēton], the schools of Democritus and Plato deny the existence of sound as well, for sound is a sensory object.
>
> (Math. VI 53=T 36)

The first sentence – "Cyrenaic philosophers hold that affections alone exist and nothing else" – is a rather peremptory statement about the exclusive existence of affections. One may guess that what is not an affection, namely the external world, is not, strictly speaking, existent. By granting existence to affections alone, the Cyrenaics, one may assume, postulate an ontological dependence of the world from us and from our affections. This impression, however, can be rapidly removed once one has gone on reading the whole of Sextus' passage. In the second sentence, we are in fact confronted with the usual dichotomy between, on the one hand, what is external and productive of the affections and, on the other, the affections themselves.

We saw in Math. VII 194 that the existence of the material world is not put under serious doubts by the Cyrenaics, at least on the basis of the interpretation of that passage I have argued for. The sentence about what "is perhaps a being" has been understood as a dialectical concession in the context of the whole argument about altered affections that Sextus developed at VII 192–3. In the same way, I believe that the peremptory remark about the exclusive existence of the affections for the Cyrenaics we find at the beginning of VI 53 is just a polemical concession Sextus makes in the interest of his own argument, purported to show the absurdity of the view of those who deny the existence of sound. In short, what Sextus does at VI 53 is show that, on the basis of the view some philosophers maintained, the existence of sound could, absurdly, be denied.

An alternative reading of Sextus' passage is available. Sextus' passage about sound ends by relating the view of the Cyrenaics to that of Democritus and Plato: according to Sextus, all these philosophers denied the existence of sensory objects. How are we to interpret the non-existence of sensory objects in Cyrenaic philosophy? Once the idealist interpretation is ruled out, as I have just done, what option will be left for us to interpret the denial of the existence of sensory objects the Cyrenaics appear to have endorsed? My answer here is that that denial points towards indeterminacy and that the Cyrenaics are best understood not as idealists but as philosophers committed to indeterminacy.[4]

INDETERMINACY

One may maintain that sensory objects are not existent either because objects are dependent on us for their existence (as any idealist would say), or because there are indeed no objects *as such* in the world out there. The metaphysical view I take Sextus as ascribing to the Cyrenaics (*Math.* VI 53) is the latter. On the basis of this view, we are effectively confronted with an undifferentiated lump of matter. Although being existent and independent of us for its own existence, this lump of matter is, however, not made up of objects, since these, as such, do not exist in a proper sense. What this metaphysical view asserts is that the world, despite its being independent of us for its existence, is undifferentiated and indeterminate.[5] At first sight indeterminacy seems a quite bizarre view, even a view with little philosophical cogency.[6] It has difficulties and internal problems that cannot be dealt with in the context of this book. For now, it is enough to anticipate that indeterminacy is a metaphysical view shared by some Greek philosophers. Both Plato (in the *Theaetetus*) and Aristotle (in *Metaphysics* Gamma, sections 4–6) have identified indeterminacy as the target of their metaphysical and logical attacks, thus granting to it a philosophical importance that scholars of ancient philosophy have often neglected.

It has been objected that the Cyrenaics cannot be committed to indeterminacy (or, for that matter, they can't hold any metaphysics) because this would be in striking contrast with their claim that human beings know only the way they are affected by things, not things as they actually are. If they held the view that things are indeterminate, the Cyrenaics would actually say something about the nature of things and this would contradict their claim that only affections are knowable. I answer this objection as follows. The statement that things are indeterminate is a very particular statement about the nature of things. To hold that things are indeterminate does not amount to saying that things have a determinate nature, that is, that things are so and so. Indeterminacy is a very special case of determinacy, in so far as indeterminacy is a matter of in-determinacy. So to hold that things are indeterminate is a very special claim about things. This claim cannot be legitimately interpreted as a standard philosophical statement about the essence of objects in the world, such as "Things are always determinately coloured and of a certain shape".

My point is that here we are on the same slippery terrain on which other ancient philosophers, such as Protagoras or the Sceptics, had walked. Protagoras claimed that perceptual truth is relative to each human being. Plato soon objected to the sophist about the epistemological status of Protagoras' statement. Is the statement that truth is relative a statement affirming a universal truth? If it is so, Protagoras' view will be self-refuting. One cannot coherently hold that truth is relative without violating the very claim of relative truth exactly when truth is universally (and objectively) proclaimed to be relative. I have argued elsewhere that a possible way out from the self-refutation problem for Protagoras is to claim a special epistemological status for his own claim that truth is relative.[7] A similar move can be adopted by the Sceptics, when they maintained that we cannot know how things really are but only how they appear to us, a claim that is very similar to that of the Cyrenaics. And ancient sources are keen to group Protagoras' relativism, Cyrenaic subjectivism and ancient scepticism into the same philosophical family (see Cic. *Acad. Pr.* II 46, 142; Euseb. *Praep. evang.* 14.2.4).

I therefore see no inconsistency between the Cyrenaic view that only affections are knowable and the claim that things are indeterminate, once it has been made clear that the latter claim is a very peculiar claim about the (indeterminate) nature of things. Such a claim cannot be legitimately understood as a claim about things being so and so. Rather, it is a claim about a very paradoxical case of determinacy, that is, a case of in-determinacy. Accordingly, the Cyrenaics could well maintain that only affections are knowable because we cannot really know how things are in themselves, that is, if they are really hot, sweet, dark and so on. That is why ancient sources tell us that the Cyrenaics say that we cannot arrive at the very nature of things. This, in turn, is so because there is a further, more fundamental, explanation of this view. We can know only how things affect us and not how things are in themselves, because things are indeterminate, that is, they do not possess any intrinsic and truly determinate feature on their own. In Cyrenaic philosophy, the epistemological view that only affections are knowable is not the unhappy consequence of our epistemological deficiency as human beings, but it is rooted into the metaphysical structure of the world.

In addition, if one still detected an inconsistency between the attribution of indeterminacy to the Cyrenaics and their epistemology, it could be replied that this inconsistency may have belonged to Cyrenaic philosophy as this was historically developed. This does not mean that, because indeterminacy appears (on some disputable grounds) to be inconsistent with Cyrenaic epistemology, the Cyrenaics were not committed to indeterminacy. Protagoras will remain a relativist and a philosopher who defended relativism even if one sees an inconsistency between his claim that truth is relative and his maintaining that truth is universally relative for all human beings.

THE CYRENAICS AND INDETERMINACY I:
THE *THEAETETUS* AGAIN

On the basis of what evidence can indeterminacy be ascribed to the Cyrenaics? Sextus' passage on sound offers the first fragile evidence that the denial of the existence of sensory objects attributed to the Cyrenaics may be interpreted as a metaphysical claim about things being indeterminate. There is further evidence strengthening the view that the Cyrenaics were committed to indeterminacy. I now begin with the weakest textual evidence, and proceed towards the strongest. I will conclude with an argument about a certain development in Greek metaphysics purported to show that the fact that Cyrenaics were committed to indeterminacy is not a mere historical accident, but is rooted in a lively metaphysical tradition of ancient Greece.

The weakest textual evidence comes from Plato's *Theaetetus*. In the preceding chapter, I made the best possible case I could to identify the subtler thinkers of *Theaetetus* 156a3 as Aristippus and the early Cyrenaics. Since the identity of the subtler thinkers is still open to question, the evidence deriving from the *Theaetetus* cannot be conclusively considered unshakable on some aspects and features of Cyrenaic philosophy. Bearing in mind that the identification between the subtler thinkers of the *Theaetetus* and the early Cyrenaics I have provided is likely but not certain, we may, however, maintain that the subtler thinkers' theory of perception offers significant echoes with the passage in Sextus about sounds. According to Sextus, the Cyrenaics denied the existence of the sensory object. The term Sextus uses to designate the sensory object is *aisthēton*, which literally means "object of perception". The term has been widely used by Plato in the *Theaetetus* in connection with the theory of perception endorsed by the subtler thinkers, where *aisthēton* is one of the two exclusive elements on which the correlative process of perception is construed.

Exactly at the point when he begins expounding the core of the subtler thinkers' theory of perception, Socrates remarks that in the context of that theory:

> There are two kinds of movement, each unlimited in number, the one having the power of acting [*poiein*] and the other the power of being acted upon [*paschein*]. From their intercourse, and their friction against one another, there come to be offspring, unlimited in number but coming in pairs of twins, of which one is a perceived thing [*to aisthēton*] and the other a perception, which is on every occasion generated and brought to birth together with the perceived thing [*tou aisthētou*]. (*Tht.* 156a5–b2)

Perception is here seen as arising when a causal encounter between a perceiving subject and a perceived object occurs. The object of perception will exist if and only if it is perceived by a subject. Strictly speaking, the existence of the perceived object is dependent on a perceiver, but not in the sense that only the object of perception depends for its own existence on the perceiver perceiving it at a given time (the time when the actual perceptual process occurs). That would constitute a case of explicit idealism, which I have just argued to be extraneous to Cyrenaic philosophy. That idealism should also be an extraneous element in the context of the theory of perception endorsed by the subtler thinkers of the *Theaetetus*, if the identification between the early Cyrenaics and *hoi kompsoteroi* were correct.

In the subtler thinkers' theory of perception, the existence of the perceived object is dependent on a perceiver, but the opposite also holds: the very existence of the actual perception is dependent on the perceived object. Plato is clear on this when he says that perceptions and perceived objects always come as twin births (*Tht.* 156a7–b2).[8] If things are so, the existence of the perceiver will also depend on the perceptual process taking place and, in the last instance, on the perceived object (*qua* being perceived). That is the ultimate reason why the subtler thinkers hold that perception is always correlative. The existence of both the perceived thing and the perceiving subject is mutually interdependent. Socrates remarks, in fact, that we had better not speak of "man" (i.e. the term indicating the perceiving subject) or "stone" (i.e. the term designating a perceived object), since these terms do not designate anything concrete and ontologically unitary in the world, but more simply aggregates (*hathroisma*) of parts we usually name "man" or "stone" (*Tht.* 157c1–3).

The lack of ontological unitarity of both perceived objects and perceiving subjects is instantaneous and persists over time. In the very moment the perceptual process takes place, the perceived object is exclusively identified by means of the perceptual qualities (redness, hotness and so on) the perceiving subject recognizes (on that occasion) as belonging to that aggregate of parts we term "a stone". In the same way, the aggregate we qualify as the perceiving subject is identified by means of the perception (of red, hot and so on) she has (on that particular occasion) with reference to the perceived object. There is no further essence, more ontologically fundamental, to be grasped that could objectively identify the perceived object and the perceiving subject. In Platonic or Aristotelian terms, this ontological deficiency applies to things and persons even more over time, where the identity of objects can be posthumously reconstructed by listing all the possible secondary qualities the aggregate of parts we identify as the perceived object has displayed in its different perceptual encounters. On the same basis, all the perceptual affections that the aggregate of parts we qualify as the perceiving subject has produced in the context of the same encounters constitute the only way we have to identify her.

The correlativity of perception and the lack of ontological unitarity of things and persons are exemplarily witnessed by Plato, when he concludes the fascinating section of the *Theaetetus* about the subtler thinkers:

> [Socrates speaking]: What we are left with [after having heard the theories and doctrines ascribed to the subtler thinkers], I think, is that it is for each other that we are, if we are, or come to be, if we come to be, since necessity ties our being together, but does not tie it to anything else, or indeed to ourselves. So what we are left with is that we are tied to each other. It follows that, whether one uses "be" or "come to be" of something, one should speak of it as being, or coming to be, for someone or of something or in relation to something. As for speaking of a thing as being or coming to be to be anything just by itself, one should not do that oneself, and one should not accept it from anyone else either. That is what is indicated by the argument we have been setting out.   (*Tht.* 160b5–c2)

Here Plato explicitly reaffirms that in perceptual processes both the subject and the object of perception do not exist just by themselves. In the kind of metaphysics Plato is sketching in this passage, each item is tied neither to anything else nor, indeed, to itself. Things and individuals are not unitary items, which can be identified and re-identified over time with accuracy and precision.[9] Strictly speaking, things and individuals are not items at all, for their existence is the mere product of a causal encounter. Things and individuals are more appropriately described as aggregates of parts arising from processes.

In light of the theory endorsed by the subtler thinkers of the *Theaetetus* (at least on the interpretation I recommend), sensory objects in the material world do not exist as such. The sensory object and the corresponding perceiving subject are the two poles of a correlative process, which is casual, temporary and evanescing. Both poles of the process are not best described as unitary items persisting over time with a stable and well-defined ontological structure but are best seen as aggregates of parts (with no unitary essence) that keep modifying over time. The metaphysical core of this view is the lack of any unitary essence for things and individuals in the world: "nothing is one thing just by itself, but things are always coming to be for someone" (*Tht.* 157a8–b1).

The *Theaetetus* thus has much to offer in helping to interpret the denial of the existence of sensory objects that Sextus attaches to the Cyrenaics (and to Plato himself, perhaps, on the basis of the evidence of the passages of the *Theaetetus* on which we have so far been concentrating) on the basis of indeterminacy. Sensory objects do not exist because they are not, strictly speaking, independent and unitary objects. I suggest that for those who are persuaded that the subtler thinkers' doctrines are consistent with Cyrenaic philosophy, the evidence provided by Plato's *Theaetetus* that the Cyrenaics were committed to indeterminacy is rather strong, the theory of the subtler thinkers providing an illuminating picture of what indeterminacy really consists in.

THE CYRENAICS AND INDETERMINACY II: THE ANONYMOUS COMMENTATOR AND PHILODEMUS

The second passage that is decisively important for someone who aims to commit the Cyrenaics to indeterminacy is the anonymous commentator on the *Theaetetus*. The commentator *clearly* ascribes indeterminacy to the Cyrenaics. When he comments on the example of the blowing wind that Socrates puts forward in Plato's *Theaetetus* (152b1–3) to show the proper meaning of Protagoras' relativism, he says:

> Something is the agent, something else is the patient. But, if people undergo affections that are opposed to the thing in

itself, they will agree that the intrinsic feature of the agent is not defined [*mē einai hōrismenēn tēn tou poiēsantos idiotēta*]; if it were so, the same thing at the same time will not produce different affections. Because of this, the Cyrenaics say that only affections are apprehensible, while external things are not. That I am being burnt – they say – I apprehend; that the fire is such as to burn is obscure. If it were such, all things will be burnt by it.

(col. LXV, 19–35=T 1)

By suggesting a linkage, both terminological and conceptual, with the active and passive elements that are so central in the theory of perception endorsed by the subtler thinkers at *Theaetetus* 156a–157c, the commentator remarks that, by being affected by the same object in different ways, it has to follow that "the intrinsic feature of the agent is not defined". Objects, therefore, are not ontologically determinate in their structures, since the object (the wind of Socrates' example) may appear cold to someone and not-cold to someone else. The wind in itself is neither cold nor not-cold. It is simply neutral, that is, it does not possess any ontological feature of its own. On the basis of this explanation, the Cyrenaic view that affections alone are apprehensible relies on external objects in the world being inapprehensible because ontologically indeterminate. The fire in itself is not caustic, because, if it were so, everybody would be burnt by it.[10]

There is another source that has been brought to light by Tsouna as possibly containing reference to the Cyrenaics. The passage in question does not name the Cyrenaics directly. However, Tsouna believes (correctly, I think) that the passage refers to the Cyrenaics. The passage in question is by Philodemus of Gadara, an Epicurean philosopher (possibly first century BCE), whose work *On Choices and Avoidances* (the title is conjectural) is preserved in a papyrus found in Herculaneum (PHerc. 1251, 23 columns). The papyrus was first edited by the Italian philologist Domenico Comparetti and is now readable in the edition prepared by Giovanni Indelli and Tsouna (1995). The papyrus is badly damaged so reconstruction by editors is often difficult. Philodemus probably wrote his treatise on choices in the first half of the first century BCE, when the Cyrenaic school had already been dead for at least a century. A sensitive philosopher like Philodemus is capable of indicating the various developments the Cyrenaic school encountered in the elaboration of its philosophy over the space of more than two centuries. This is particularly probable in so far as the Cyrenaics, especially the later sects of the school, extensively rivalled the Epicureans with their theories on pleasure and the end. The doctrines of the later sects of the Cyrenaic school are likely to have been well known by those Epicureans, like Philodemus, who aimed to argue against Cyrenaic tenets.

The main point Philodemus seems to be addressing in his text is a root-and-branch rejection of those philosophical doctrines that do not relate choices about actions to rational calculation and knowledge. In his attack against what he believes are irrational views that ground decisions for acting on factors that have nothing to do with reason and knowledge, Philodemus singles out a family of doctrines that are undoubtedly Cyrenaic in their core. The passage goes thus:

(Col. II) They claim that as for truth no judgement is superior to any other. They believe in fact that the great *pathos* of the soul occurs as a result of pain and that thus we make our choices and avoidances by observing both bodily and mental pain ...

(Col. III) Some people denied that it is possible to know anything. They also added that if nothing on whose basis one should make an immediate choice is present, one should not choose immediately. Some other people made affections [*pathē*] of the soul as the moral ends and as not in need of any additional judgement based on further criteria. In doing so they granted to everybody an authority, which was not accountable, to get pleasure in whatever they cared to name and to do whatever contributed to it. Others held the view that what our school calls grief or joy are totally empty notions because of the manifest indeterminacy of things.

(*On Choices and Avoidances*, cols II and III=T28 & 29)

The view that the affections of the soul are the ends of life (col. III) is the kernel of Cyrenaic ethics. At the same time, Philodemus' words that affections are "not in need of any additional judgement based on further criteria" is an explicit reference to the Cyrenaic idea that only affections are knowable and perfectly legitimate in their own epistemological rights.[11] In linking Cyrenaic ethics and epistemology in the way he does in this passage, Philodemus is concerned about the conceptual linkage he sees as operating between the ethics and the epistemology of the Cyrenaics. Since they maintain that affections people experience are their only source of knowledge, it will be correct for the Cyrenaics to postulate that people decide what course of action they will follow in light of the affections they have. Given his rationalistic approach to ethics and knowledge, that one decides what action to perform on the basis of one's affections is a problematic view to adopt for Philodemus. While discussing these views, he also refers to a third group of people who appear to have criticized the Epicureans on the ground that what the Epicureans call grief or joy are "totally empty notions because of the manifest indeterminacy of things" (end of col. III).

Philodemus' attribution to the Cyrenaics of the view that things are indeterminate is quite remarkable. No other source, apart from the anonymous commentator, provides the same kind of explicit attribution of indeterminacy to the Cyrenaics. Philodemus attributes such indeterminacy to the Cyrenaics by making an example that has to do with ethical concepts, such as joy or grief, on which the Epicureans centred their ethical speculation. Although the attribution of indeterminacy to the Cyrenaics is made by suggesting an ethical example central to

Epicurean thinking, Philodemus' attribution need not to be restricted to ethical cases at all.

The attribution of the view that things are manifestly indeterminate comes at the end of Philodemus' reasoning against the Cyrenaics. The attribution appears to be the almost natural outcome of the overall argument purported to criticize the philosophical views of the Cyrenaics that Philodemus has been constructing in cols II and III. I take such an argument to be the following: the Cyrenaics ground knowledge on affections; such affections cannot be further elaborated by reason and so are purely subjective. In being so, these affections grant to each of us the authority to take pleasure in whatever we believe – quite incorrectly, according to Philodemus – to be pleasurable. We thus decide on a particular course of action on the basis of our subjective affections. This is possible – that is the conclusive point when indeterminacy comes in – because things in the world are manifestly indeterminate, that is, they are not in themselves pleasurable or painful, white or black and so on. On the basis of the conceptual reconstruction of Cyrenaic philosophy that Philodemus provides us with, affections are the basis of knowledge and the guide for action because things in the world are ultimately indeterminate.

THE CYRENAICS AND INDETERMINACY III: COLOTES

The last textual evidence under scrutiny is Colotes' account of Cyrenaic philosophy as preserved by Plutarch. Like Philodemus, Colotes of Lampsacus is an Epicurean philosopher, apparently a very young student of Epicurus, when the latter held his school in that city (310–306 BCE). Colotes wrote a book entitled "On the point that conformity to the views of the other philosophers actually makes it impossible to live", where a vigorous attack against the philosophers of the past and of his own time (the Cyrenaics and the Academics) was carried out. Colotes' book perished at some point, but Plutarch epitomized some important parts of it and provided a critical assessment of Colotes' views. Among other things, Colotes offers an account of Cyrenaic epistemology and metaphysics. Plutarch says:

He [Colotes] aims, I suspect, to refute the Cyrenaics first, and then the Academy of Arcesilaus. The latter school was of those who suspended judgement on everything; whereas the former, placing all affections and sense-impressions within themselves, thought that the evidence derived from them was not enough, as far as assertions on external objects are concerned. Distancing themselves from external objects, they shut themselves up within their affections as in a siege. In doing so, they adopted the locution "it appears" but refused to say in addition that "it is" with regard to external objects. This is the reason why – Colotes says – the Cyrenaics cannot live or cope with things. In addition, he says (making fun of them), that "these men do not say that a man or a horse or a wall is, but that they themselves are being walled or horsed or manned [*toichousthai kai hippousthai kai anthrōpousthai*]". (*Adv. Col.* 1120c–d=T 16)

After having reported Colotes' main argument about the Cyrenaics, Plutarch himself provides further information on Cyrenaic thinking and raises objection to Colotes:

In the first place, Colotes uses these expressions maliciously, just as a professional denouncer would do. These consequences among others will follow without any doubt from the teachings of the Cyrenaics. He should however have presented their doctrine in the actual form in which those philosophers taught it. They say we are being sweetened and bittered and chilled and warmed and illuminated and darkened. Each of these affections has within itself its own evidence, which is intrinsic to it and unchallenged.

But whether the honey is sweet or the young olive-shoot bitter or the hail chilly or the unmixed wine warm or the sun luminous or the night air dark is contested by many witnesses (wild and domesticated animals and humans too). Some in fact dislike honey, others like olive-shoots or are burned off by hail or are chilled by the wine or go blind in the sunlight and see well at night. When opinion stays close to the affection it therefore preserves its infallibility. On the contrary, when it oversteps them and mixes up with judgements and statements about external objects, it often disturbs itself and makes a fight against other people, who receive from the same objects contrary affections and different sense-impressions.   (*Adv. Col.* 1120e–f=T 17)

Commenting on the passage, Tsouna writes:

> although the Cyrenaics left unquestioned the basic assumption of objectivity, the evidence is divided as to what exactly they took reality to be: an undifferentiated substratum affecting us in various ways …, or a world of ordinary things or states of affairs, such as fire, iron, honey, night and light.   (1998: 82–3)

She argues for the latter option, whereas I will defend the former. I argue in fact that, on the basis of Colotes' evidence, one may interpret the Cyrenaics as committed to indeterminacy. We have earlier seen that for the adherent of indeterminacy there are no unitary objects as such. Plutarch, followed by some scholars, suggests that Colotes has been malicious in attributing to the Cyrenaics such expressions as "to be walled" and so on. This, however, misses the point, for I take Colotes to be here addressing an important philosophical point. The Cyrenaics famously invented neologisms of the kind "I am being whitened, sweetened" and so on. In these neologisms there is exclusive reference to secondary qualities of perceived objects, for example colour or taste. There is no direct reference at all to objects and items. This lack is the missing part Colotes emphasizes when he suggests to the Cyrenaics the use of more appropriate expressions such as "to be walled, or horsed". The Cyrenaics had better restore in their neologisms – and, for that matter, in their philosophy – a reference to objects in the world, Colotes warns. Otherwise, their philosophy would become untenable, for it would get rid of objects as such by admitting of secondary qualities alone. And this, Colotes tells us, is an absurd view to adopt.

But to avoid any reference to objects as such and to refer to the world of undifferentiated matter we are confronted with by indicating only secondary properties is the best philosophical characterization of indeterminacy, not only according to the definition of it I have provided in this chapter but, more importantly, according to what Aristotle says in *Metaphysics* Gamma, sections 5 and 6. When he deals with those who deny the principle of non-contradiction, Aristotle clearly indicates that the principle of non-contradiction can be denied coherently only by those who assume that reality is ontologically indeterminate.[12] He suggests that those who deny the principle of non-contradiction and assume that reality is indeterminate get rid of, among other things, the notions of essence and substance, thus maintaining that everything is said *per accidens*. As Aristotle puts it, with his usual insight:

And in general those who use this argument [i.e. those who deny the principle of non-contradiction] do away with substance and essence. For they must say that all attributes are accidents, and that there is no such thing as being essentially man or animal. For if there is to be any such thing as being essentially man this will not be being not-man or not being a man (yet these are negations of it); for there was some one thing which it meant, and this was the substance of something. And denoting the substance of a thing means that the essence of the thing is nothing else. But if its being

97

essentially man is to be the same as either being essentially not-man or essentially not being a man, then its essence will be something else. Therefore our opponents must say that there cannot be such a definition of anything, but that all attributes are accidental; for this is the distinction between substance and accident – white is accidental to man, because though he is white, whiteness is not his essence. But if all statements are accidental, there will be nothing primary about which they are made, if the accidental always implies predication about a subject.   (Γ 5 1007a21–b1)

Like Colotes, Aristotle rebuts the view that it is possible to do away with objects and essences. There is room, I claim, for explaining Colotes' mockery as a serious warning for the Cyrenaics. To make their views at least intelligible, the Cyrenaics should have adopted neologisms where an explicit reference to objects (and not to secondary properties alone) is made. Of course, Colotes may have highlighted the absurdity of the view that objects as such are not existent exactly in light of what Aristotle himself had said about indeterminacy in *Metaphysics* Gamma.[13] And with this remark we arrive at the last argument I wish to produce to claim that the Cyrenaics may have been committed to indeterminacy.[14]

THE EVIDENCE FROM HISTORY

In the course of this chapter, I have often referred to Plato's *Theaetetus* and to Aristotle' *Metaphysics* Gamma as the two *loci classici* where indeterminacy is actually recognized as a philosophical position of widespread currency in Greek philosophy. Aristotle, in particular, by suggesting that indeterminacy is the fundamental view behind the negation of the principle of non-contradiction, makes it a central tenet in Greek metaphysics.[15] In his treatment of the principle of non-contradiction, Aristotle makes clear that indeterminacy was a view shared by most thinkers before Socrates, thinkers who centred their epistemologies almost exclusively on perception. And in the interpretation of Plato's *Theaetetus* I have sketched in Chapter 3, there is much room for arguing that the ultimate aim of the dialogue is confutative of the various theories of knowledge endorsed by Protagoras and by the Socratic thinkers. This is so exactly because those theories, being all based on perceptions, ultimately rest on indeterminacy.

Beyond the textual evidence I have provided to maintain that the Cyrenaics may have been committed to indeterminacy, an indirect argument on the pervasiveness of indeterminacy in Greek philosophy can now be formulated. Plato and Aristotle witness the presence of indeterminacy in Greek philosophy in Presocratic philosophy, but also in their own times. The very fact that they actually wrote about indeterminacy is a clear sign that it was a view debated in the fourth century BCE. Protagoras and his relativism could be interpreted as summing up for the first time in Greek philosophy the original tradition of indeterminacy one may find at the origins in Anaxagoras' theory of secondary qualities, in Democritus' theory of the world and even in Gorgias' controversial claim that nothing is. On the other hand, Pyrrho's philosophy has been persuasively interpreted as a philosophy of indeterminacy. There is large agreement among scholars that, for a correct interpretation of the philosophy of Pyrrho, one has to rely on the fundamental passage of Aristocles of Messene reporting what Timon says of Pyrrho. The passage goes like this:

He [Pyrrho] left nothing in writing; his pupil Timon, however, says that the person who is to be happy must look at these three points: first, what are things by nature? Second, in what way ought we to be disposed towards them? And, finally, what will be the result for those who are so disposed? He [Timon] says that he [Pyrrho] reveals that things are equally indifferent, unstable and indeterminate [*ep'isēs adiaphora kai astathmēta kai anepikrita*]; for this reason, neither our sensations nor our opinions tell the truth or lie. For this reason then, we should not trust them, but should be without opinions and inclinations and without wavering, saying about each single thing that it no more is than is not or both is and is not or neither is nor is not.

(Euseb. *Praep. evang.*14.18.2–3=F4 Chiesara)

The statement that things are equally indifferent, unstable and indeterminate has to be taken, obviously enough, as the answer to the first of Timon's questions: "what are things by nature?" On Timon's account, Aristocles reports, Pyrrho holds that things are indeterminate. On this metaphysical view, Richard Bett (2000: esp. 14–62, 114–22) has recently developed an interpretation of Pyrrho's philosophy as centred on such indeterminacy.[16]

We have therefore an initial tradition about indeterminacy that groups Anaxagoras, Democritus and Gorgias, and of which Protagoras is perhaps the most philosophically sophisticated exponent. We have Plato and Aristotle clearly marking the importance of indeterminacy – although both rejecting its philosophical plausibility – in the context of Greek metaphysics. And almost at the end of the fourth century BCE we see Pyrrho grounding his philosophy on indeterminacy. What happened in-between? Is there any room for arguing that the Cyrenaics, often grouped by ancient authors and modern scholarship with Protagoras and Pyrrho,[17] may have shared with the latter thinkers the metaphysical view that things are indeterminate? The interpretation of the textual evidence I have provided at length in this chapter allows one to answer yes to this question. On the other hand, the philosophical context I have just sketched makes it clear that the interest for indeterminacy the Cyrenaics showed is not a peculiar episode in the history of Greek thought, but it is deeply rooted in a lively metaphysical tradition of classical antiquity.

5

PERSONS, OBJECTS
AND KNOWLEDGE

In Chapter 1 I advocated a minimalist view on the basis of which the Cyrenaics are Socratics because the founder of the school was an associate of Socrates. I have also warned that at a later stage I would give a more committed meaning for the adjective "Socratic" when attached to the Cyrenaics. I do so now in so far as I claim that the interest in epistemology the Cyrenaics clearly had is clear evidence of their Socratic legacy. Socrates' philosophy (whatever interpretation one may offer of it) rests on the assumption that the ethical enquiries that are so typical of Socrates' dialogical activity coincide with an epistemological search for moral knowledge. In Socrates there is an isomorphic coincidence between epistemology and ethics.

THE CYRENAICS AS SOCRATICS ONCE AGAIN

In a fully Socratic spirit, the Cyrenaics conceived of epistemology and ethics as parts of philosophy that are the two undividable faces of the same coin. Both Cyrenaic ethics and epistemology are centred on the crucial notion of affection (*pathos*), which serves as the epistemological factor for human knowledge and, at the same time, as the ethical key element of human behaviour. In the philosophy of Socrates, it is arbitrary to postulate a

THE CYRENAICS

predominance of the ethical above the epistemological, in so far as the former presupposes and rests on the latter. In the same way, for the Cyrenaics it is unnatural to assume that the epistemological derives from the ethical.[1] In the world of Socrates, the true answer to the *ti esti* question ("What is X?", where X can be "virtue", "courage", "friendship", "knowledge" and so on) is the basis of moral knowledge and the guide of practical conduct. Likewise, the notion of affection in Cyrenaic thinking provides the same insight into knowledge and ethics that the true answer to the *ti esti* question guarantees in Socrates' philosophy.

That the views of the Cyrenaics on knowledge and ethics are best seen as part of their Socratic legacy and that the Socratic origin of Cyrenaic doctrines applies independently to the ethics and epistemology of the school are clear enough from a remark by Sextus. Before reporting in detail what the Cyrenaics held on knowledge and pleasure at *Math.* VII 191–200, Sextus observes:

But now that the Academics' story has been told, from Plato onward, it is perhaps not beside the point to review the position of the Cyrenaics. For the school of these philosophers seems to have emerged from the discourse of Socrates, from which also the Platonist tradition arose.   (VII 190)

Sextus' account of Cyrenaic thought is divided into two parts. The first deals with the question of the criterion of truth (VII 191–8) and is centred on the fundamental view that only our affections are knowable to us. The second part (VII 199–200) is about the end. In the latter part, Sextus observes, "What these philosophers [the Cyrenaics] say about the criteria correspond to what they say about ends. For affections do extend to ends too" (VII 199). It is evident that in these passages Sextus does not suggest any derivation of the epistemological from the ethical in Cyrenaic thinking. On the contrary, he seems to believe that the epistemological and ethical doctrines of the Cyrenaics stem, like Plato's, from the philosophy of Socrates. And this is so without

102

any predominance of ethics over epistemology. It is, therefore, arbitrary to maintain that Cyrenaic epistemology is modelled on Cyrenaic ethics, as much as it is misleading to affirm that Socratic epistemology depends on Socratic ethics. Both Cyrenaic epistemology and ethics are contextually based on the crucial notion of *pathos* (affection). To this notion we now revert.

A *pathos* has, for the Cyrenaics, both a physical part and a mental counterpart. Sextus says, "Cyrenaic doctrine differs from Scepticism in so much as it says that the end is pleasure and the smooth motion of the flesh" (*Pyr.* I 215=T 30). Pleasure, the key ethical affection for the Cyrenaics, is a smooth motion of the flesh. Diogenes himself insists on the point when he says, "they [the Cyrenaics] said there are two kinds of affection, pleasure and pain, the former a smooth, the latter a rough motion" (DL II 86). Whenever we are affected pleasurably or painfully, we experience a physical alteration in our body (smooth and rough, respectively). Is this alteration enough for us to really *feel* pleasure and pain? Does the physical alteration need a mental counterpart that could grant the individual undergoing the alteration with the mental awareness that she is really feeling that very pain or pleasure? The Cyrenaics hold that the physical alteration needs a mental equivalent. This is witnessed by some passages. The first is Diogenes Laertius II 85, where the view that the end is pleasure is ascribed to Aristippus the Elder. The passage goes like this: "he [Aristippus] proclaimed as the end the smooth motion resulting in perception". For the Cyrenaics affections (in this case the affection of pleasure) are smooth motions that result in sensations, namely in the awareness that we are actually feeling that very affection.

The same point is illustrated by a remark by Clement of Alexandria: "they [the Cyrenaics] say that pleasure in itself is a

103

smooth and gentle motion, with some perception" (*Strom.* II 20 106, 3=*SSR* IV A 175). Another passage that is crucial for this aspect is that by Aristocles/Eusebius:

> He [Aristippus the Younger] clearly defined pleasure as the end, inserting into his doctrine the concept of pleasure related to motion. For he said, there are three conditions [*katastasesis*] of our temperament: one, in which we are in pain, is like a storm at sea; another, in which we experience pleasure and which can be compared to a gentle wave, for pleasure is a gentle movement, similar to a fair wind; and the third is an intermediate condition, in which we experience neither pain nor pleasure, which is like a calm. He said we have perception of these affections alone [*toutōn de kai ephaske tōn pathōn monōn hēmas tēn aisthēsin echein*].
>
> (F5 Chiesara=*SSR* IV A 173 and B5=T 4)

On the basis of the last sentence of Aristocles' passage, Cyrenaic epistemology seems to endorse the view that we are aware of the content of our affections, initially felt through an alteration of the body. A point Aristocles' passage raises is about the relations between what we may term "affective feelings" (such as pleasure and pain) and "representational feelings" (such as perceptions of white, hot and so on). Does Aristocles' passage tell us that, since only affective feelings are closely tied up with movements, the third intermediate state – not being itself a movement and hence being potentially different from the other two states – is not a proper affection? Do we need to read Aristocles' last sentence that "we have perception of these affections alone" as simply referred to the proper affections generated by movements, namely to pleasure and pain?

In the latter case, Aristocles' passage would appear to exclude the possibility that there are representational feelings. Since on this interpretation we would have perceptions of feelings of pleasure and pain alone, which are generated by movements, and since we conceive of intermediate states as not being generated by any movements and, thus, as not properly featuring any affections, we would have to conclude that representational feelings in Cyrenaic epistemology need to be explained as a particular case of affective feelings. Think, for example, of someone who loves ice cream and who is now tasting a vanilla ice cream: the affection she is feeling at the moment is a case of pleasure but it is also an affection of white. The affective feeling (pleasure) is also, on this occasion, a representational feeling (the sensation of white).

The latter explanation is favoured by Jacques Brunschwig (1999: 255–6) and makes Cyrenaic epistemology fully dependent on Cyrenaic ethics, in so far as it makes the *pathos* to which the Cyrenaics always refer be primarily an ethical concept that, only in a derivative sense, has an epistemological meaning. This explanation is obviously philosophically problematic, since all the cases of epistemological affections need explaining as cases of ethical affections. But this is hardly true: we all experience many cases of epistemological affections that are not cases of ethical affections. I see my desk as green, but I do not feel any sensation of pleasure or pain in connection with my perception of green. It helps little to postulate that the Cyrenaics may have been interested only in those ethical affections that also have an epistemological counterpart because this would restrict their epistemology to an extremely narrow field of enquiry, thus reducing a highly original theory of knowledge to a rather unimpressive epistemology (see Tsouna 1998: 14–15). But, and this is the essential point, Brunschwig's interpretation is discharged by another source on Cyrenaic epistemology, Sextus *Math.* 199–200, as follows:

(199) What these philosophers [the Cyrenaics] hold about the criteria [of truth] seems to correspond to what they say about ends. For affections [*pathē*] do extend to ends too. Some of the affections are pleasant, others are painful and others are intermediate [*ta de metaxu*]. The painful ones are, they say, bad and their end is pain, whereas the pleasant ones

are good, whose unmistakable end is pleasure. The intermediates are neither good nor bad, whose end is neither good
nor bad, which is an affection in between pleasure and pain
(200[=T 35]).

Sextus makes clear that what Aristocles calls intermediate
states are affections in their own rights. The dubious expression
of Aristocles ("we have perception of these affections alone") is
probably intended to be referring to all the three states mentioned
earlier in Aristocles' text.[2] On the basis of Sextus' passage, intermediate states are affections in themselves, which are neither
pleasurable nor painful but are most likely to be mere representational feelings. The overall picture of Cyrenaic thinking about
pathē is thus one in which there are affections that are purely
ethical (carrying pleasure or pain). On the other hand, there are
intermediate affections that are neutral from an ethical standpoint (as Sextus observes, these affections are neither pleasant
nor painful) but that may be thought of as being exclusively epistemological, that is, affections providing us with some kind of
knowledge.

On the basis of the conceptual analogy between affective and
representational affections, in the absence of any textual element
in Aristocles and Sextus that may prevent us from assuming so,
one may well postulate that in Cyrenaic philosophy intermediate
states too are somehow related to motion. The alteration our
bodies undergo when we are affected epistemologically may be
understood as the result of a perceptual movement intervening
between the world and us. When we see an object as white (or
when we are whitened, to use the Cyrenaic jargon), our sense
organs are altered in such a way that we see whiteness. There is
a brief passage of Plutarch that speaks of movement with reference to a representational affection. In comparing the Cyrenaics
with the Epicureans, in his attempt to defend the former from
Colotes' criticism, Plutarch asks rhetorically whether "they [the
Cyrenaics] do not say that the external object is sweet, but that an

affection or a movement of this kind related to taste has occurred [*pathos de ti kai kinēma peri autēn gegonenai toiouton*]" (*Adv. Col.* 1121b). A representational feeling (of sweet) is here openly described as a movement related to taste.

Pathos is, therefore, one central concept of Cyrenaic philosophy, both in ethics and epistemology. The Cyrenaics thought that every *pathos* begins with a physical alteration in our body and ends with our mental awareness of that alteration. A last feature of affections (as the Cyrenaics conceived of them) is their occurring at one given, and definite, time. The fundamental passage for this feature of Cyrenaic *pathē* is by Athenaeus, which goes thus:

> Having approved of the affection of pleasure, he [Aristippus the Elder] claimed that pleasure is the end of life, and that happiness is based on it. He added that pleasure occupies one temporal unit [*monochronon*], since he believed, as profligates do, that the memory of past enjoyments nor the expectation of a future one be important for him. Judging the good in light of the present alone, he considered that what he enjoyed in the past and will enjoy in the future be not important for him, the former because it exists no more, the latter because it does not yet exist and is not manifest.
> (*Deipnosophists* XII 544a–b=SSR IV A 174=T 8)

A usual translation for the adjective *monochronos* is "short-lived", "momentary". Following Tsouna (who translates it as "uni-temporal"; Tsouna 1998: 15–17), I suggest translating *monochronos* as "occupying one temporal unit". The crucial idea that Athenaeus reports in his passage is that every affection has its own temporal unit, which is defined by the time the affection lasts before evanescing forever. What is really meant when Aristippus is reported to speak of affections that occupy one temporal unit is not that these affections last for a short time. It is truly possible that I will be having a feeling of pleasure all morning if I am reading a novel I like. The point is rather that these affections have specific and time-limited lives, that is, they exactly last the time in which they are actually felt by us. Before that time and after it, these affections do not have any life in us. In the Cyrenaic world, we are thus confronted with perishing affections that do not survive (the limits of) the present, however long this may be.

The Cyrenaics centred their ethics on the affection of pleasure and restricted the scope and space of that affection to the present, for they believed that what one had already enjoyed and what one will enjoy are not present, and hence are nothing. Diogenes reports the same point of Athenaeus, when he says, "Nor do they [the Cyrenaics] admit that pleasure is derived from the memory or expectation of the good ..., for they assert that the movement affecting the mind dies away with time" (DL II 89–90). Affections are confined to the present because of their nature; the movements from which Cyrenaic affections originate inevitably perish over time. The idea that affections are confined to the present is traditionally given crucial importance as far as Cyrenaic ethics is concerned, for it may tell us something about the possible relationship the Cyrenaics envisaged between pleasure and happiness. If our affections of pleasure last only when they are actually felt by us, what will the relationship between pleasure and happiness be? Is happiness to be conceived as the sum of past, present and future enjoyments? In addition, if affections are time limited, this will concern not only the ethics of the Cyrenaics but also their epistemology, in so far as representational affections too are related to motions and movements.

The time-limitedness I attach to Cyrenaic affections is something that concerns even things and persons of the Cyrenaic world. The Cyrenaics, on my interpretation, are committed to indeterminacy and thus question the existence over time of both objects and subjects, thus conceiving of the former as not-unitary items and the latter, in a Humean fashion, as bundles of affections with no inner unity (I shall shortly return to this point in more detail). Time-limitedness is therefore a central factor of

Cyrenaic philosophy as a whole. Now that we have a general overview of the features of Cyrenaic affections, we can move on to the details of Cyrenaic epistemology. We shall do so by using – as an excellent starting-point for the whole discussion – the critique Aristocles of Messene advances on Cyrenaic philosophy.

ARISTOCLES' CRITICISM

Because of its relevance, I quote Aristocles' text almost fully, although I shall do so by adding my own comments. I begin with the initial paragraph of Aristocles' text:

> Next would be those who say that affections alone are apprehensible. This view was adopted by some of the philosophers from Cyrene. As if oppressed by a kind of torpor, they maintained that they knew nothing at all, unless someone standing beside them struck and pricked them. They said that, when burnt or cut, they knew that they were affected by something [*kaiomenoi gar elegon ē temnomenoi gnōrizein hoti paschoien ti*]. But whether the thing which is burning them is fire, or that which cut them is iron, they could not tell [*poteron de to kaion eiē pur ē to temnon sidēros, ouk echein eipein*].
> (F5 Chiesara=Euseb. *Praep. evang.* 14.19.1=T 5)

What is peculiar in Aristocles' passage is that, while expounding Cyrenaic views, he actually refers to the example of the fire the anonymous commentator himself uses when he compares Cyrenaic epistemology with Protagoras' relativism (see col. XLV, 32–5).[3] Since things are not intrinsically defined, the commentator says, "the Cyrenaics say that affections alone are apprehensible, while external things are not. That I am being burnt – they say – I apprehend; that the fire is such as to burn is obscure. If it were such, all things will be burnt by it" (col. LXV, 26–32).

The commentator's point is that for the Cyrenaics only affections are apprehensible (epistemological position) because we cannot know how external things really are. This is so because external things have no intrinsic feature on their own, namely things are indeterminate (metaphysical position). The example of the fire collapses the two positions (the epistemological and the metaphysical) into the same picture. I know that I am being burnt, so I undeniably know the affection of hot I am now feeling. What I do not know, however, is whether what causes my feeling of hot is hot in itself. In light of the awareness that the agent does not possess any intrinsic feature of its own, I do not know whether the fire is intrinsically hot, because "if it were such, all things will be burnt by it".

The same combination of epistemological and ontological views is to be found in Aristocles' text. After having stated that for the Cyrenaics what can be effectively known is how things affect us, Aristocles says that the Cyrenaics are perfectly aware that one can be affected in certain ways (the epistemological position), but "whether the thing which is burning them is fire ... they could not tell" (the metaphysical position). The anonymous commentator says that for the Cyrenaics we cannot know whether an object like the fire possesses in itself the feature of hotness. In Aristocles' passage, what the Cyrenaics appear to be saying is not that one cannot know whether the fire does in itself possess a secondary quality (the hotness). For Aristocles, the Cyrenaics hold the view that, while knowing that they are feeling hot when they are burnt, they cannot say that what burns them is actually a fire. Differently from the anonymous commentator, who placed the reason for Cyrenaic subjectivism in the impossibility of knowing whether a thing possesses an intrinsic feature (i.e. a secondary quality, such as the hotness), Aristocles seems to be placing the reason for that subjectivism in the impossibility of knowing the real identity of things *causing the affections*.

This brings us back to indeterminacy. According to Aristocles' testimony, for the Cyrenaics we are incorrigibly aware of our affections because we are unable to know the real identity of the thing that appears to cause in us the affection we feel at present. We do not know whether the affection of hot we are now feeling is really caused by a fire or by something else. This hints at the view that objects as such may indeed be non-existent. The Cyrenaics do away with objects as unitary and temporally stable items because they cannot even know what objects, if any, are in the world. In short, what I suggest is that in his passage Aristocles expresses the same point about the non-existence of objects as unitary items Colotes is reported to have formulated, when he suggests to the Cyrenaics to employ such expressions as "to be walled, manned" and so on.[4] Moreover, what Aristocles observes in the prosecution of his argument confirms the reference to indeterminacy I have just proposed. He says, as if he is actually continuing the initial part of his argument:

> Three things must necessarily exist at the same time: the affection itself, what causes it, and what undergoes it. The person who apprehends an affection must necessarily perceive also what undergoes it. It cannot be the case that, if someone is for example warm, one will know that one is being warmed without knowing whether it is himself or a neighbour, now or last year, in Athens or Egypt, someone alive or dead, a man or a stone. One will therefore know too what one is affected by, for people know one another and the roads, cities, the food they eat. Likewise, craftsmen know their tools, doctors and sailors infer by means of signs what will happen, and dogs discover the tracks of wild animals.
> (F5 Chiesara=Euseb. *Praep. evang.* 14.19.3–4=T 6)[5]

The core of Aristocles' criticism in this passage is that in sensing an affection the individual has to be aware that *she* is sensing an affection and, hence, she has to be provided with a clear understanding of her own identity (if she is a human being or a stone, alive or dead, in Athens or in Egypt and so on). At the same time, the individual undergoing an affection has to be aware of what causes it. She has to be fully aware of the *identity* of the objects she happens to be confronted with. She has to be able to recognize other people, roads, cities and so on. According to Aristocles, the double awareness (of one's own identity and of the causes of affections) is impossible for the Cyrenaics. Nor can they tell if what causes the affection of hot in them is a fire or if they are human beings. In elaborating such a critique of Cyrenaic views, I take Aristocles to be identifying a Cyrenaic position that ultimately rests on the view that things in the world are indeterminate. Aristocles' text is thus important, in so far as it places Cyrenaic epistemology on a par with Cyrenaic metaphysics and, in particular, with the view that in the Cyrenaic world objects and persons have no stable identity.

Now, what does it mean to hold that only affections are knowable in the context of a metaphysical view that conceives of objects and persons not as unitary items? If items in the world are neither unitary nor equipped with a stable identity, how could we conceive of items, such as persons or objects? One option would be the one we explored in Chapter 4: objects and persons are simply aggregates. In the Cyrenaic world, both objects and persons are best interpreted as bundles of some episodic and temporary features. Since they are not equipped with a stable ontological essence, objects and persons are best thought of as being under perennial change and as moving from one episode of their fragmented life to the subsequent one with no possible interruption. Objects and persons are, for the Cyrenaics, aggregates immersed in a perennial process of transformation and modification.

The only conceptual alternative to a metaphysics of objects is, in fact, a metaphysics of processes. We do not have any direct and strong textual evidence that the kind of indeterminate metaphysics that, on my interpretation, the Cyrenaics endorse is linked to a metaphysics of processes. The kind of indeterminacy I see at the roots of Cyrenaic philosophy will seem to make good sense philosophically only if it is placed within a metaphysics of processes, exactly like the one Plato illustrates at length in the *Theaetetus* (in connection with the subtler thinkers' theory of perception). There are two textual hints pointing us towards the idea that the Cyrenaics may have endorsed a metaphysics of processes in connection with indeterminacy. The first hint is the adjective *monochronos*, as referred to the kind of affections the Cyrenaics are interested in. I have earlier suggested translating *monochronos* as "occupying one temporal unit". This translation aims to convey the idea that each *pathos* lasts only for the time in which it is actually felt. This means that affections have a limited life and can be legitimately taken to be arising from an encounter between the subject feeling the affection and something else causing the affection. When one of the two poles of the relationship breaks away, the affection perishes. Hence, we can conceive of affections as the concrete results of a process of interaction between a subject and an object. In addition, we have observed that for the Cyrenaics an affection is itself a movement. But each movement is inevitably a process from the state of quietness to its opposite. So the metaphysics of indeterminacy as contemplated by the Cyrenaics could be well accommodated – at least in principle – by a metaphysics of processes.

SELVES AND OBJECTS

What *sense* can we ultimately make of a world where objects and persons do not have a stable and definable identity? My immediate answer is that although the philosophical views attributed to the Cyrenaics we have been discussing so far may appear strange at first, they are quite respectable philosophical views and views that may seem true when carefully considered. Let us think of persons. In the Cyrenaic picture I am drawing, persons do not have any deep metaphysical essence. So how are we to explain our being the same person over time? How are we to explain personal identity if, in the Cyrenaic world, there is no identity of persons at all? David Hume, for instance, put forward a conception of persons and personal identity that is very close, if not identical, to the one the Cyrenaics may have held.

Hume has described such a conception in the following way:

For my part, when I enter most intimately into what I call myself, I always stumble on some particular perception or other, of heat or cold, light or shade, love or hatred, pain or pleasure. I never can catch myself at any time without a perception, and never can observe any thing but the perception. When my perceptions are removed for any time, as by sound sleep; so long am I insensible of myself, and may truly be said not to exist. And were all my perceptions removed by death and could I neither think, nor feel, nor see, nor love, nor hate after the dissolution of my body, I should be entirely annihilated, nor do I conceive what is farther requisite to make me a perfect non-entity …

I may venture to affirm of the rest of mankind, that they are nothing but a bundle or collection of different perceptions, which succeed each other with an unconceivable rapidity, and are in a perpetual flux and movement. Our eyes cannot turn in their sockets without varying our perceptions. Our thought is still more variable than our sight; and all our other senses and faculties contribute to this change; nor is there any single power of the soul, which remains unalterably the same, perhaps for one moment. The mind is a kind of theatre, where several perceptions successively make their appearance; pass, re-pass, glide away, and mingle in an infinite variety of postures and situations. There is properly no simplicity in it at one time, nor identity in different; whatever natural propension we may have to imagine that simplicity and identity. The comparison of the theatre must not mislead us. They are the successive perceptions only, that constitute the mind; nor have we the most distant notion of the place, where these scenes are represented, or of the materials, of which it is composed.

(1888: bk I, §VI, 252–3)[6]

Hume's words constitute an impeccable exposition of the view about persons and personal identity I claim can be ascribed to the Cyrenaics. Persons are best seen as bundles or collections of their own changing perceptions/affections. In this picture, there is no self that may function as a substratum surviving changes and modifications over time and that, because of this, represents our true and full "I". One may raise the objection that there are no ancient sources on the Cyrenaics openly dealing with the question of persons and personal identity. Nonetheless, it is also true that on my interpretation the Cyrenaics appear to have endorsed indeterminacy. And indeterminacy concerns all things in the world, both objects and persons, who in the context of that metaphysical view are seen as not-unitary and fragmented items.

In addition, there is also indirect evidence that may support the claim about persons I am proposing in connection with the Cyrenaics. The problem of persons and personal identity is not foreign to Greek philosophy. It is a rather old problem that was still aired at the time of the Cyrenaics. The evidence of Plato's *Theaetetus* confirms this: in that dialogue persons are seen exactly as bundles of perceptions (esp. *Tht.* 157b8–c3) and as not equipped with a further identity persisting over time (esp. *Tht.* 159a6–160a6, where the problem of the two Socrateses is discussed). That Plato, a contemporary of Aristippus, was well aware of the problem of persons and personal identity is evident also from a famous passage of the *Symposium* (207d5–208e4), where the identity of persons is truly regarded as an apparent fact. But the problem of persons and their identity is older than Plato. There is evidence that Epicharmus, a Pythagorean thinker of the fifth century BCE, formulated an argument called the Growing Argument (*Auxanomenos Logos*), which purported to show that every change in a subject implies the existence of a new subject. To show the full implication of his argument, Epicharmus is reported to have written a comedy in which a borrower refuses to give money back to his lender on the ground that she is no longer the same person who originally borrowed the money.[7] Nothing prevents us from assuming that the Cyrenaics were aware of the philosophical problem of persons and of their identity over time. They may well have suggested their own solution for it.

One may now wonder what sense we could make of Cyrenaic epistemology if we maintained that the Cyrenaics conceived of persons as mere bundles of affections, with no further inner identity. So far we have seen that the fundamental tenet of Cyrenaic epistemology is that only affections are apprehensible. The affections the Cyrenaics speak of are always and necessarily referred to the subject having those affections. I have quoted the Cyrenaic neologism "I am being whitened", where the "I" in such an expression refers to the subject undergoing the affection of white. What sense will we make of this "I" and of the epistemological infallibility connected to it in the context of Cyrenaic epistemology if there is no proper "I"? What sense will we make of Cyrenaic subjectivism if there is no proper subject in the Cyrenaic world?[8]

To answer this objection, perhaps we need to revise our deepest conceptions about persons and their identity in light of the clarifications on the concept of "person" Derek Parfit has developed in his groundbreaking *Reasons and Persons* (1984). By rehearsing Hume's approach to the question of persons as bundles of perceptions, Parfit suggests that personal identity is not an all-or-nothing view. As far as the identity of persons is concerned, we are not confined to the two alternatives we are usually faced with: either that the self is a deep further fact that persists over time among inevitable changes and modifications or that the self is so fragmented in isolated episodes as to be effectively non-existent. Parfit suggests a view between the other two, hence rejecting the alternative "all or nothing". The view Parfit advocates is that personal identity is not what really matters. What really matters is a sort of psychological connectedness linking the various selves we experience to be in our life. That connectedness is radically different from a persisting self, which as such survives any temporal modification and ontological change.[9]

The psychological connectedness Parfit refers to may be compared to a sort of loose self. This loose self is different both from the kind of self intended as a deep further fact and from an annihilated "I" (i.e. the view that the temporary and fragmented episodes of our psychological life are radically independent one from the other, so that we are really doomed to experience no connection at all between them). The loose self is what allows us to speak of a self even in those cases – such as the ones Parfit himself scrutinizes, Hume's bundles of perceptions, the supposedly Cyrenaic collections of affections – that we have recently reviewed. The philosophical view about persons and their identity that I ascribe to the Cyrenaics is that of a loose self, which can be regarded as the referent of the expression "I" in the Cyrenaic neologism "I am being whitened". This is enough for the view about persons that I, relying on some evident features of Cyrenaic philosophy illustrated earlier, believe can be accommodated into the philosophical outlook of Aristippus and his followers. In the Cyrenaic world, persons are best seen as collections of affections. What about objects in that world?

On the basis of the metaphysics of indeterminacy I have ascribed to the Cyrenaics, there are no proper objects as such in the world. For the Cyrenaics there is a real substratum, mind-independent, and made up of an undifferentiated lump of matter. Such a substratum is not constituted by objects as single, unitary items, since what we conventionally term "objects" are no more than collections of secondary qualities. Since a metaphysics of indeterminacy cannot be a metaphysics of objects, we may reinterpret it as a metaphysics of processes, where the bundle of perceptions constituting the perceiving subject and the collection of secondary qualities constituting the perceived object are best seen as the result of temporary processes that casually put the former in touch with the latter. Is the idea that in our everyday life we are not confronted with a world of discrete objects – as common sense usually tells us – so shocking? Is this idea more shocking than the one telling us that we are just a loosely inter-related bundle of psychologically interconnected selves?

I am not quite sure which of the two views appears to be more disturbing at first sight, but Parfit could be right when he says that we may find these views ultimately consoling. There is no space here to deal fully with a metaphysics of indeterminacy and with the view that the world is made up of an undifferenti-ated lump of matter, where processes take place and where the products of these processes are interactions between a subject (more appropriately a bundle of mental states) and an object (more appropriately a collection of secondary qualities). For now it may be noted that the common-sense metaphysical view that the world around us is populated by objects is generally regarded to be so firm because it is supposed to be grounded on science.

But even this more comfortable belief needs to be revised. Scientific research has made clear that objects are not what they appear to be at a first sight. We see a table and believe that the object we are seeing is really a table. We cannot be deceived about the fact that what we are actually seeing is a table. Yet, on a scientific level, what we believe to be a table is, more essentially, a compound of molecules, equipped with a certain balance of forces. On a scientific outlook, what we see as a table is thus not strictly speaking a table, but something else. Our way to think of objects is more primitive than the ones adopted by science and *cannot* rest on science, at least not on the kind of science predom-inant today, that is mostly governed by quantum mechanics and physics. One of the most enduring theoretical effects of quantum physics is that reality, in its ultimate version, is indeterminate. Werner Heisenberg elaborated a principle, called the uncertainty principle, or principle of indeterminacy, which goes thus: "In the field of reality whose connexions are formulated by the quantum-theory, natural laws do not lead to a complete determination of what happens in space and time; what happens ... depends instead on the game of fortune" (1926; my trans.).

Heisenberg observes that the ultimate constituent of reality, namely the elementary particle, is indeterminate. We cannot identify the ontological nature and the behaviour of the elementary particle by using the usual space–time dichotomy, since there are two clear elements of indeterminacy in the picture: the duality wave–particle and its non-locality (in more scientific terms, its entanglement). On the basis of Heisenberg's view, because of the substantial indeterminacy of the behaviour of elementary particles, classical physics is unable to explain most of the phenomena of reality. Heisenberg's views about indeterminacy have been given wide circulation in philosophy by Thomas Kuhn and Paul Feyerabend. Feyerabend especially has argued for a view of reality as indeterminate and variably determined by incommensurable conceptual schemes, belonging to different cultural outlooks and perspectives (Feyerabend 1975: esp. ch. 17). One of Feyerabend's heirs, John Dupré, has recently defended with success a non-reductive, indeterminate metaphysics (Dupré 1993). In one of the most prominent works of contemporary metaphysics, Peter Van Inwagen has defended a powerful ontology of material beings: existing things are either a simple (i.e. a molecular constituent of reality) or a living organism. Since simples are the basic elements of every material object, things such as tables and chairs, composed of simples arranged in a particular fashion, cannot be truly regarded as existing items.[10]

What I ultimately suggest is that both the view that we are not more than bundles of loosely interconnected psychological states and the related view that the world is made up of an undifferentiated lump of matter where what we term objects are best seen as collections of secondary qualities are views of which we can make sense, however radically shocking they may appear at first sight. In addition, they can even be views that are true views. We resist them only because they are in radical contrast to some of our deepest assumptions. To appreciate the novelty of such radical views, we need to revise profoundly our beliefs about what we are and about how the world is.

For the Cyrenaics only our affections are knowable to us.[11] How can this expression be interpreted in the picture about persons and objects I have been drawing so far? In the Cyrenaic world the loose subject is confronted with a substratum of undifferentiated matter. When the loose subject comes into touch with the substratum, what she is able to know is how she is affected by that substratum. Since the loose subject is not confronted with a substratum that is made up of objects, that subject can be affected only by registering secondary qualities. The Cyrenaic neologism "I am being whitened" now makes full sense. The "I" of the expression refers to the loose subject undergoing the particular affection of white, at the time when the process of interaction with the undifferentiated substratum occurs. Accordingly, "to be whitened" refers to the quality of the affection, which is, on this occasion, an affection of white. In Cyrenaic neologisms no reference at all is made to what we usually term the "object" causing the affection because, strictly speaking, there is no unitary item in the world out there. When the "I" referred to in the Cyrenaic neologism gets in touch with the undifferentiated substratum, an interaction between that "I" and the substratum appearing white occurs. In this interaction, the perceiving subject is provided with an affection of white, which is private to her and which constitutes for the Cyrenaics the exclusive basis for knowledge.

A point that is worth highlighting in this connection is the privacy of one's affections and their absolute incorrigibility. The point is clearly marked by Sextus: "it is possible, they [the Cyrenaics] say to assert infallibly and truly and firmly and incorrigibly that we are being whitened or sweetened" (*Math.* VII 191).

In Cyrenaic epistemology, the perceiving subject is the fulcrum from which knowledge radiates. The subject is the epistemological authority from which knowledge arises, in so far as the subject is the only element epistemologically allowed to report how she is affected in the very moment when the perceptual process takes place. No one else is allowed to do so on her behalf. Differently from all other Greek philosophers, the Cyrenaics placed the *locus* of knowledge within the boundaries of the subject, however fragmented this could be. Consequently, while not rejecting the existence of the external world in an idealist sense, they made the truth dependent on the internal mental states of the perceiving subject, thus dissolving the view – at the roots of Greek epistemology – that truth is always and exclusively a truth of external objects.

Although signalling differences between them, ancient sources often pair Cyrenaic epistemology with Protagoras' relativism and Pyrrho's scepticism (and also with Epicurean epistemology). Eusebius says, "Pyrrho and his followers maintain that human beings can know nothing, Aristippus and his followers that only our affections are knowable, whereas the pupils of Metrodorus and Protagoras hold that we must trust to the perceptions of the body alone" (*Praep. evang.* 14.2.4=*SSR* IV A 216). Cicero adds:

> One criterion is that of Protagoras, who holds that what appears true to someone is really true for that person; another is that of the Cyrenaics, who believe that there is no criterion whatsoever beyond inmost affections, another is that of Epicurus, who places the criterion of truth into the senses and in the primary notions of things and in pleasure. (*Acad. Pr.* II 46, 142=*SSR* IV A 209)

There are surely differences between the Cyrenaics, Protagoras and Pyrrho, as far as their epistemologies are concerned. Nonetheless, such differences are less important than their affinities (but see Tsouna 1998: ch. 10). Protagoras claimed that all appearances are true for those who have them. If I feel the wind as hot and you as cold, it will be the case that the wind is hot for me and cold for you. In Protagoras' relativism, the main concern is on the relativity of perception. Each perception is true relatively to a perceiver. In Cyrenaic epistemology there is no explicit reference to relativity. Yet, the Cyrenaics are not so distant from Protagoras; for them, each affection is the source of individual knowledge. To reuse Protagoras' example, in the presence of a blowing wind, one of us could claim, in Cyrenaic jargon, to be warmed and another to be colded. One is, once again, incorrigibly correct in one's own affections. And, although relativity is nowhere mentioned in connection with Cyrenaic epistemology, the best way to account philosophically for the view that all affections are true (Cyrenaic subjectivism) is to interpret that view as ultimately reducible to relativism. In *Metaphysics* Gamma, sections 5–6, Aristotle shows in fact that one could legitimately hold the view that all appearances are true if one were prepared to maintain that all appearances are relative (*Metaph.* Γ 6.1011a17–24; see also Politis 2004: ch. 6, §4). While retaining the same dichotomy between appearances and the world, Pyrrho reversed the epistemological optimism of the Cyrenaics and of Protagoras when he suggested that appearances could not tell us anything true. The distance between Pyrrho's view on knowledge and the Cyrenaics' appears therefore to be greater than that between the latter and Protagoras.

BEYOND AFFECTIONS

One may wonder whether Cyrenaic epistemology ends with affections. When Aristocles says that for the Cyrenaics we can have perceptions of affections, does he mean that perception is merely the individual's mental assent to (her awareness of) the affection initially felt through a modification of the body? Does "perception" in Cyrenaic philosophy mean exclusively the individual's mental awareness of the corresponding bodily affection? There are two sources that show that for the Cyrenaics a perception is (also) something different from the mere awareness of a bodily alteration. One is Plutarch, *Against Colotes* 1120f, when he amends Colotes' account by telling us what the Cyrenaics had really said. In commenting on Cyrenaic epistemology, Plutarch remarks:

> When opinion stays close to the affection it therefore preserves its infallibility. On the contrary, when it oversteps them and mixes up with judgements and statements about external objects, it often disturbs itself and makes a fight against other people, who receive from the same objects contrary affections and different sense-impressions.
>
> (*Adv. Col.* 1120f=T 17)

While affection is always infallible for the Cyrenaics (since each affection has its evidence, intrinsic to it and irreversible), opinion is all right when it stays close to affection. On the other hand, when opinion oversteps affections by trying to tell how things really are, opinion goes wrong. The main point Plutarch raises in the passage is the distinction between appearance and reality, a distinction that may suit the Cyrenaics, too, when they distinguish between the apprehensibility of affections and the un-apprehensibility of things. But what is important for us in Plutarch's account is that, while commenting on Cyrenaic epistemology, he draws a clear distinction between affections (and their cognitive infallibility) and opinions (and their related fallibility).

The second passage is by Diogenes Laertius: "They [the Cyrenaics] say that one may feel a pain greater than another and that perceptions do not fully speak the truth" (II 93=T 27). As in Plutarch's passage, Diogenes too may be suggesting a distinction between the epistemological power of affections and the possible epistemological failure of perceptions. This interpretation seems to be confirmed by the sentence immediately preceding the one about perceptions not always speaking the truth, where Diogenes points out that the Cyrenaics affirmed that a pain could be greater than another. Since Diogenes has insisted at II 87 that for the Cyrenaics "pleasure does not differ from pleasure nor is one pleasure more pleasant than another", I interpret his remark that a pain could be greater than another to be suggesting that the Cyrenaics believed it possible to reflect upon pleasures. This, in turn, will be the case if there is something more than affections in Cyrenaic epistemology. It may be noted that Diogenes' remark about a pain being greater than another could mean that either the same individual is able to say that a pain she is now feeling is greater than another she has already felt; or that an individual can say that the pleasure she is feeling is greater than the one another individual is feeling or has felt. In both cases, an extra-affective capacity should be admitted of to compare different pleasures. Likewise, when the Cyrenaics claimed that happiness is the sum of all pleasures, past, present and future (DL II 87), they must have claimed that one can say one is happy when one is able to assess, compare and evaluate pleasures enjoyed over different periods of time. I see no conceptual way to do so by relying on "pure" affections.

Beyond the textual evidence on which we have so far focused, there are other elements on whose basis one may conjecture that the Cyrenaics could have admitted of extra-affective (more judgemental) capacities. Like all other philosophers, the Cyrenaics argued for philosophical views. When they say that pleasure is the end or that affections only are knowable, these are two statements that are neither affections in themselves nor easily derivable from affections. So how are the Cyrenaics able to explain the legitimacy of these two statements by relying on a theory of knowledge that is exclusively centred on the infallibility of one's affections? Second, the Cyrenaics invented neologisms of the kind "I am being X-ed" to express the infallibility of one's affections. They maintained that an affection could be formulated and communicated through a linguistic expression. But, as Aristocles points out (Euseb. *Praep. evang.* 14.19.2), "I am being X-ed" is not an affection, but a statement.

The Cyrenaics are attributed with an original theory of language, which argues for the view that language is the only thing that is common to human beings. If language is meaningful and if affections can be translated into meaningful statements, how are the Cyrenaics to account for these two *phainomena* in the context of an epistemology that *prima facie* appears to be admitting of affections only? In Chapter 6, especially § "Wittgenstein", I shall argue that the theory of language and meaning endorsed by the Cyrenaics is coherent in so far as it presupposes that Cyrenaic individuals are able to perform epistemological activities not reducible simply to affections. Otherwise, their semantics would become completely untenable. In short, my point is whether, given the absolute prevalence of affections in Cyrenaic epistemology, there is room in that epistemology for judgemental activities that are extra-affective. My suggestion is that although I am more than ready to insist that the peculiarity of Cyrenaic epistemology lies in their theory of affections, the Cyrenaics may have allowed for a more judgemental activity that could explain those aspects of their epistemology that do not appear reducible to affections.

INTERNAL TOUCH

One possible way to assess the claim that the Cyrenaics could have admitted of extra-affective activities in their epistemology is to understand Cicero's doctrine of internal touch. Cicero has twice spoken of an internal touch with reference to the Cyrenaics. The first passage goes like this:

What about the Cyrenaics, by no means contemptible philosophers? They deny that anything can be perceived from the outside, while they do say to perceive only those things they experience by means of an internal touch, like pain and pleasure; they cannot know whose sound or colour something is, but to sense only to be affected in a certain way.

(*Acad. Pr.* II 24.76=*SSR* IV A 209=T 11)

In another passage, Cicero says, "What about touch, of that touch philosophers call interior, of either pleasure or pain, in which the Cyrenaics believe that only there is the criterion of truth [*iudicium*], because it is perceived by means of the senses?" (*Acad. Pr.* II 7, 20=*SSR* IV A 209=T 10).

Both of Cicero's passages insist on the fact that the Cyrenaics placed the boundaries of truth within the individual by denying that anything can be perceived from the outside and by suggesting that the criterion of truth lies in internal touch. What is internal touch? And how does it work? When we have been faced with the first details of the theory of affections of the Cyrenaics, I have suggested that affection (*pathos*) has a double meaning in Cyrenaic philosophy. First, it refers to the bodily alteration we feel through the modification of our sense organs. When I am whitened, my eyes are altered so that I have an affection of white. After the bodily alteration through the appropriate sense organs, the mental awareness of that alteration follows. In this picture the sense organ (the touch, for instance) is what, through the appropriate alteration of our body, provides the essential information for us to be aware that we have a certain affection of soft or hard. Correspondingly, an internal touch could be the proper judgemental organ that, differently from the other physical sense organs, is not outside us but, to use Cicero's image, wholly inside us. Once we are provided with the cognitive infallibility our affections grant us, we may elaborate on those affections, on the conceptual relations among them, by means of the internal touch.

The kind of judgemental activity I believe can be carried out by internal touch is such as to be in perfect harmony with the Cyrenaic theory of affections, in so far as the judgements we can formulate by means of the internal touch are best interpreted as subjective appearances. In place of an organizing mind that is able to supervene on perceptions and deal with those judgements that are mostly detached from the senses (see Ch. 3, § "The wooden horse"), the Cyrenaics spoke of touch as the internal sense aimed to provide subjective judgements on affections. This seems to suggest that there is a strict parallelism between outer and inner senses. Whereas the former provide us with those bodily alterations ultimately resulting in the mental awareness to be affected in a certain way, the latter register the modifications caused by affections in one's mind, so that we can create a second-order, higher level of mental activity enabling us to form subjective, yet refutable and fallible, judgements. For such judgements the Cyrenaics may well have employed the term "perceptions". This term and the related verb "to perceive" are used by Cicero himself and can also be found in those sources on the Cyrenaics, such as Plutarch and Diogenes Laertius, where a distinction is drawn between affections and perceptions.

A possible analogy between the Cyrenaics and the Epicureans may appropriately be drawn here. In their canon, the Epicureans set out sensations and preconceptions (and feelings) as criteria of truth. For them, sensations are understood as the reception of impressions from the environment and are said to be all true. There are thus close affinities between the Epicurean view that all sensations are true and the Cyrenaic doctrine that affections alone are apprehended and infallible. For the Epicureans, once it has often repeated itself a sensation gives rise to preconceptions, which are extra-perceptual concepts. Those basic concepts are further elaborated by the mind through analogy and similarity into more complex ideas. Now, one may imagine that the extra-affective activities the Cyrenaics appear to have admitted of in their epistemology could operate in a way similar to Epicurean preconceptions. Once the Cyrenaic individual has individuated some affections that keep recurring, she may fix them into more stable concepts. These perceptions are best interpreted as subjective and fallible appearances that may ideally constitute a web of judgemental items in addition to affections.[12]

ARISTIPPUS THE YOUNGER

If there is a Cyrenaic philosopher who could have been responsible for the introduction of extra-affective activities into the core of Cyrenaic epistemology, that could be Aristippus the Younger. He lived at a time when the Epicureans and the Cyrenaics discussed their rival hedonistic theories. It would be no surprise that their cognate, yet competing, epistemologies could be interpreted as reflecting shared inclinations and as influencing each other. Obviously, when one speaks of the role of Aristippus the Younger in the proper elaboration of Cyrenaic philosophy, the terrain becomes muddy. I do not oppose the usual exegetical scheme on whose basis Aristippus the Elder had no proper role in the elaboration of Cyrenaic doctrines (whereas his grandson is philosophically responsible for the formulation of those doctrines) to the contrary view that Aristippus the Elder was solely responsible for the elaboration of Cyrenaic doctrines (whereas his grandson played a very limited role in that formulation). We had better go on by relying on the few certainties we have on the question.

I argued earlier that on the basis of Diogenes' account one may ascribe to Aristippus the Elder the initial formulation of the main ethical and epistemological tenets of the Cyrenaic school. On the other hand, Aristippus the Younger is surely given a certain doctrinal importance in the Cyrenaic school by Aristocles' testimony (=T 4). In addition, Aristippus the Younger lived at a time when, on my interpretation, the Cyrenaic school had already elaborated its doctrines and was already recognized as a proper school. In addition, he also lived at a time when Cyrenaic philosophy (already identified as a proper body of philosophical views) was surely under attack either from schools that elaborated

rival views (such as Epicurus') or under the solicitation of philosophers, such as Pyrrho, who put forward metaphysical views
cognate to those of the Cyrenaics. What I mean is that Aristippus
the Younger could well have been in philosophical need to revise
the doctrinal coherence of the body of doctrines that, on my
understanding, his grandfather initially formulated.

All these elements force me to believe that Aristippus the
Younger is likely to have systematized into a coherent, or more
systematic whole, the body of doctrines his grandfather elaborated, in response to the philosophical challenges, friendly
or unfriendly, that Pyrrho and the Epicureans posed to the
Cyrenaics. If I have to indicate at least one conceptual element that
I believe can be correctly attributed to Aristippus the Younger, it
is the famous Cyrenaic neologisms of the kind "I am being X-ed",
of which there are no traces in the sources on the thought of
Aristippus the Elder. The invention of a neologism is in accordance with the conceptual systematization of a whole philosophical
system. Once the philosopher dealing with the systematization
has done the job, she may well suggest a new language able to
capture the philosophical innovations of the body of doctrines
she has newly organized. In the case of Cyrenaic philosophy, a
new language was actually needed to show the full import of a
philosophy that cannot be labelled as only barely innovative for
Greek philosophy.

6

LANGUAGE AND MEANING

THE CYRENAICS ON LANGUAGE

Among the sources on the Cyrenaics, Sextus is the only one who reports a rather interesting Cyrenaic argument on language. I quote Sextus' passage in full:

They [the Cyrenaics] say that no criterion is common to human beings, common names are assigned to objects [*onomata de koina tithesthai tois chrēmasin*]. (196) All in common in fact call something white or sweet, but they do not have something common that is white or sweet. Each human being is aware of his own private affection. One cannot say, however, whether this affection occurs in oneself and in one's neighbour from a white object, since one cannot grasp the affection of the neighbour, nor can his neighbour, since he cannot feel the affection of that other person. (197) And since no affection is common to us all, it is hasty to declare that what appears to me a certain way appears the same way to my neighbour as well. Perhaps I am constituted so as to be whitened by the external object when it comes into contact with my senses, while another person has the senses constructed so as to have been disposed differently. In any case, the *phainomenon* is absolutely not common to us

131

all [*ou pantōs oun koinon esti to phainomenon hēmin*]. (198)
That we really are not all affected in the same way because
of different dispositions of our senses is clear from the cases
of people who suffer from jaundice or ophthalmia and from
those who are in a natural condition. Just as the first group of
persons are affected yellowly, the second redly and the third
whitely from the same thing, so it is also probable that those
who are in a natural condition are not affected in the same
way by the same things because of the different construction
of their senses, but rather that the person with grey eyes is
affected in one way, the one with blue eyes in another, and
the one with black eyes in another yet different way. It follows
that the names we assign to things are common [*hōste koina
men hēmas onomata tithenai tois pragmasin*], but that we
have private affections [*pathē de ge echein idia*].

(*Math.* VII 196–8=T 34)

In this passage Sextus constructs an argument about the meaningfulness of language in the context of Cyrenaic philosophy, the
full import of which has not yet been recognized.[1] Sextus contrasts
the privacy of one's affections and the commonality of language
in Cyrenaic thinking. In the overall construction of Cyrenaic
philosophy that I have so far offered, nothing is common: things
in the world are not common, since strictly speaking there are
no proper things as unitary items. Affections are not common,
since each of us is affected in a peculiarly subjective and hardly
transferable way. The fact that Sextus makes the Cyrenaics claim
that language is common is thus something that strikes us. What
does it mean that "common names are assigned to objects" or that
"all people in common call something white or sweet"?

In the passage Sextus says twice that "common names are
assigned to things" (or to objects): at the beginning and at the
end of the extract I have quoted. While in the latter case, there
are no doubts that the word used by Sextus to mean "thing"
is *pragma*, in the former case there are some textual variants,

spanning from *chrēmasin* (Natorp and Mannebach), to *pragmasin* (Kayser, thus duplicating exactly the same final sentence at *Math.* VII 198), *krimasin* (Bekker) or *sunkrimasin* (Mutschmann and Giannantoni). In any case, as Tsouna (1998: 106) has correctly suggested, all the textual variants for the sentence at VII 196 (as well as *pragma* at VII 198) may refer to either external objects or affections. But the examples Sextus gives in the passage are always of secondary qualities, such as sweet and white, and never of "objects", such as horse and stone. When he says that for the Cyrenaics common names are assigned to things, what Sextus has in mind is that for the Cyrenaics common names are given to those secondary qualities we experience when we are affected in a certain way.

In the argument about language Sextus attributes to the Cyrenaics, how is it possible to have private affections of white (which are always infallibly subjective and cannot be transferred to anyone else) and, at the same time, a common understanding of the term "white"? Sextus warns that for the Cyrenaics "all people in common call something white or sweet". All people have a common "meaning" for the term white or sweet. "But they do not have something common that is white or sweet": the same people have private and subjective affections of white and sweet. Sextus later insists on the privacy of our affections, when he remarks, "In any case, the *phainomenon* is absolutely not common to us all". What is in focus here is exactly how it is possible to account for the meaningfulness of language in a kind of epistemology centred on private and non-transferable affections.

This is a problem precisely because, as Sextus' argument shows, the Cyrenaics allow for common names in the absence of absolutely shared objects and in the presence of absolutely private affections. If the Cyrenaics admitted of a world of common objects, the meaningfulness of language would not be under any threat. Words would have (as their meanings) the things in the world to which they would refer: as in any referential semantics, including the Greek one, the meaning of a term would be the object in the world for which the term stands. On my interpretation, the Cyrenaics are committed to inde-terminacy and do not admit of objects as unitary items. That is the reason why, for the Cyrenaics, words such as "white" or "sweet" always refer to private affections. They could not refer to anything else, indeed not to objects in the world. That is why they have to explain how it is possible that language is mean-ingful in their world of private affections.

ARISTOTLE

Sextus has seen that, given their epistemological and metaphys-ical commitments, there is a problem for the Cyrenaics as far as their theory of language and meaning is concerned. He focuses on the kernel of the problem when he contrasts common names and uncommon (i.e. private) affections. Sextus provides the solution to this problem when he says that the Cyrenaics held that common names have to be assigned to things (i.e. to those secondary quali-ties the individual privately experiences when she is infallibly affected). Nonetheless Sextus does not say how the transition between private affections and common names could be carried out for the Cyrenaics. Tsouna (1998: 107), for instance, insists on the point that, on the basis of Sextus' passage, common names *are assigned* (*tithesthai*) to objects, thus suggesting that convention-alism is behind the theory of meaning of the Cyrenaics. Since we all experience the affection of white in different contexts, we all decide the convention to call "white" what we believe to be one and the same colour. But the fact that the Cyrenaics could have been conventionalists does not in itself explain how words are meaningful in the Cyrenaic world, where common names always refer to private affections. To say that we all decide the convention to call "white" what we believe to be one and the same colour does not fully explain how we effectively move from private affections of white to the common name of "white". Conventionalism may appear to be the most reasonable explanation one can find in the end, after having tried to make good sense of the philosophical details of the Cyrenaic theory of language and meaning, as Sextus expounds it. Conventionalism in itself, however, does not say anything that could be immediately helpful in shedding light on the very details of Cyrenaic semantics.

To find a plausible answer as to how the Cyrenaics defended their theory of language and meaning, we should pause for a while and see how such a theory is in sharp contrast with the classical theory of meaning Aristotle has summed up in the semantic triangle he illustrates at the beginning of *De Interpretatione*. Here Aristotle says:

> Now spoken sounds [*ta en tēi phōnēi*] are symbols of affections in the soul [*tōn en tēi psuchēi pathēmatōn sumbola*], and written marks symbols of spoken sounds. And just as written marks are not the same for all men, neither are spoken sounds. But what these are in first place signs of – affections of the soul – are the same for all; and what these affections are likenesses of – actual things – are also the same [*hōn mentoi tauta sēmeia proton, tauta pasi pathēmata tēs psuchēs, kai hōn tauta homoiōmata pragmata ēdē tauta*].
>
> (*Int.* 16a4–8)

Let us for the moment isolate three elements in Aristotle's passage: spoken sounds, affections and actual things. In the final sentence of the passage, Aristotle holds that the spoken sounds stand for (are signs of) the affections of the soul, which he maintains to be the same for all (I take him to be saying here that when one of us says "white", the same affection of white arises in each of us). But, Aristotle adds, the affections of the soul are images of the things in the world, which are, like affections, already the same (I take him to be saying that the affections of white we really have correspond to actual white things in the world, which are, in turn, white for us all). The crucial term in this semantic triangle is "affection": affections both refer to the spoken sounds (which are their signs) and to the things in the world (of which they are the images).

Aristotle insists on the absolute isomorphism between things, words and affections in so far as he defends a referential account of meaning: for someone to understand the meaning of "white" is to link mentally the affection of white he undergoes to the actual white thing.[2] For Aristotle, each of us has the same affection of white, with reference to the word "white" and to actual white things. On the other hand, the Cyrenaics accept only one of the two relations of Aristotle's triangle: that between words and affections. They cannot accept the other relation of Aristotle's triangle – that between affections and things in the worlds – because for them there is no common world (of objects) out there to be shared. In accepting just the relations between affections and words, the Cyrenaics seriously jeopardize the conditions of meaningfulness for words, since affections for them are not images of actual things. On their account, affections cannot be the instruments through which words and things get in touch, hence words cannot get their meaningfulness from affections actually corresponding to things. The Cyrenaics thus retain the Aristotelian view that words refer to affections, but affections are seen to be private and not corresponding to actual things. How could the Cyrenaics explain the fact that words will have shared meanings, to be understood by any speaker of a language, if words refer exclusively to private affections and not to actual things? This is the most urgent problem to be answered, if we want to ascribe to the Cyrenaics a credible theory of meaning and language.

GORGIAS

Although in striking contrast with the rest of Greek semantics, the Cyrenaics' views did not come out of the blue. Before them, Gorgias defended a similar conception of meaning and initiated a trend of ideas in ancient philosophy of language, but I see the Cyrenaics as the front-runners in Hellenism. I first show how Gorgias and the Cyrenaics defend the view that, to be meaningful, a term can even not refer to a thing in the world. Second, I shall deal with Gorgias' behavioural resolution to the problem of meaning, thus suggesting that this solution is the one that, at least in principle, could have been available to the Cyrenaics. I shall also argue that the behavioural solution is implicit, or at least presupposed, by other aspects of Cyrenaic philosophy.

Gorgias' approach to language can be detected in the last section on incommunicability in *On What Is Not* (DK82B3=Sextus, *Math.* VII 83–7), which shortly precedes Sextus' own account of Cyrenaic philosophy of language (=*Math.* VII 196–8, the section on which we have been concentrating so far). Gorgias' argument goes thus:

> The means by which we indicate are words, and words are not identical with the things that really are. Therefore, we do not indicate to our neighbour the things that exist but only words, which are other than what really is. Just as the visible things will not become audible (and vice versa), so too, since the things that are exist externally, it will not become identical with our words. Not being words, it cannot be revealed to another person.
>
> Words, he [Gorgias] asserts, are formed from the impressions caused by external objects, that is, by sensory objects [*ho ge mēn logos, phēsin, apo tōn exōthen prospiptontōn hēmin pragmatōn sunistatai, toutesti tōn aisthētōn*]. From the occurrence of flavour there is in fact produced in us the word uttered concerning this quality, and by the incidence of colour the word concerning that colour. And if this be so, it would not be the word that mirrors the external object, but the external object that is indicative for the word [*ouch ho logos tou ektos parastatikos estin, alla to ektos tou logou mēnutikon ginetai*]. (*Math.* VII 84–5)

In this passage, Gorgias rejects the (Aristotelian) idea that there is a linkage between words and objects, such as that the meaning of a word is the object in the world for which the word stands. What about the other half of Aristotle's triangle, the relation between words and affections? This relation is at the basis of the Cyrenaic theory of language as it has been so far reconstructed. Gorgias observes that words cannot derive their meanings from affections and perceptions: each of us has, in fact, her own subjective and private sensations. This argument is put forward in the pseudo-Aristotelian pamphlet *On Melissus, Xenophanes and Gorgias*, which preserves an alternative edition of Gorgias' *On What Is Not*:

> Even if it is possible to know and read a word, how can the hearer have a conception of the same thing? For it is impossible for the same thing to exist at the same time in a number of separate people; for then the one would be two. But even if the same thing was in a number of different people, nothing would stop it from appearing differently in them, given that they are not completely alike, nor in the same place; for if there was such a thing, it would be one and not two. But not even the same man appears to perceive similar things in himself at the same time, but different things with his hearing and with his sight, and different again at the precise moment and in the past, so that one man can hardly perceive the same as another. Thus it is impossible, if anything exists, for it to be known; and, if it is known, no one could reveal it to another; for the reason that things are not words, and because no one has the same conception as another [*dia te to mē einai ta pragmata logous, kai hoti oudeis heteron heterōi tauton ennoei*].   (980b9–22)

The last two lines of this extract from *On Melissus, Xenophanes and Gorgias* significantly exemplify Gorgias' views on language. First, things are not words. Between things and words there is always an insuperable gulf and words cannot signify things. Second, words cannot derive their meanings from their being linked with affections, since each of us has private and subjective ways to perceive things. If it were not so, each of us would have the same perception, even at different times, under different circumstances and so on. Yet, words *do* have shared meanings. For someone like Gorgias and the Cyrenaics, who are aware that the semantic linkage between words and affections is under the threat of privacy and subjectivism, the only way to account for the meaningfulness of words is to accept a behavioural theory of meaning. A behavioural approach to meaning is exactly that of Gorgias, at least according to the interpretation of Alexander Mourelatos (1987) and G. B. Kerferd (1981a, 1984), which I share.[3]

Gorgias' behavioural approach to the apparently inexplicable fact that words have meanings for those who reject the view that the meaning of a word is its referent can be found in the following sentence:

> from the occurrence of flavour there is produced in us the word uttered concerning this quality, and by the incidence of colour the word concerning that colour. And if this be so, it would not be the word that mirrors the external object, but the external object that is indicative for the word.
>
> (*Math.* VII 85)

We learn the meaning of words by combining the sensations we have (of colours, flavours and so on) with the way words interact with one another and with the way things are "indicative" (*mēnutikon*) of the words. As Mourelatos puts it, "it is rather uncanny how closely the vocabulary of section 85 [of *Math.* VII] resembles the vocabulary of modern behaviourist theory. External objects … 'fall upon us' or 'make an impact on us' or 'impinge upon us' [*prospiptontōn hēmin, hupoptōseōs*]" (1987: 163). Other works by Gorgias reinforce the idea that he explained the meaningfulness of words by endorsing a behavioural theory of meaning. Gorgias holds that a word always has an effect on other speakers of the same language when he says, "in response to the happy and unhappy occurrences affecting things and bodies, the soul comes itself to experience a certain emotion, through *logos*" (*Hel.* 9); or when by comparing words and drugs he remarks, "just as different drugs draw different humours from the body ... so too with words" (*Hel.* 14). Again, with reference to these passages, Mourelatos says, "if only we changed the archaic expression 'drawing out humours' to the behaviourist idiom of 'eliciting a physiological reaction' this sentence could just as well have been written by such advocates of the stimulus–response conception of meaning as Leonard Bloomfield or B.F. Skinner" (1987: 158). It is exactly in the context of such a behavioural theory of meaning that the linkage between words and affections is no longer problematic. We relate the words we use and the affections we feel by learning how to cope with other people's reactions to linguistic stimuli and by observing how words are indicative of things. Gorgias' theory of meaning shows how it is possible that we learn the meaning of words indicating colours and flavours by relating them to our affections of those colours and flavours. By experiencing the practice of language (how words are used, how other people react to words), we eventually learn the meaning of terms, such as "white" or "sweet", as well as how these terms are related to our sensations.

By providing fresher strength for a suggestion Rodolfo Mondolfo (1953) put forward some years ago, what I suggest is that the Cyrenaics may well have derived their theory of meaning from Gorgias. When we are faced with the account of language Sextus attributes to the Cyrenaics, we realize that there is a gap, both conceptual and explanatory, in that account. The Cyrenaics contrast private affections with common names, when they are reported to say, "all people in common call something white or sweet, but they do not have something common that is white or sweet" (*Math.* VII 196). Yet, in Sextus' account, it is not explained how it is possible for the Cyrenaics to move from private affections

to common names. For all those philosophers not adopting a
referential semantics on whose basis the meaning of a term is its
referent in the world, the *only* conceptual way to account for a credible theory of meaning is behaviourism, in whatever fashion one
may want to adopt it. When the Cyrenaics maintain that words are
commonly used and meaningful, they thus have to invoke some
sort of behavioural theory of meaning. There is nothing in Sextus'
account to prevent us from assuming that the Cyrenaics may
have maintained that we learn the meaning of the words "sweet"
or "white" by seeing how other people use those terms and how
they react to them. More particularly, in Sextus' passage there is a
crucial sentence that can now be fully given its true interpretation.
I have earlier argued that the things in the expression "common
names are assigned [*tithesthai*] to things" (*Math.* VII 196, 198)
are affections of secondary qualities. Now, under the light of the
behavioural interpretation I attribute to the Cyrenaics, the verb "to
assign" does not express any sort of conventionalism where people
in common linguistically christen things and where the meanings
of words are decided by convention. In my interpretation, the verb
"to assign" refers to the personal act of naming an affection. This
act will be performed by an individual who, after having learned
the meaning of words by interacting with other speakers of her
language, is able to link an occurrence of a linguistic item to an
affection she feels.

WITTGENSTEIN

At this point, there is a philosophical comparison that naturally
comes to mind and that may shed further light on the philosophy
of language of the Cyrenaics and on their philosophy as a whole.
I refer to Wittgenstein's conception of meaning as set forth in the
Philosophical Investigations. Wittgenstein's idea that the meaning
of a word is its use in the language goes along with a rejection
of a referential theory of meaning and with the parallel rejection

of the possibility of a private language for naming sensations. The ultimate ground on which Wittgenstein's theory of language rests is behaviourism. There are therefore striking philosophical similarities between the conception of meaning I have attributed to Gorgias and to the Cyrenaics and that of Wittgenstein. In particular, I claim that Wittgenstein's argument about the naming of sensations is of great help in assessing the full implication of some important aspects of Cyrenaic philosophy.

In the first paragraph of the *Philosophical Investigations*, Wittgenstein – wrongly – identifies Augustine's conception of language as the polemical target of his theory of meaning. After having quoted a passage from the *Confessions*, where the learning of language is described,[4] Wittgenstein observes:

> these words, it seems to me, give us a particular picture of the essence of human language. It is this: the individual words in language name objects – sentences are combinations of such names. – In this picture of language we find the roots of the following idea: Every word has a meaning. This meaning is correlated with the word. It is the object for which the word stands. (1953: §1)

To such a referential theory of meaning, Wittgenstein opposes his own, where to learn a language means to become accustomed to the rules of those language games that constitute that language.

How does this theory of meaning work in those cases where sensations are involved? Wittgenstein asks. He focuses on "pain", one of the two polar affections of Cyrenaic ethics (*ibid.*: §244). How does a person know that what she feels is pain? Is a semantic linkage between the word "pain" and the feeling of pain (the affection of pain, in Cyrenaic terms) at all possible? This is exactly the problem about meaning the Cyrenaics had faced: having got rid of the world as a determinate entity made up of distinct objects, how is it possible to refer meaningful words to affections that are ineluctably private and subjective? Wittgenstein argues that it is impossible for one to have a private language for naming one's sensations, on the ground that, if provided with a private language, one would not be offered *any* criterion to assess the correct re-identification of one's sensation.[5]

Wittgenstein argues for the same kind of behavioural answer to the problem about the meaning of "pain" (and of all other words indicating sensations) the Cyrenaics (and Gorgias) seem to have argued for. For Wittgenstein, we learn the meaning of the word "pain" by learning the pain-behaviour (see *ibid.*: §§244, 245, 384). What is, however, important for us here is that in his argument about pain Wittgenstein distinguishes between what we may call the privacy of the owner and epistemological privacy:

> In what sense are my sensations *private*? – Well, only I can know whether I am really in pain; another person can only surmise it. – In one way this is wrong, and in another nonsense. If we are using the word "to know" as it is normally used (and how else are we to use it?), then other people very often know when I am in pain. – Yes, but all the same not with the certainty with which I know it myself! – It can't be said of me at all (except perhaps as a joke) that I *know* I am in pain. What is it supposed to mean – except perhaps that I *am* in pain?
>
> Other people cannot be said to learn of my sensations *only* from my behaviour, – for I cannot be said to learn of them. I *have* them.
>
> The truth is: it makes sense to say about other people that they doubt whether I am in pain; but not to say it about myself.   (*Ibid.*: §246)

In Wittgenstein's argument about sensations, there is a sense in which the subject feeling the sensation of pain is in a privileged condition. The subject *has* the sensation of pain (while others do not have *her* sensation of pain). The subject who feels the sensation of pain cannot be in doubt that she is really feeling pain. This means that, as far as her sensations are concerned, the subject experiences a privacy that is the privacy of the owner. In a fundamental sense, the subject *owns* her sensations. In conceptual terms, such an ownership is easily translatable into the same kind of privacy of affections the Cyrenaics themselves defended. In both pictures – that is, the Cyrenaics' and Wittgenstein's – the subject is exclusively aware of being affected in the way she is actually affected. That is why in the passage of the *Philosophical Investigations* just quoted, Wittgenstein observes, "It can't be said of me at all (except perhaps as a joke) that I *know* I am in pain". The use of the verb "to know" with reference to the expression "I am in pain" is a nonsense, in so far as the subject uttering the sentence "I am in pain" is aware of being in pain, with no possibility to be mistaken about that (see also *ibid.*: §408).

The exclusive privacy of affections is also the basis of the Cyrenaics' epistemological view that only affections are knowable. On the contrary, Wittgenstein does not claim that we know only our sensations and that these are the exclusive source of knowledge. Yet, both Wittgenstein and the Cyrenaics insist – although with different emphasis – on the peculiarity of "I"-states and "I"-reports. The other aspect to which Wittgenstein (*ibid.*: §246) draws our attention is that we come to understand our sensations not by relying on a private language but, as it were, by learning the language-game (and the related grammar) of pain. And this can be done by observing other people' pain-behaviours. When he remarks that it is wrong to say that "only I can know whether I am really in pain; another person can only surmise it", Wittgenstein refers to the argument developed at length (*ibid.*: §§243–71) that we ourselves arrive at the understanding that we feel pain only by means of the acquisition of the (public) grammar of the word "pain", namely by understanding how this word is used by all speakers of the same language. There is no way, no private language, by means of which we can arrive at a private understanding of our sensations and of their very nature.

This is the kind of *epistemological privacy* Wittgenstein does not believe to be possible, as far as sensations are concerned.

If Wittgenstein's overall argument is correct, this will mean that none of us will make sense of our sensations and affections if not by relying on rules and behaviours that are public and publicly shared. In the absence of such rules, we would not be able to make *any* sense of *any* of our sensations. This argument will apply, at least in principle, to Cyrenaic affections too. The Cyrenaics could coherently claim that we will know our affections if there are common rules and shared behaviours that ultimately allow us to come to terms with the very nature and content of our affections. It has to be noted that the fact that we come to terms with our affections only by means of public rules and behaviours does not prejudice the peculiarity of affections the Cyrenaics wholeheartedly endorsed. Affections remain private events carrying wholly subjective features. In the Cyrenaic world I am unmistakably aware that I am being whitened or that I am feeling pain at this moment, although I have learned the meaning of "white" and "pain" by observing others using the same word in different circumstances.

In his argument about the Cyrenaics' theory of meaning, Sextus says:

> Each human being is aware of his own private affection. One cannot say, however, whether this affection occurs in oneself and in one's neighbour from a white object, since one cannot grasp the affection of the neighbour, nor can his neighbour, since he cannot feel the affection of that other person. (*Math.* VII 196)

Sextus' remark can be interpreted along the lines of the Wittgensteinian argument I have been reconstructing so far. The Cyrenaic individual is aware of her own affections in a way that is wholly peculiar to her. She cannot submit to the affections of others who, like her, are aware of their affections in their own inevitably subjective way (this point recalls Wittgenstein's privacy of the owner). At the same time, there is nothing in Sextus' passage that prevents us from assuming that Cyrenaic individuals, although incapable of having access to the affections of others, have learned how to use words such as "white", "pain" and so on by observing the (public) grammar of such words in the language they all share.

On the contrary, the behavioural solution to the problem of meaning I have suggested as one possible solution the Cyrenaics may have adopted makes it probable that they could have endorsed the kind of (Wittgensteinian) distinction between epistemological privacy and privacy of the owner. Of course, the Cyrenaics did not elaborate the problem in the terms Wittgenstein himself employed, but I interpret Sextus' insistence that the Cyrenaics singled out language as the exclusive element that is common in their world of fragmented selves and unstable objects as evidence that they indeed recognized language as the only public medium human beings have to make sense of themselves and of their inner world. Perhaps we do not wish to grant the Cyrenaics the full elaboration of the distinction between a private and a more public aspect of affections. On the basis of the evidence on Cyrenaic philosophy we are offered by ancient sources, one is, however, allowed to suggest that the Cyrenaic views about language and meaning would be understandable only if the Cyrenaics were prepared to accept the view that we conceptually come to terms with our sensations by means of a public and shared language. This view is, in turn, implicit in Sextus' crucial passage on which we have focused our attention in this chapter, at least if we want to make sense of it. If they did not endorse this view, the Cyrenaics could not even claim to be able to deal conceptually with those affections they made the epistemological and ethical fulcrum of their philosophy.

There are two important consequences for Cyrenaic philosophy. The first is that both the alleged behavioural solution to the problem of meaning the Cyrenaics may well have endorsed and the indispensable commonality they grant to language both presuppose that there are other people in the world beyond the single individual. In the behavioural theory of meaning the Cyrenaics are likely to have endorsed, the individual learns the meaning of words by understanding how language is spoken by other people, whose existence is thus presupposed. Again, language will be common if it is spoken by many people, not by a single individual. Because of this, those who suggest that the Cyrenaics may have raised the problem of other minds are on the wrong track (see Tsouna 1998: 89–104).

Second, the behavioural solution to the problem of meaning the Cyrenaics are likely to have endorsed and the indispensable commonality they grant to language both presuppose that the Cyrenaic individual is capable of carrying out an epistemological activity that is truly extra-affective. The idea that we learn the meaning of words not by relating the object in the world for which the word stands to the word itself but by interpreting how other people use those words requires that we are able to use epistemological capacities that are not ultimately reducible to affections. Such capacities will be required to an even greater extent if what lies behind the commonality of language is the view that we come to terms with the nature of our affections by means of shared linguistic rules and behaviours. If I can catalogue the sensation I am feeling at the moment as a case of pain only by relying on a shared understanding of common rules and behaviours, that understanding will require epistemological skills that are not easily derivable from affections. This shows that, although ineluctably central to Cyrenaic thinking, affections are not the only epistemological items the Cyrenaics admitted of.

7

PLEASURE AND HAPPINESS

As far as Cyrenaic ethics is concerned, the most relevant source is Diogenes Laertius:

> The end is not the same as happiness, since the end is particular pleasure [*telos men gar einai tēn kata meros ēdonēn*], whereas happiness is a collection made out of particular pleasures [*eudaimonian de to ek tōn merikōn ēdonōn sustēma*]. Among these both past and future pleasures are counted together. Particular pleasure is desirable because of itself. On the other hand, happiness is desirable not because of itself, but because of the particular pleasures.
>
> (II 87–8=T 20)

We are immediately given the kernel of Cyrenaic ethics: pleasure is the end and pleasure is desirable in virtue of itself. On the other hand, the importance of happiness is derivative of pleasure, since happiness is not desirable for itself but in virtue of particular pleasures. In light of the predominance of pleasure over happiness, it has been claimed – quite correctly – that the Cyrenaics constitute the only exception to Greek eudaemonism: the view, absolutely central to Greek ethics, that happiness is the end of life.[1] Later, while still endorsing the claim that the Cyrenaics are anti-eudaemonists, I shall restrict the scope of

Cyrenaic hedonism by describing the secondary, yet proper role of happiness in the ethics of the Cyrenaics. For the moment, let us concentrate on the kernel of Cyrenaic hedonism, namely on the view that pleasure is the end.

CYRENAIC HEDONISM

We have seen at length that the Cyrenaics posit pleasure and pain as the two central feelings of their ethics. As Diogenes says, for the Cyrenaics pleasure is a smooth motion: "they [the Cyrenaics] said that there are two kinds of affection, pleasure and pain, the former a smooth, the latter a rough motion" (DL II 86; see also Sextus *Pyr.* I 215; Clement of Alexandria [=*SSR* IV A 175]). As with all other *pathē*, for the Cyrenaics pleasure has a physical part (i.e. the physical alteration in the body) and a mental counterpart (i.e. the mental awareness of the bodily alteration). When they claim that pleasure is a smooth motion of the flesh, the Cyrenaics suggest that like all other Cyrenaic affections, pleasure begins with a smooth alteration in our body. To avoid the kind of objection Socrates makes to Philebus at the beginning of the dialogue bearing that name, one has to be mentally aware to be affected pleasurably; if not, one could not even know to feel pleasure (*Phlb.* 11b–c).[2] On the ground of the same argument, the Cyrenaics claim that after the initial alteration of the body (the smooth motion) one becomes mentally aware of that alteration. It is at this point that pleasure – "the smooth motion resulting in perception" (DL II 85) – becomes the end for the Cyrenaics.

Once the double aspect (both physical and mental) of Cyrenaic pleasure has been highlighted, we may revert to another important claim of Cyrenaic ethics. The kind of pleasure the Cyrenaics make the goal of one's life is bodily pleasure. As Diogenes puts it, "the pleasure [the Cyrenaics talk about] is bodily pleasure [*tou sōmatos*], which is the end" (II 87). How shall we understand this claim? Are we to understand that the only pleasure worth pursuing is that of the body? I do not believe that the Cyrenaics actually claimed that the only pleasure that is worth pursuing is exclusively that of the body. According to Diogenes, the Cyrenaics openly admitted of pleasures that are not bodily, but of the soul: "[for the Cyrenaics] not all mental pleasures and pains are derived from bodily pleasures and pain" (II 89). Even pleasures of the soul are spoken of as if they are pleasures worth pursuing for their own sake and as ends (see DL II 90, 96). When they are reported to claim – on the basis of Diogenes' testimony – that the kind of the pleasure that is the goal of life is the pleasure of the body, the Cyrenaics are simply holding, I suggest, that pleasure always starts off in the body.

Let us take a basic pleasure: the one we feel when we drink fresh water on a hot summer day. Through the initial alteration of the appropriate sense organ, we become aware of feeling pleasure when we drink that water. Things may become more complicated when we take a less basic pleasure, such as sexual pleasure. Contrary to commonsensical assumptions, sexual pleasure is not a simple pleasure, since it involves much more than the mere physical excitement and ends with much more than a physical gratification. Sexual pleasure begins with an undeniable excitement of the body. When such an excitement is actually felt, however, it is immediately mixed up, in a way that is so typical of genuine human relationship, with a vast array of emotions as well as concern for the benefit of the other. Further, the excitement one feels when one makes love with the person one is in love with is channelled and shaped by one's own beliefs about love and sex. It is only in the context of one's beliefs about love and sex that sexual acts gain the actual meaning one subjectively attaches to them. If, for instance, a lover believes that when he is making love with his beloved he is actually recreating the sort of original unity of separate halves that are always in search of each other that Plato speaks of in the *Symposium* (189d–193d), the kind of pleasure he feels is not at all reducible to a mere physical gratification. It involves a rather thick emotional aspect that is openly predominant over that gratification.

Even in the case of sexual pleasure, which may represent for us the paradigmatic case of a bodily pleasure, there is an element transcending the boundaries of the body, in the way in which that pleasure is both conceived of and experienced. There is, therefore, an important aspect in every pleasure that is imputable to the role that beliefs play in the formation of (and in the experience of) those pleasures. If with a basic pleasure such as the satisfaction of a summer thirst the role of our pleasure beliefs (that is, our beliefs about pleasure) is minimal, in less basic pleasures (such as sexual pleasure) the role played by our pleasure beliefs will amount to a bit more than the mere awareness of feeling that very pleasure. In the latter cases our pleasure beliefs can be understood as shaping the way in which pleasure is conceived of and actually felt.

BODILY AND MENTAL PLEASURES

The Cyrenaics show their awareness that our beliefs play a proper role when we experience pleasures. They say, for instance, that some are incapable of feeling any pleasure because their minds are perverted.[3] In addition, the Cyrenaics recognize the existence of pleasures of the soul, that is, of pleasures deriving from friendship, from honouring the parents and the country (see DL II 89, 96). These pleasures cannot be properly explained by exclusive reference to a physical ingredient. Although it is not desirable in itself but in virtue of its consequences, the Cyrenaics also value prudence as a good (II 91). The Cyrenaics also insist that although pleasure is always desirable in itself, "there are things productive of certain pleasures that are often of painful nature and are the opposite of pleasure, so that the accumulation of pleasures that does not produce happiness is difficult" (see DL II 90). We shall return to this passage but, even at a first sight, it shows that for the Cyrenaics it is possible to speak of pleasures that have a painful cause and of others that have different causes. This passage surely implies that the Cyrenaics allow for the possibility of discerning between pleasures and the related causes. This could be done only if we were equipped by a judgemental capacity that is epistemologically independent of pleasures and that allows us to form our own beliefs on pleasure.

It has to be noted that when I speak of a judging capacity and of the role it plays in the way we conceive of and experience pleasures, I do not intend to speak of a capacity that can provide us either with objective judgements on the goodness of pleasures or with rationally grounded beliefs on how, for instance, sexual pleasure has to be universally experienced. The kind of judgemental capacity I claim could be accommodated in the Cyrenaics' ethics of pleasure is purely subjective and is perfectly explicable in terms of that epistemology of subjective appearances that I illustrated in Chapter 5 (§ "Beyond affections"). To go back to the example of sex, in the context of Cyrenaic thinking the beliefs that shape the way in which sexual pleasure is conceived of and experienced are formed only in a subjective way, that is, only in relation to how things appear to the subject being sexually affected.

Summing up, for the Cyrenaics pleasure is the end. For them pleasure has both a physical and a mental ingredient. The latter shifts from the mere awareness of actually feeling a pleasure in basic pleasures (thirst) to more elaborate cases where our own beliefs on pleasure play an important role in the actual way we experience it. When they claim that the pleasure that is the end is the pleasure of the body, the Cyrenaics may well have meant that each and every pleasure begins with an alteration of the body. The alteration of the body, however, is inevitably followed by a mental counterpart, more or less elaborate, according to the different types of pleasure we experience. This characterization includes many pleasures we daily experience and does not rule out any kind of pleasure we could in principle recognize as "non-bodily".

Even the pleasure one derives from realizing that one's country is prosperous may be conceived of as beginning with a bodily alteration. For a start, one may get pleasure (for one's soul) from the prosperity of one's country, once one has actually seen *with one's eyes* that one's country is indeed prosperous. One goes around in one's country; one's eyes are altered in such a way that one can see large parts of the country to be in wonderful economic, social and natural conditions. Second, one may get pleasure (for one's soul) from the prosperity of one's country, once one has actually *realized* that there are large parts of it that are in wonderful economic, social and natural conditions. This could be done only if one were able to form a judgement about the economic, social and natural conditions in which one's country finds itself to be. For the Cyrenaics, however, extra-affective judgements can only be formulated as subjective appearances, namely by transferring to the activity of the mind the kind of perceptual scheme we use when external sense organs are involved. The Cyrenaics speak of a special internal touch, which I interpreted earlier as the means by which Cyrenaic individuals construct their own, extra-affective and subjective beliefs. Strictly speaking, one may well assume that even in those cases where a pleasure of the soul is concerned, there is an alteration of the body as the basis of that pleasure, namely the alteration caused by the internal touch in our minds. And the two examples Cicero gives when he refers to the Cyrenaic doctrine of the internal touch are, in effect, pleasure and pain (see Ch. 5, § "Internal touch").

On the basis of this argument, even pleasures of the soul can be catalogued as bodily pleasures. This is so because even in the case of pleasures that at first sight we may label "non-bodily", there is an alteration of the body, namely that caused by the internal touch into our mind. In light of this, the Cyrenaics can be understood as endorsing a full-scale hedonism, spanning from simpler bodily pleasures to more sophisticated types of mental pleasures. This argument is not aimed to undermine the view – surely ascribable to the Cyrenaics – that in Cyrenaic ethics there is a preference of bodily "bodily" pleasures over mental ones. On the point Diogenes observes, "they [the Cyrenaics] claim that bodily pleasures are better than mental ones and that bodily pains are worse than mental ones. This is the reason why offenders are punished with the former" (DL II 90). We may suggest that bodily "bodily" pleasures are preferable in so far as they retain more perspicuously the immediacy of the physical ingredient of pleasure (see O'Keefe 2010: 118). Yet the overall point I wish to make when I attribute to the Cyrenaics the view that mental pleasures too can be ultimately explained as cases of bodily pleasures is that, although preferring bodily "bodily" pleasures, the Cyrenaics embrace in their hedonism all kinds of pleasures.

PLEASURE AS *MONOCHRONOS*

We move on to another important feature of Cyrenaic hedonism: the time-limitedness of pleasure. Athenaeus says:

> Having approved of the affection of pleasure, he claimed that pleasure is the end of life, and that happiness is based on it. He added that pleasure occupies one temporal unit [*monochronon*], since he believed, as profligates do, that neither the memory of past enjoyments nor the expectation of future ones be important for him. Judging the good in light of the present alone, he considered that what he enjoyed in the past and will enjoy in the future be not important for him, the former because it exists no more, the latter because it does not yet exist and is not manifest.
> (*Deipnosophists* XII 544a–b=*SSR* IV A 174=T 8)

I argued earlier for the translation of *monochronos* as "occupying one temporal unit". The crucial idea behind the translation is that, like all other affections, for the Cyrenaics pleasure has its own temporal unit, which is defined by the time the affection of pleasure lasts before evanescing forever. I equate the meaning of *monochronos* in Athenaeus' passage with that of *merikos* (particular) in Diogenes' line that for the Cyrenaics the end is the particular pleasure (DL II 87). In both passages, what is highlighted is that the kind of pleasure the Cyrenaics hold to be the end is the time-limited pleasure that, in being such, is also particular and partial. Like all other Cyrenaic affections, pleasure dies away with time. The goal of life is exactly the particular pleasure the individual is feeling at the present time.

The irrelevance of past and future pleasure is a point Diogenes himself remarks on when he says, "They [the Cyrenaics] deny that pleasure consists in the memory or expectation of the good, as Epicurus held" (II 89). Athenaeus is, however, the one who gives us more details on the crucial difference between past and future pleasures and present ones in Cyrenaic ethics. The Cyrenaics do not deny that future and past pleasures exist, since they claim that these pleasures, in addition to present ones, are counted together to reach happiness (II 88). What they claim – and this is the point that both Athenaeus and Diogenes make – is that past and future pleasures do not count as the end on the ground that these pleasures cannot actually be experienced in the present. The goal of life is instead the particular and uni-temporal pleasure of the present: what one has enjoyed in the past exists no more, whereas what one will enjoy in the future does not exist yet and is not manifest.

Cyrenaic ethics and epistemology can be regarded as perfectly complementary, in so far as they are both rooted in the funda-mental (Cyrenaic) concept of affection. Without postulating any predominance of one over the other, the Cyrenaics centre both their ethics and epistemology on the idea that what is essentially important are those transient affections (of white or of pleasure) of which human beings are infallibly aware, and which consti-tute the basis for both the epistemological and ethical life of the Cyrenaic individual. Diogenes reports a version of a famous argument – the Cradle argument – to show how the Cyrenaics argued for their hedonism.[4] He says, "That pleasure is the end is proved by the fact that, from our youth onwards, we are instinctively attracted to it, and, once we obtain it, we seek for nothing more and avoid nothing so much as its opposite, pain" (II 88). The Cradle argument provides, I claim, a secondary reason why the Cyrenaics may have historically defended their hedonism. My point is rather that the ultimate reasoning behind Cyrenaic ethics is grounded on the notion of affection that the Cyrenaics so vividly place at the centre of their philosophy.

THE CYRENAICS AND EPICURUS

At this point one may wonder whether the kind of hedonism centred on the pleasure of the present that the Cyrenaics adopted can account for a credible ethics. As Tim O'Keefe puts it:

Why do they [the Cyrenaics] reject planning for the future …? This seems like a good strategy for leading an *unpleasant* life. If I blow all my money jetting off to Vegas and indulging in drinking bouts, gambling, orgies and enjoying fish, then I'll probably end up on the street impoverished, and ill.

(2002: 396)

This is an essential question to ask in order to assess the credibility of Cyrenaic ethics more fully. We shall be in a good position to answer it once we deal with a preliminary question, namely about the difference between the hedonism of the Cyrenaics and that of Epicurus. For reasons of space, I shall deal with this question very briefly by focusing only on the main points of divergence between the ethics of Epicurus and that of the Cyrenaics that Diogenes himself identifies.[5] Diogenes raises two points in connection with his treatment of the ethics of Epicurus (book X of the *Lives*) and that of the Cyrenaics (book II): (i) the distinction between *katastēmatic* (static) pleasures and pleasures *kata kinēsin* (in motion); and (ii) the difference between bodily and mental pleasures (and the related importance of past and future pleasures as opposed to present ones).

On the first point, as Diogenes puts it, "Epicurus differs from the Cyrenaics with regard to pleasure. The latter do not consider pleasure the kind of pleasure that derives from a state of rest, but only that which consists in motion. Epicurus admits both" (X 136). In support of this view, Diogenes quotes a passage from Epicurus: "Peace of mind and freedom from pain are pleasures implying a state of rest; joy and delight are understood to consist in motion and activity" (*ibid.*, quoting Epicurus, *On Choice*). The same point is pressed by Diogenes when he deals with Cyrenaic ethics: "pleasure of the body which is the end is not the static pleasure following the removal of pains or, as it were, the freedom from discomfort, which Epicurus accepts and maintains to be the end" (II 87). This is no surprise for us. As shown at length, the Cyrenaics hold that the kind of pleasure that is the end is the pleasure of the present, which in turn begins with a smooth movement of the flesh. Since they link pleasure and movement so tightly, the Cyrenaics could not admit of any pleasure that implies a state of rest.[6]

The second point of divergence between Epicurus and the Cyrenaics is about bodily and mental pleasures. Diogenes says:

> Further, Epicurus disagrees with the Cyrenaics in that they hold that pains of the body are worse than mental pains. Those performing bad actions are made to suffer bodily punishment whereas Epicurus holds the pains of the mind to be the worse. The flesh in fact endures the storms of the present alone, the mind those of the past and future as well as the present. In this way also he holds that mental pleasures are greater than those of the body. (X 137)

Diogenes informs us that Epicurus believes that mental pains are greater than bodily ones, hence arguing against the Cyrenaic view on whose basis bodily pleasures are greater than mental ones because offenders are punished with the former (II 90). Epicurus does not actually say that the Cyrenaics did not admit of mental pleasures, but that they simply valued bodily pleasures more highly than mental ones. I have earlier suggested that this may be so because bodily (bodily "bodily", to use my label) pleasures retain more perspicuously the immediacy of the physical ingredient (of the affection) that, together with the less immediate mental one, constitute the actual pleasure we feel. Diogenes adds a further argument in support of Epicurus' view that mental pleasures are superior to bodily ones. The argument is this: mental pleasures are able to combine past, present and future pleasure in a kind of unitary item, while the body can be concerned about the present alone. Because of this, mental pleasures are superior to bodily ones.

On the basis of Diogenes' argument, Terence Irwin (1991: 61) has suggested that the Cyrenaics valued bodily pleasures more than mental ones exactly because they do not recognize pleasures of memory and anticipation, as these are, for instance, clearly admitted of in Plato's *Philebus*. Although not exactly amounting to the same argument, both Diogenes' and Irwin's arguments make Cyrenaic hedonism far too down-to-earth than usually allowed. I have earlier provided an argument showing that mental pleasures too could be regarded by the Cyrenaics as special cases of bodily pleasures. How does this argument fit with Diogenes' and Irwin's? Is the view that the Cyrenaics admit of mental pleasures seriously threatened by what Diogenes and Irwin say? For a start, even bodily "bodily" pleasures are composed by a mental counterpart, that is, the awareness that we are actually being affected pleasurably. Without the awareness that one is being affected pleasurably, one is not even able to recognize pleasure as such and give any sense to the bodily alteration one experiences. The kind of mental pleasures the Cyrenaics admit of, such as the one derivable from realizing that our country is prosperous, is explicable by conceiving of those pleasures as composed by a mere physical and a more mental part. Are these mental pleasures augmented or diminished by the memory of the past and/or the expectation of the future? It can be so when, for instance, the pleasure derived from my country being in prosperity is augmented by the well-grounded prevision that my country will get even more prosperous (for instance, because new policies of integration and social welfare are being introduced). The mental pleasure derivable from the awareness that my country is prosperous will, however, remain mental, even if it is not linked with any memory of the past or expectation of the future.

On the other hand, the body itself has a memory in so far as it offers the same instinctual reaction when it is solicited by the same external factor. The following example could be enlightening. When I was a professional 400m runner, I was used to training in a particularly useful way. In almost every key performance I had a crisis after 300m, so my trainer set up a practice in which I repeatedly simulated that part of the event. I was trained to run it at a slower pace, to contrast the diminishing speed and the effects of the brutal emergence of tiredness. My trainer, who had much experience in the field, told me that the body has a memory and could reproduce that particular pace and reaction in the key event, at the appropriate moment, without any internal or mental input. I soon learned how right he was.

The idea that for the Cyrenaics bodily pleasures are superior to mental ones because they do not recognize pleasures of memory and anticipation is therefore not wholly plausible. In addition, although the Cyrenaics surely hold that what is essential is the pleasure of the present and, hence, do not recognize any *great* value to the memory of past pleasures and to the expectation of future ones, there is a passage by Cicero that shows that for the Cyrenaics too anticipation matters:

> The Cyrenaics believe that pain is produced not by every kind of evil, but by an evil that has not been looked for or expected. That has no little weight in increasing a pain;

for all unexpected things appear to be more serious ....
This anticipation [*praemeditatio*] of future evils softens the
arrival of those that one has seen coming from afar.

(*Tusc.* 3.13.28–9=*SSR* IV A 208=T 14)

The Cyrenaics believe that the anticipation of a future pain
could influence the way we actually feel that very pain when it
comes. They thus recognize that the mind plays a role in the way
we feel our pleasure and pains. What makes them differ from
the Epicureans is in understanding how important that role is.
This is the main point of Diogenes' argument at X 137. Epicurus
places great weight on the memory of past pleasures and the
expectation of future ones in so far as he grants the mind an
essential power in the elaboration and fruition of pleasures. In
short, Epicurus recognizes that both memory of the past and
expectation of the future shape the actual ways we feel pleasure.
Differently from Epicurus, the Cyrenaics base their hedonism
on the affections of the present. But this does not mean that
they do not recognize any role for the mind in the way in which
we experience pain and pleasure. Compared to the Epicureans,
such a role is more restricted, given the overall commitment to
present pleasures Cyrenaic ethics displays. At the same time,
when they attribute more importance to bodily pleasures, the
Cyrenaics are not committed to the view that bodily pleasures
are the only important ones because the mind has no role in
experiencing them.

THE ETHICS OF THE LOOSE SUBJECT

How credible will Cyrenaic ethics be if it is grounded on the
perishing pleasure of the present? First, Cyrenaic hedonism is
perfectly functional using the concept of the loose subject that I
claim is central to Cyrenaic philosophy. In the Cyrenaic world, the
subject is best conceived of as a bundle of affections, temporally

divided, but psychologically interconnected in a loose way. At the same time, the Cyrenaic loose subject is also different from *nothing*. Although being different from a truly determinate self, this subject is the bearer of those infallible affections that are the basis of the Cyrenaics' theory of knowledge. Despite being so fundamentally grounded on infallible and transient affections, Cyrenaic theory of knowledge can also admit of an epistemology of subjective appearances. The loose subject is thus not only responsible for infallible affections but also responsible for the elaboration of appearances. This is so in light of a psychological connectedness that allows the loose subject to go beyond the strict limits of mere affective episodes. I have more than once remarked how I see Cyrenaic epistemology and ethics to be closely interrelated, in such a way that it is possible to extend the model I use in making sense of the former to explain the latter (and vice versa). On the basis of such a tight analogy, I make the loose subject the inevitable referent for those experiences of pleasure the Cyrenaics make the end. The loose subject experiences the pleasure of the present and makes it the goal of its life. The pleasure of the present is bodily, in so far as for the Cyrenaics each and every pleasure begins with an alteration of the body.

A case has been made to conceive of mental pleasures – which the Cyrenaics openly admit of – as particular cases of bodily pleasures. The loose subject experiences perishing affections of pleasure that, being either bodily "bodily" or (bodily) mental, are the end as the Cyrenaics conceive of it. At the same time, the Cyrenaics do not grant great importance to both memory of past pleasures and anticipation of future ones. This, however, does not exclude that the Cyrenaics recognize the role our subjective beliefs could have in the actual way we conceive of and, consequently, experience the pleasures we feel. The psychological connectedness I attribute to the Cyrenaic loose subject is ultimately responsible for the production and elaboration of those extra-affective, belief-related activities that influence the actual way in which we experience pleasure.

If this is so, Cyrenaic ethics will show itself to be something more complete and less down-to-earth than it is normally believed to be (as much as Cyrenaic epistemology is something more captivating than a mere epistemology of infallible affections). At the same time, by granting to Cyrenaic ethics a more complete level of cogency and appeal than usually expected, we would also be in a better condition to understand the Cyrenaic claim about happiness. According to Diogenes, the Cyrenaics conceive of happiness as "a collection [sustēma] made out of particular pleasures. Among these both past and future pleasures are counted together" (II 87; see also Ath. *Deipnosophists* 544 A–B=SSR IV A 174). Diogenes also speaks of happiness as "accumulation [hathroismos]" of pleasures (II 90).[7] Given the metaphysics of indeterminacy that, on my interpretation, the Cyrenaics endorse, subjects and objects are not provided with any stable and unitary essence that allows one to identify and re-identify them over time with objective accuracy. In the Cyrenaic world subjects and objects can be only identified as, respectively, loose subjects and collections of secondary qualities. By transferring such concepts of things and persons to Cyrenaic ethics, happiness cannot be properly regarded as the end, since that would presuppose an idea of life as a single and determinate item, such as the one that is implied in, for instance, Aristotle's eudaemonist ethics.

In the Cyrenaic world, happiness, like those subjects and objects that populate it, is best described as the imperfect collection of transient episodes of pleasure. Only by conceiving it in this way does happiness gain a meaning for the Cyrenaics. The importance of happiness could be derived only by linking all the episodes of past, present and future pleasures that the Cyrenaic individual happens to have experienced in her life. Happiness is thus imperfectly, yet surely, present in Cyrenaic ethics. Irwin (1991: 70–75) argues that, since the Cyrenaics rejected the idea of a continuing self over time, they make the pleasure of the present the only goal of life, thus discharging happiness as a whole. But the fact that the Cyrenaics rejected the idea of a continuing self over time does not mean that the self is nothing, as I have argued. The psychological connectedness that I have recognized as fully belonging to the Cyrenaic loose subject is what allows the Cyrenaic individual to link pleasure (which remains the end) and happiness (i.e. a collection of pleasures) in the way ancient sources on Cyrenaic ethics actually do. Hence, although remaining full hedonists, the Cyrenaics are not indifferent to happiness.

By being provided with a psychological connectedness, the loose subject can link mentally past, present and future pleasures, which are all counted together in happiness. In this picture, past and future pleasures are fully there, because they contribute, together with the present ones, to the formation of one's happiness. So, again, past and future pleasures are not discharged in Cyrenaic ethics because Cyrenaic individuals cannot transcend in any way the limit of the affections of the present. The notion of happiness that the Cyrenaics appear to be proposing shows that for them it is possible to conceive of happiness not only in terms of present affections of pleasures but also in terms of a collection of past and future pleasures with present ones. Being past and future, the former pleasures are not present now, when, drinking a glass of wine, we are experiencing a pleasurable affection. Because of this absence, past and future pleasures are discharged by the Cyrenaics as contributing nothing to the pleasure of the moment. Yet, they are valued in so far as one can make sense of them in terms of happiness, which is a less evanescent event in one's life.[8]

<h2 style="text-align:center">THE PHILEBUS</h2>

One traditional interpretation of the Cyrenaics has been centred on the absolute predominance in Cyrenaic thought of ethical speculation over other branches of philosophy. Accordingly, many scholars, both of the Cyrenaics and of Plato, have attempted to find echoes of Cyrenaic hedonism in the *Philebus*. Zeller defended the view that Aristippus is the polemical target of the whole dialogue with the following argument. After having shown that the crucial passage of the *Philebus* (53c4–6) has to be read as a passage referring to a hedonistic thesis, Zeller (1923: II 1, 352) argues that, since Protagoras did not elaborate any hedonistic ethics out of his perceptual relativism, the only philosopher Plato could have had in mind in that passage was Aristippus.[9] Zeller's view has been highly influential and is shared by most historians of ancient philosophy in the last century. In particular, Auguste Diès (1949: *Notice*, LIII) has defended the view that the dialogue is directed against the hedonism of Aristippus and Eudoxus of Cnidus, the mathematician and astronomer, follower of Plato, who was well known for the kind of hedonistic ethics he professed.[10] Diès identifies in the *Philebus* three main hedonistic theses: (i) pleasure is the *summum bonum*; (ii) pleasure is simply the termination of pain; and (iii) pleasure is a process of becoming. While he believes that the second hedonistic thesis is surely ascribable to Speusippus, the first and third theses are surely attributable to Aristippus (and, as far as the first thesis is concerned, to Eudoxus too). Diès argues quite correctly that pleasure was a hotly debated topic in the Academy. Plato is highly likely to have written a dialogue where he rejects all the kind of hedonisms he saw flourishing in and around his own school. One of the main gains of Diès's interpretation of the *Philebus* is to have shown that the thesis on whose basis pleasure is a process of becoming (*Phlb.* 53c) is not an anti-hedonistic view at all, although Plato uses it in the context of an argument purported to argue against pleasure. Nothing prevents us from assuming that Plato argues against pleasure by also relying on the view that pleasure is a process of becoming. This in itself, however, does not commit those holding that view to be anti-hedonists.

Socrates says, "Have we not been told that pleasure is always a process of becoming, and that there is no being at all of pleasure? There are some subtler thinkers who have tried to pass on this doctrine to us, and we ought to be grateful to them"

(*Phlb.* 53c4–6). Among the few scholars who have most reso-
lutely tried to interpret this reference to pleasure as a process of
becoming as an anti-hedonist move by Plato (hence discharging
any possible reference, in that passage, to the hedonism of the
Cyrenaics) is Giannantoni. He has argued that the theory that
pleasure is a process of becoming has to be interpreted as an anti-
hedonistic view in light of what Aristotle says in the *Nicomachean
Ethics*. When he deals with pleasure in books VII and X of the
Nicomachean Ethics, Aristotle, Giannantoni argues, clearly
treats the view that pleasure is a process of becoming as a view
advanced by rivals of pleasure. In addition, in his own analysis
of pleasure as a candidate for the highest good Aristotle always
refers to Eudoxus and never to Aristippus.[11] This ought to imply,
Giannantoni concludes, that Aristippus did not elaborate any
credible ethical theory. Hence, *Philebus* 53c4–6 cannot offer a
reference to Aristippus' theory of pleasure.[12]

Giannantoni's arguments are, however, hardly cogent. The fact
that Aristotle is silent on Aristippus in the *Nicomachean Ethics*
when he elaborates his own critique of the view that pleasure is
the highest good does not in itself prove that Aristippus did not
hold any hedonistic theory. But, Giannantoni insists, Aristotle
uses the view that pleasure is a process of becoming as a critique
of pleasure, so that view ought to be an anti-hedonist view (hence,
it cannot be attributed to the Cyrenaics, well-known hedonists). Like Plato in the *Philebus* (at least on the basis of some
interpretations), even Aristotle in the *Nicomachean Ethics* may,
however, have used a hedonistic view to contrast hedonism. Plato
and Aristotle may have believed that to maintain that pleasure
is always a process of becoming (and not a proper ontological
item, with a well-defined essence) is in itself an argument not in
favour of hedonism but against it. Both Plato in the *Philebus* and
Aristotle in the *Nicomachean Ethics* are concentrating on what
mostly matters in human life. Given their shared concern, they
both insist that what matters in human life must belong to the
realm of essences: of what is such just in virtue of itself and not

in relation to any other thing. If it is conceived of as a process of becoming, pleasure cannot possibly count as the target of human life. That is why those who held that pleasure is a process of becoming were ultimately committed, for Plato and Aristotle, to a kind of internal refutation of hedonism.

The view that pleasure is a process of becoming can be, however, a hedonist view. If pleasure is defined as a process of becoming, this will make it the best possible candidate for the human good for those philosophers, like the Cyrenaics, who accept a metaphysics of indeterminacy. If pleasure is a process of becoming, this will mean that pleasure is, in a fundamental sense, intrinsically dependent on the particular conditions of the individual experiencing it (at a given time and under particularly subjective conditions). This does not prevent Plato and Aristotle, who adopt an opposite metaphysics of, respectively, Forms and essences, from interpreting such a view as a step in an argument against hedonism. The difference of approaches on pleasure between, on the one hand, Plato and Aristotle and, on the other, those holding the view that pleasure is a process of becoming (on my interpretation, the Cyrenaics) is clear from the very start of the *Philebus*.

In this dialogue Plato makes Socrates catalogue pleasure as belonging to the unlimited (*apeiron*), when he says, "reason is akin to cause and is part of that family, while pleasure itself is unlimited (*apeiron*) and belongs to the kind that in and by itself neither possesses nor will ever possess a beginning, middle or end" (*Phlb.* 31a7–10). Pleasure is ranked as unlimited by Socrates together with perceptual qualities, such as hot, cold and so on.[13] On the other hand, reason and knowledge are classified within the genus of the limited (*peras*).[14] Whatever interpretation one may want to offer of the limited–unlimited dichotomy through which Plato suggests we read reality in the *Philebus*, it is clear that the inclusion of pleasure (and of perceptual qualities too) in the category of the unlimited points towards the notion of indeterminacy on which, in my interpretation, the Cyrenaics centred their view of the world. Before reporting the view that pleasure is movement and a process of becoming (*Eth. Nic.* X 1173a28-30), Aristotle states the view that while the good is determinate, pleasure is indeterminate, because it admits of more and less (1173a15-16). Since in the passages on pleasure just reported – as well as in the whole initial section of Book X of the *Nicomachean Ethics* – he often refers to Plato's own treatment of pleasure in the *Philebus* (see e.g. *Eth. Nic.* 1172b28-36), Aristotle is most likely to be translating Plato's concept of unlimitedness of pleasure into his notion of indeterminacy of pleasure (see Broadie & Rowe 2002).

I take Aristotle's equation between unlimitedness and indeterminacy of pleasure as strengthening the suggestion that in putting pleasure into the category of the unlimited in the *Philebus*, Plato has exactly in mind the Cyrenaics, who, I have claimed throughout, were fully committed to indeterminacy. Pleasure cannot be the target of human life for Plato in the *Philebus* (and for Aristotle in the *Nicomachean Ethics*) for a variety of reasons, including the fact that pleasure is an indeterminate item. But, if one rejects a metaphysics of Forms and essences and, consequently, assumes indeterminacy as a viable metaphysical option, the view put forward by some subtler thinkers at *Philebus* 53c4-6, that pleasure is best described as a process of becoming, is a fully hedonistic view. Those subtler thinkers may well be the Cyrenaics. This identification is possible on the ground that the view ascribed to the subtler thinkers at *Philebus* 53c4-6, that pleasure is always a process of becoming, is fully compatible with the Cyrenaic idea of pleasure. As we know, one of the basic claims of Cyrenaic ethics is that pleasure and pain are definable as, respectively, a smooth and rough movement of the flesh. Now, a movement is in itself a process of becoming, that is, a process from a state of rest to a state of motion. Aristotle himself, when he deals with pleasure in *Nicomachean Ethics* (X 1173a28-31), assimilates quite naturally the idea that pleasure is movement with the view that pleasure is a process of becoming.

In addition, the relation between *kinēsis* (movement) and *genēsis* (process of becoming) was already established by Plato in the section of the *Theaetetus* where the subtler thinkers are the protagonists. Just after having given details on Protagoras' Secrete Doctrine – the view that nothing is one thing just by itself and that everything is subject to motion (*Tht.* 152d1–e1) – Socrates points out that this doctrine is corroborated by the fact that coming to be (*genēsis*) and being are both produced by movement (*kinēsis*) (153a5–10). By saying that being is also produced by movement, Socrates is just anticipating the theory of perception of the subtler thinkers, where (as we saw in Chapter 3) the being of an object is defined exclusively within the limits of the perceptual encounter between the perceiving subject and the perceived object. As Socrates puts it when he illustrates the details of the subtler thinkers' theory of perception, a stone is really white for the person who sees it as white only when this person gets in touch with the perceived object (*Tht.* 156e1–7).

What is peculiar in the subtler thinkers' theory of perception is that when he shows the symmetrical correlativity that is inevitably central to that theory, Socrates lists a series of perceptions that are representative of such correlativity. Among these, he lists "seeings, hearings, smellings, feelings of cold and heat; also what are called pleasures, pains, desires, fears and others" (*Tht.* 156b2–5). Nonetheless, pleasure (and pain) had not appeared as a proper perception up to that point of the *Theaetetus* and, after that brief appearance, they disappear in the rest of that dialogue. In the subtler thinkers' theory of perception, pleasure is regarded (like all other perceptions) as arising from movement and generation (from *kinēsis* and *genesis*), but it is not offered a lengthier treatment in the *Theaetetus*. It is given such a treatment in the *Philebus*, especially in connection with the view (*Phlb.* 53c4–6) that pleasure is always a process of becoming. Plato explicitly mentions that view by ascribing it to some subtle thinkers. A clear allusion to the subtler thinkers of the *Theaetetus* is evident: in both cases, thinkers named as subtler philosophers defend similar, if not identical, views about perceptions and pleasures. This is to confirm my suggestion that when he refers to thinkers he qualifies as subtler in the *Theaetetus* and in the *Philebus*, Plato appears to be identifying philosophical views that we are ready to interpret as Cyrenaic views, that is, as views expounding the philosophical commitments of Aristippus the Elder and his early followers.

III
CONCLUSION

8

CYRENAIC PHILOSOPHY
AND ITS LATER EPIGONI

CYRENAIC PHILOSOPHY

In this book I have tried to amplify the field of interests of the Cyrenaics by adding metaphysics and philosophy of language to ethics and epistemology. In so doing, I have also offered an ambitious interpretation of the Cyrenaic school by showing that, in addition to the school, there is a *Cyrenaic philosophy* for us to account for. By Cyrenaic philosophy I mean a coherent set of philosophical views (ethical, epistemological, metaphysical and semantic). I say that the set of philosophical views I see as representing Cyrenaic philosophy is coherent because I take Cyrenaic ethics to be perfectly organic with the epistemology and metaphysics of the school, as much as epistemology and metaphysics are in perfect accordance with the semantic approached adopted by the Cyrenaics.

The cardinal concept for Cyrenaic ethics and epistemology is that of affection (*pathos*). The two ethical key affections for the Cyrenaics are pleasure and pain, while they admit of an (epistemological) affection that is neutral from the ethical point of view and is purely representational. Cyrenaic *pathē* – both affective and representational – are best interpreted as originating from movements and alterations in us. In Cyrenaic philosophy, affections are wholly subjective. If I see a table as white, on the basis of Cyrenaic epistemology, I can be said to be whitened. What can be known for sure in the example of me seeing a table is that I am absolutely certain that I see the table as white and that I cannot be mistaken about this. Only affections can be known for the Cyrenaics: we can get subjective knowledge of how things appear to us. The same idea applies to Cyrenaic ethics. Pleasure is the end. How each individual experiences pleasure is a wholly subjective matter and there is no intrinsic difference among pleasures. (Although I have focused my understanding of Cyrenaic epistemology and ethics on the centrality of affections, I have, however, suggested that the Cyrenaics admit of an extra-affective capacity allowing us to construct subjective judgements out of affections.)

Cyrenaic epistemology and ethics are subjective in so far as they both rest on a metaphysics of indeterminacy. In their epistemology, the Cyrenaics concentrate on the way we are affected by the external world because, for them, there is no real way to arrive at a real understanding of how the world actually is. This is so, in turn, because things in the world are indeterminate, that is, they do not have a stable, unified and unitary essence. By adopting such a metaphysical view, the Cyrenaics conceive of objects as collections of qualities and as subjects (as particular items in the world), as bundles of momentary affections. I have also shown that the Cyrenaics are committed to indeterminacy in line with an ontological tradition starting at least with Protagoras and ending up with Pyrrho, the initiator of ancient scepticism. When I ascribe metaphysical indeterminacy to the Cyrenaics, I do not suggest that they speculated at length on that concept or defended it with particular subtle arguments. In the passages we have gone through to ascribe indeterminacy to the Cyrenaics, in fact, little information is available for us to reconstruct the actual way they argued for indeterminacy. Nonetheless, a commitment to indeterminacy (and this is the point I wish to underline) could have been rather natural for the Cyrenaics, indeed much more natural than it is for us today. In his defence of the principle of non-contradiction in *Metaphysics* Gamma, sections 4–6, Aristotle openly ascribes the view that things are indeterminate to almost all the thinkers before or coeval with him, because all of them defended a conception of knowledge exclusively based on perception and on subjective appearances.

As for language, another underestimated philosophical interest of the Cyrenaics, the behavioural solution I have suggested the Cyrenaics may have adopted in their theory of meaning has its ultimate reason in indeterminacy. Since, for the Cyrenaics, there are no objects as such in the world, the usual semantic triangle affection–word–thing-in-the-world cannot be adopted to explain why words have shared meanings. By making the referential nexus between words and things recede, the Cyrenaics make words refer to our affections alone. Since the latter are private, numerous and always changing, the Cyrenaics have to let in a sort of behaviourism, on whose basis each person can understand the meaning of "white" despite the fact that people have rather different affections of white. In adopting such a behavioural solution for the problem of meaning, the Cyrenaics developed to a fuller and perhaps more radical extent the semantic approach initially adopted by Gorgias in *On What Is Not*.

We are therefore far from the traditional picture of the Cyrenaics as a minor Socratic school with a restricted philosophical interest in ethics alone. In addition to hedonism, the Cyrenaics not only developed an original epistemology, but were also committed to indeterminacy in metaphysics and to behaviourism in the philosophy of language. This makes the Cyrenaic school a proper philosophical school, with a clear and sophisticated theoretical agenda. On the ground of this more positively oriented interpretation of the Cyrenaic school (and, by extension, of the other two Socratic schools of the Megarics and the Cynics about which there is still much to learn), Plato and Aristotle appear to have been not giants in a philosophical desert, but two great philosophers in good company. The Socratic schools were minor up to a certain point.

The reader is well aware now that in the reconstruction of the Cyrenaic school and philosophy I have provided here I have often integrated the philosophical evidence deriving from ancient sources with current (or in any case more modern) philosophical insights. This, however, does not need to be taken as an unreasonable intrusion of the contemporary into the ancient. Rather, I have in some cases adopted a contemporary approach better to clarify the philosophical scope of the arguments ancient sources attribute to the Cyrenaics. Those arguments were, however, already there and could be interpreted coherently even in the absence of contemporary aids. Just as an example, I have ascribed to the Cyrenaics a concept of the self as a bundle of affections. I have done so on the basis of the evidence deriving from (an interpretation of) ancient sources. That could have been enough for us to gain an understanding of the Cyrenaic concept of the self. By providing tight analogies between that concept and the concept of the self as this has been understood by Hume and Parfit, my aim was to help the reader to get a more profound philosophical comprehension of the philosophical issues the Cyrenaics are likely to have dealt with.

A last point to be addressed is the historical development of Cyrenaic philosophy. In this concluding chapter I have spoken of a Cyrenaic philosophy, intended as a coherent body of philosophical views, to be attributed to the Cyrenaic school and to its exponents and members. By speaking of a Cyrenaic philosophy, I have meant to suggest that the views on ethics, epistemology, metaphysics and language that have been ascribed in this book to the Cyrenaics are views representing the philosophical core of the Cyrenaic school. From a more historical standpoint, however, one may wonder whether such views were historically stable views, to be shared as such by all the members of the Cyrenaic school, whose entire life spanned more than two centuries. I am inclined to suggest that both the early members of the school and its later sects adhered (more or less firmly, surely with different emphasis) to the philosophical views I have just briefly referred to. This is not to deny that Cyrenaic philosophy, like all other philosophies and human artefacts, was subject to change.

One of the claims I have been defending throughout the book is that Aristippus the Elder may be properly regarded as responsible for the initial elaboration of some of the doctrinal views of the Cyrenaic school. I have made such a claim on the basis of those sources that openly ascribe to Aristippus the Elder some cardinal views of Cyrenaic ethics and epistemology, as well as on the basis of Plato's testimony. I am more than ready to admit that Aristippus the Elder did not fully develop Cyrenaic philosophy because some theoretical refinements or innovations of that philosophy were introduced at a later stage. Those refinements and innovations were, however, such as not to prejudice a sort of doctrinal continuity between the philosophical views of Aristippus the Elder and his successors. I take Cyrenaic philosophy as defined in this chapter – and, for that matter, in the whole of this book – to be grounded on such doctrinal continuity.

A doctrinal continuity can also be invoked between the traditional body of Cyrenaic views and the later epigoni of the school, namely the followers of Hegesias, Annniceris and also of Theodorus (although the Godless deserves a more autonomous approach). Even if there is more than one point on which these later sects differed from traditional Cyrenaic doctrines, still those key ideas that constitute the particular philosophy of the Cyrenaics were shared by the later members of the school. Again, this is not to deny that, by reacting to different philosophical solicitations posed by a cultural environment that was rapidly and drastically changing, the later sects of the Cyrenaic school introduced new views into the body of its traditional doctrines. Despite some philosophical innovations, the later sects of the school, in fact, were openly recognized by ancient sources as sects of philosophers still belonging to the Cyrenaic school.[1] We now briefly look at those sects.

HEGESIAS AND ANNICERIS

As far as the later sects of the Cyrenaic school are concerned, the fundamental source is still book II of Diogenes Laertius' *Lives*. Let us start our brief survey into the later epigoni of the Cyrenaic school with Hegesias. He was known by the nickname "death-persuader" (*peisithanatos*) and, according to Cicero (*Tusc.* I 34, 84=*SSR* IV F4), he wrote a book entitled "*Apokarterōn*" (On a man starving himself to death).[2] He was also so eloquent when he spoke on death that, according to Valerius Maximus (*SSR* IV F 5), the king Ptolomaeus forbade him to speak on death anywhere and at any time to prevent people from committing suicide. The pessimistic approach to life of Hegesias appears not to have been in contrast with the fundamental view of Cyrenaic ethics.[3] The continuity between the Cyrenaics proper and the Hegesians is attested by Diogenes himself, who opens his account of the latter (DL II 93–6) by remarking, "Hegesias' followers had the same ends [as the Cyrenaics proper], that is pleasure and pain" (II 93). By relying on the fundamental affections of pleasure and pain, the Hegesians appear to have strengthened the commitment to anti-eudaemonism that can be seen as typical of the Cyrenaics. The Hegesians say, "It is impossible to reach happiness, for the body is infected with much suffering, the soul suffers with the body and it is disturbed by it …. It follows that happiness does not exist. Life and death are, in turn, each desirable" (II 94).

As far as pleasure and pain are concerned, the Hegesians seem to have fully endorsed the subjectivity that is so intrinsic to Cyrenaic ethics and, for that matter, to Cyrenaic thought as a whole. Diogenes, once again, informs us:

They believed that there is nothing pleasant or unpleasant by nature. When one happens to feel pleasure in something or disgust for something else, this is due to lack or rarity or overabundance. Poverty and wealth contribute nothing to the calculus of pleasure, since the rich and the poor do not feel pleasure differently. Slavery and freedom, nobility and low birth, glory and dishonour are equally indifferent to the measure of pleasure.   (II 94 end)[4]

Like the proper Cyrenaics, the Hegesians insist that an affection is the basis of human knowledge and conduct when they are reported to remark that "allowance should be made for errors, for none errs voluntarily but under the constraint of some affections" (II 95). Accordingly, "we should not hate men, but teach them better" (*ibid.*). This ought to imply that affections can be supervened by another epistemological capacity and replaced with more suitable affections or appearances.[5] The Hegesians appear thus to be reflecting the same distinction between the epistemological role of affections and that of appearances in Cyrenaic epistemology that I referred to earlier. The same point surfaces when they are made to report not having approved of perceptions since these latter do not lead to accurate knowledge: the Hegesians are said to have done whatever appears to be rational (*tōn t'eulogōs phainomenōn panta prattein*: II 95 end).

Let us now briefly concentrate on Anniceris and his own followers. From Diogenes' account (II 96–7), we gain the picture of a sect far less pessimistic than the Hegesians. Anniceris' followers openly value friendship, gratitude, and respect for parents and the country. It appears that they were prepared to tolerate uncomfortable inconveniences to defend friendship. As Diogenes puts it:

A friend has to be cherished not merely for his utility (for, if that fails, we should no longer be friends with him), but for benevolence, for the sake of which we are prepared even to endure suffering. And in fact, although we make pleasure the end and we are annoyed when we are deprived of it, we should tolerate it because of the love for our friend.   (II 97)

This passage makes clear not only that the Annicerians valued friendship but that their appreciation of it is not in contrast with Cyrenaic hedonism. The Annicerians are still fully committed to the major tenets of the Cyrenaic school. In particular, the Annicerians retain pleasure as the end, as Diogenes himself notes in the passage just quoted and as another important passage tells us:

> The Annicerians maintained that there is no definite end of the whole of life, but claimed that there is a special end for each action – the pleasure resulting from the action. These Cyrenaics repudiate Epicurus' account of pleasure as the removal of pain, denouncing it as a condition of a corpse. We take pleasure not only in pleasures but also in the company of others and in ambition.
>
> (Clem. Al. *Strom*. II, 21 130, 7–8[=*SSR* IV G 4])

Anniceris and his followers not only retain the core Cyrenaic view that pleasure is the end but also conceive of such an end as the kind of pleasure deriving from every single pleasurable action. In so doing, they perhaps emphasize the absolute singularity of every affection of pleasure that is already central to the traditional body of Cyrenaic hedonism. The rejection of Epicurus' definition of pleasure (i.e. absence of any pain) by calling it a state of death should be interpreted as a full commitment to the Cyrenaic view that every affection is inevitably linked with movement. When there is no movement there cannot be, for the Cyrenaics, any affection. In light of this, Epicurus' view that pleasure lies in the absence of any painful disturbance could not be accepted by the Cyrenaics and by the Annicerians, who, by living at a time when the Epicureans were flourishing, had the chance – and the necessity – to reaffirm the distance in ethics between the two rivalling hedonisms.

The Annicerians appear to have admitted of pleasures that are not easily reducible to bodily pleasures, such as pleasures deriving from mental pleasures. Some scholars, such as Döring (1988: 53ff.), interpret Anniceris' evaluation of pleasures other than bodily ones as evidence of a philosophical necessity for the Cyrenaics to revise the core of their hedonism in light of a polemic with the Epicureans. Against Döring, Andre Laks (1993: esp. 39–49) has suggested that the emphasis given by the Annicerians to such mental pleasures cannot be interpreted as an original innovation of Anniceris but, more probably, as the reaffirmation of a central point of Cyrenaic hedonism against those other Cyrenaics, such as the Hegesians, who were too inclined to pessimism.[6] I fully side with Laks in crediting the proper Cyrenaics as the ones responsible for originally admitting of mental pleasures into their hedonism.

THEODORUS THE GODLESS

We now come to Theodorus, the Godless or, for *antiphasis* or auto-proclamation (see DL II 100), the God. Theodorus is an original philosopher in his own right and seems to have distanced himself more decidedly from the core of Cyrenaic philosophy than Hegesias and Anniceris did. That Theodorus was considered a philosopher of the Cyrenaic school but also viewed as a philosopher advocating other philosophical positions not fully Cyrenaic is clear from the most detailed account of Theodorus' life, works and *placita*: DL II 97–104. Diogenes' account of Theodorus is, in fact, a proper *bios*, reporting doctrinal views as well as anecdotes and ending with a list of homonyms. Scholars such as Marek Winiarczyk and Giannantoni have collected a reasonable list of sources on Theodorus, granting him a kind of philosophical visibility later Cyrenaics can rarely be credited with.[7]

Theodorus was instructed by Aristippus the Younger (and, later in his life, by Anniceris; see DL II 98). Aldo Brancacci (1982) has shown how Pyrrho seems to have influenced Theodorus' ideas and how Theodorus and Bion of Borysthenes could be regarded as the intermediaries between the original scepticism of Pyrrho and Arcesilaus' philosophy.[8] Were this hypothesis correct, the linking element of this picture of history of ancient philosophy could perhaps be indeterminacy. Pyrrho's indeterminacy thesis could have pushed Aristippus the Younger to reshape the Cyrenaics' commitment to indeterminacy along new and more aggressive lines. Taught by Aristippus the Younger, Theodorus is likely to have often heard the doctrine of indeterminacy and, hence, to have been directly attracted by the thought of Pyrrho, the philosopher of indeterminacy *par excellence*.

Of course, to test the full validity of such a philosophical genealogy we need a close scrutiny of ancient sources as well as further evidence. It is to be hoped that this could be attempted soon in order to shed more light on the conceptual parentage between important protagonists of the Greek philosophical world, such as the Cyrenaics, Pyrrho, Theodorus the Godless, Bion and Arcesilaus. If I had to indicate a text to begin with in order to assess the legitimacy of the view of Theodorus as closely committed to (and as an intermediary of) indeterminacy, it would be Philodemus' *On Choices and Avoidances*. In particular, in the last lines of col. III of Philodemus' treatise is written, "others held the view that what our school call grief or joy are totally empty notions because of the manifest indeterminacy of things". Winiarczyk and Giannantoni have included that passage of Philodemus in the list of the sources on Theodorus.[9] If in the last line of col. III of *On Choices and Avoidances*, Philodemus actually refers to Theodorus' views, the latter will be ascribed a clear and explicit commitment to indeterminacy. As suggested, in response to the solicitation of Aristippus the Younger and Pyrrho, Theodorus may have embraced the notion of indeterminacy to a fuller extent and also elaborated his own philosophy on the basis of such a metaphysical idea, which had been already permeating the core of traditional Cyrenaic metaphysics.

I have begun this brief sketch of Theodorus and of his philosophical role in the Cyrenaic school with a note on his originality, just to suggest that Theodorus is in effect an original thinker who is likely to have developed the philosophical views of the Cyrenaics, even in ways that are divergent from Cyrenaic orthodoxy. Before moving to Diogenes' account of Theodorus to find further support for the thesis about Theodorus' originality and his possible distancing from some views characteristic of the Cyrenaic school, I provide an outline of Theodorus' life on the basis of Winiarczyk's (1981: IX) conjectures:

1. Theodorus is born in Cyrene around 340 BCE; here he is taught by Aristippus the Younger.
2. Around 313 BCE, Theodorus goes to Athens.
3. 313–309 (?) BCE: Theodorus stays, for the most part, in Athens (although he often travels to other cities, such as Corinth, where he is supposed to have met the Cynic Metrocles; see DL II 102). In Athens, he has many students (among them is Bion of Borysthenes), to whom he teaches *sophistarum modo*.[10] Theodorus has the chance to converse with Stilpon, the Megaric (see DL II 100, 116).
4. 309 (?) BCE: Theodorus puts forward his atheist ideas in his book *On the Gods* and is accused of impiety. Through the intercession of Demetrius Phalereus, he leaves the city, escaping trial (see DL II 101).
5. After 309 (?) BCE, he goes to Alexandria; once there he is sent by Ptolomaeus to Lysimachus, at that time the king of Thracia (see DL II 102).
6. Theodorus returns to Cyrene, which was then governed by Ptolomaeus' brother. Here he is supposed to have founded his own school and elaborated his own doctrine, under the influence of Anniceris and in response to the challenge posed to Cyrenaic philosophy by the Epicureans.
7. 250 (?) BCE: his death.[11]

In Diogenes' account of Theodorus (DL II 97–104) we find the attribution to Theodorus of a view that is in contrast with one of the main tenets of Cyrenaic philosophy. Theodorus is reported to have claimed that the end is joy (*chara*) while grief (*lupē*) is its opposite and has to be avoided (II 98). He is also said to have maintained that practical wisdom and justice (*phronēsis* and *dikaiosunē*) are the good, their contraries the bad, while pleasure and pain are intermediates (*ibid.*). Theodorus appears not to make pleasure and pain the two key concepts of his ethics, replacing them with joy and grief. In addition, he speaks of practical wisdom and justice as the good and makes pleasure and pain intermediates. In advocating such views, Theodorus appears to be retaining the standard taxonomy of Cyrenaic affections (pleasure, pain and intermediates), but also reinterprets that taxonomy in a way that is not orthodox in Cyrenaic philosophy. In getting rid of pleasure and pain as the two polar elements of ethics and in speaking of justice and wisdom as the good, Theodorus effectively departs from traditional Cyrenaic ethics, to put forward an ethics of joy and grief that could have been perhaps more challenging for the Epicureans, whom Theodorus is likely to have confronted.

APPENDIX

CYRENAIC TESTIMONIES
IN TRANSLATION

I list the sources and testimonies on the Cyrenaics in translation in alphabetical order of the authors. The title of the work from which the passage is quoted is bracketed. The corresponding testimony in Giannantoni's *Socratis et Socraticorum Reliquiae*, if available, is indicated at the end of the passage.

THE ANONYMOUS *THEAETETUS* COMMENTATOR

1. "Something is the agent [*to poiēsan*], something else is the patient [*to paschon*]. But, if people undergo affections that are opposed to the thing in itself, they will agree that the intrinsic feature of the agent is not defined [*mē einai hōrismenēn tēn tou poiēsantos idiotēta*]; if it were so, the same thing at the same time will not produce different affections. Because of this, the Cyrenaics say that only affections are apprehensible [*mona ta pathē phasin katalēpta*], while external things are not [*ta de exōthen akatalēpta*]. That I am being burnt – they say – I apprehend; that the fire is such as to burn is obscure. If it were such, all things will be burnt by it" (col. LXV, 19–35=*SSR* IV A 214).

ARISTOCLES AND EUSEBIUS

From Eusebius, *Preparation for the Gospel*

2. "Aristippus from Cyrene maintains that the end of good things is pleasure, of bad things pain [*telos agathōn tēn ēdonēn, kakōn de tēn algēdona*]; he rejects all the other sciences of nature, saying that the only useful thing to do is to look for what is good and bad" (Euseb. *Praep. evang.* 1.8.9=*SSR* IV A 166).

3. "[Aristippus the Elder] did not clearly speak of the end [*telos*] in public. However, he said that the essence of happiness lies in particular pleasures. And, by always speaking about pleasure, he led his followers to think that he affirmed that living pleasurably is the goal of life" (Euseb. *Praep. evang.* 14.18.31=*SSR* IV A 173).

4. "Among his hearers [of Aristippus the Elder], there was his daughter Arete, who had a son and called him Aristippus. He was introduced to philosophy by her and for that he was termed 'mother-taught'. He clearly defined pleasure as the end, inserting into his doctrine the concept of pleasure related to motion. For he said, there are three conditions [*katastaseis*] of our temperament: one, in which we are in pain, is like a storm at sea; another, in which we experience pleasure and which can be compared to a gentle wave, for pleasure is a gentle movement [*leian kinēsin*], similar to a fair wind; and the third is an intermediate condition [*mesen katastasin*], in which we experience neither pain nor pleasure, which is like a calm. He said we have perception of these affections alone [*toutōn de kai ephaske tōn pathōn monōn hēmas tēn aisthēsin echein*]" (Euseb. *Praep. evang.* 14.18.32=*SSR* IV A 173 and B5).

5. "Next would be those who say that affections alone are apprehensible [*mona ta pathē katalēpta*]. This view was adopted by some of the philosophers from Cyrene. As if oppressed by a kind of torpor, they maintained that they knew nothing at all, unless

someone standing beside them struck and pricked them. They said that, when burnt or cut, they knew that they were affected by something [*kaiomenoi gar elegon ē temnomenoi gnōrizein hoti paschoien ti*]. But whether the thing which is burning them is fire, or that which cut them is iron, they could not tell [*poteron de to kaion eiē pur ē to temnon sidēros, ouk echein eipein*]" (Euseb. *Praep. evang.* 14.19.1=*SSR* IV A 218).

6. "Three things must necessarily exist at the same time: the affection itself [*to te pathos auto*], what causes it [*to poioun*], and what undergoes it [*to paschon*]. The person who apprehends the affection must necessarily perceive also what undergoes it. It cannot be the case that, if someone is for example warm, one will know that one is being warmed without knowing whether it is himself or a neighbour, now or last year, in Athens or Egypt, someone alive or dead, a man or a stone. One will therefore know too what one is affected by, for people know one another and the roads, the cities, the food they eat. Likewise, craftsmen know their tools, doctors and sailors infer by means of signs what will happen, and dogs discover the tracks of wild animals" (Euseb. *Praep. evang.* 14.19.3–4 [no corresponding testimony in *SSR*]).

7. "How will the man undergoing the affection be able to tell that this is pleasure and that pain? Or that one is affected, when one is tasting or seeing, or hearing? Or that one is tasting with his tongue, seeing with his eyes and hearing with his ears?" (Euseb. *Praep. evang.* 14.19.5 [no corresponding testimony in *SSR*]).

ATHENAEUS

8. "The Cyrenaic school began with Aristippus the Socratic; having approved of the affection of pleasure, he claimed that pleasure is the end of life, and that happiness is based on it. He added that pleasure occupies one temporal unit [*monochronon*],

since he believed, as profligates do, that neither the memory of past enjoyments nor the expectation of future ones be important for him. Judging the good in light of the present alone, he considered that what he enjoyed in the past and will enjoy in the future be not important for him, the former because it exists no more, the latter because it does not yet exist and is not manifest" (*Deipnosophists* XII 544a=*SSR* IV A 174).

AUGUSTINE

From *Against the Academics*, book III

9. "Someone when he is tasting something, can swear with good faith that he knows through his own palate that what he is tasting is sweet, or the contrary. He cannot be brought away from that knowledge by any Greek trickery. Who could in fact be so shameless as to ask when I am licking something with delight: 'Maybe you are not tasting, but this is a dream'? Do I resist? That will delight me even if I happen to be asleep. No likeness of false things can confuse what I said to know. An Epicurean philosopher or the Cyrenaics may perhaps say many other things in favour of the senses, against which I have remarked that nothing was said by the Academics" (III 11.26=*SSR* IV A 210).

CICERO

From *On Academic Scepticism*

10. "What about touch, of that touch philosophers call interior [*interiorem*], of either pleasure or pain, in which the Cyrenaics believe that only there is the criterion of truth [*iudicium*], because it is perceived by means of the senses?" (*Acad. Pr.* II 7, 20=*SSR* IV A 209).

11. "What about the Cyrenaics, by no means contemptible philosophers? They deny that anything can be perceived from the outside [*qui negant esse quicquam quod percipi posit extrinsecus*], while they do say to perceive only those things they experience by means of an internal touch [*ea sola percipere quae tactu intumo sentiant*], like pain and pleasure; they cannot know whose sound or colour something is, but to sense only to be affected in a certain way" (*Acad. Pr.* II 24, 76=SSR IV A 209).

12. "Others declare that pleasure is the end [*finem*]: among these, the most important is Aristippus, who followed Socrates and from whom the Cyrenaics all derived (*Acad. Pr.* II 42, 131=SSR IV 178).

From *On Ends*

13. "When Epicurus said that pleasure is the highest good [*summum bonum*], on the one hand he did not fully understand that idea; on the other, that idea is not his own: before him and in a better way, that idea was of Aristippus" (*Fin.* I 8, 26=SSR IV A 181).

From *Tusculan Disputations*

14. "The Cyrenaics believe that pain is produced not by every kind of evil, but by an evil that has not been looked for or expected. That has no little weight in increasing a pain: for all unexpected things appear to be more serious ... This anticipation [*praemeditatio*] of future evils softens the arrival of those that one has seen coming from afar" (*Tusc.* 3.13.28–29=SSR IV A 208).

CLEMENT OF ALEXANDRIA

15. "They [the Cyrenaics] say that pleasure in itself is a smooth and gentle motion, with some perception [*meta tinos aisthēseōs*]" (*Strom.* II 20 106, 3=SSR IV A 175).

COLOTES AND PLUTARCH

From Plutarch's *Against Colotes*

16. "He [Colotes] aims, I suspect, to refute the Cyrenaics first, and then the Academy of Arcesilaus. The latter school was of those who suspended judgement on everything; whereas the former, placing all affections and sense-impressions within themselves, thought that the evidence derived from them was not enough, as far as assertions on external objects are concerned. Distancing themselves from external objects, they shut themselves up within their affections as in a siege. In doing so, they adopted the locution 'it appears' but refused to say in addition that 'it is' with regard to external objects. This is the reason why – Colotes says – the Cyrenaics cannot live or cope with things. In addition, he says (making fun of them), that 'these men do not say that a man or a horse or a wall is, but that they themselves are being walled or horsed or manned' [*toichousthai kai hippousthai kai anthrōpousthai*]" (*Adv. Col.* 1120c–d=*SSR* IV A 211).

17. "In the first place, Colotes uses these expressions maliciously, just as a professional denouncer would do. These consequences among others will follow without any doubt from the teachings of the Cyrenaics. He should however have presented their doctrine in the actual form in which those philosophers taught it. They say we are being sweetened and bittered and chilled and warmed and illuminated and darkened [*glukainesthai gar legousi kai pikrainesthai kai psuchesthai kai thermainesthai kai phōtizesthai kai skotizesthai*]. Each of these affections has within itself its own evidence, which is intrinsic to it and unchallenged [*tōn pathōn toutōn hekastou tēn enargeian oikeian en hautōi kai aperispaston echontos*]. But whether the honey is sweet or the young olive-shoot bitter or the hail chilly or the unmixed wine warm or the sun luminous or the night air dark is contested by many witnesses (wild and domesticated animals and humans too). Some in fact

dislike honey, others like olive-shoots or are burned off by hail or are chilled by the wine or go blind in the sunlight and see well at night. When opinion stays close to the affection it therefore preserves its infallibility [*hothen emmenousa tois pathesin hē doxa diatērei to anamartēton*]. On the contrary, when it oversteps them and mixes up with judgements and statements about external objects, it often disturbs itself and makes a fight against other people, who receive from the same objects contrary affections and different sense-impressions" (*Adv. Col.* 1120e–f=*SSR* IV A 211).

DIOGENES LAERTIUS

From book II of *The Lives of Eminent Philosophers*

18. "He [Aristippus] proclaimed as the end the smooth motion resulting in perception [*tēn leian kinēsin eis aisthēsin anadidomenēn*]" (II 85=*SSR* IV A 175).

19. "They [the Cyrenaics] said there are two kinds of affection, pleasure and pain, the former a smooth, the latter a rough motion [*tēn men leian kinēsin, tēn hēdonēn, ton de ponon tracheian kinēsin*]" (II 86=*SSR* IV A 172).

20. "The end is not the same as happiness, since the end is particular pleasure [*telos men gar einai tēn kata meros hēdonēn*], whereas happiness is a collection made out of particular pleasures [*eudaimonian de to ek tōn merikōn hēdonōn sustēma*]. Among these both past and future pleasures are counted together [*hais sunarithmountai kai hai parōichēkuiai kai hai mellousai*]. Particular pleasure is desirable because of itself [*einai te tēn merikēn hēdonēn di'hautēn hairetēn*]. On the other hand, happiness is desirable not because of itself, but because of the particular pleasures" (II 87–8=*SSR* IV A 172).

THE CYRENAICS

21. "Pleasure of the body which is the end is not the static pleasure following the removal of pains or, as it were, the freedom from discomfort, which Epicurus accepts and maintains to be the end" (II 87=*SSR* IV A 172).

22. "That pleasure is the end is proved by the fact that, from our youth onwards, we are instinctively attracted to it, and, once we obtain it, we seek for nothing more and avoid nothing so much as its opposite, pain" (II 88=*SSR* IV A 172).

23. "[For the Cyrenaics] not all mental pleasures and pains are derived from bodily pleasures and pain [*ou pasas mentoi tas psuchikas hēdonas kai algēdonas epi sōmatikais hēdonais kai algēdosi ginesthai*]" (II 89=*SSR* IV A 172).

24. "They [the Cyrenaics] deny that pleasure consists in the memory or expectation of the good, as Epicurus held, for they assert that the movement affecting the mind dies away with time" (II 89–90=*SSR* IV A 172).

25. "There are things productive of certain pleasures that are often of painful nature and are the opposite of pleasure, so that the accumulation of pleasures that does not produce happiness is difficult [*hōs duskolōtaton autois phainesthai to athroismon tōn hēdonōn eudaimonian mē poiounta*]" (II 90=*SSR* IV A 172).

26. "They [the Cyrenaics] claim that bodily pleasures are better than mental ones and that bodily pains are worse than mental ones. This is the reason why offenders are punished with the former" (II 90=*SSR* IV A 172).

27. "They [the Cyrenaics] say that one may feel a pain greater than another and that perceptions do not fully speak the truth [*tas aisthēseis mē pantote alētheuein*]" (II 93=*SSR* IV F 1).

PHILODEMUS

From *On Choices and Avoidances*

28. "They claim that as for truth no judgement is superior to any other. They believe in fact that the great *pathos* of the soul occurs as a result of pain and that thus we make our choices and avoidances by observing both bodily and mental pain" (col. II=*SSR* IV H 30).

29. "Some people denied that it is possible to know anything. They also added that if nothing on whose basis one should make an immediate choice is present, one should not choose immediately. Some other people made affections [*pathē*] of the soul as the moral ends and as not in need of any additional judgement based on further criteria. In doing so they granted to everybody an authority, which was not accountable, to get pleasure in whatever they cared to name and to do whatever contributed to it. Others held the view that what our school calls grief or joy are totally empty notions because of the manifest indeterminacy of things [*hoi de dia tēn emphainomenēn aoristian hapasan kenēn tēn lupēn kai tēn charan, hēn hēmeis dē legomen, edogmatisan*]" (Col. III=*SSR* IV H 30).

SEXTUS EMPIRICUS

From *Outlines of Pyrrhonism*, book I

30. "Cyrenaic doctrine differs from Scepticism in so much as it says that the end is pleasure and the smooth motion of the flesh [*tēn leian tēs sarkos kinēsin*]" (I 215=*SSR* IV A 212).

From *Against the Mathematicians*, book VII

31. "(11) The Cyrenaics appear to confine themselves to ethics only, and to dismiss physics and logic as contributing nothing to the happiness of our life. Some, however, have suggested that this view about them is actually refuted by the very fact that the Cyrenaics divided ethics into sub-branches: one, having to do with what has to be done or avoided; another dealing with affections; a third one on actions; the fourth concerned with causes; and a final one dealing with arguments" (=*SSR* IV A 168; see also Sen. *Ep. ad. Lucilium* XIV 1, 12=*SSR* IV A 165).

32. "(191) The Cyrenaics hold that affections [*pathē*] are the criteria [of truth] and that they alone are apprehended and are infallible [*kai mona katalambanesthai kai adiapseusta tunchanein*]. None of the things that have caused the affections [*tōn de pepoiēkotōn ta pathē*] is, on the contrary, apprehensible or infallible. They say that it is possible to state infallibly and truly and firmly and incorrigibly that we are being whitened or sweetened [*oti men gar leuikanometha, phasi, kai glukazometha, dunaton legein adiapseustōs kai bebaiōs kai alēthōs kai anexelenktōs*]. It is not possible however to say that the thing productive of our affection [*to empoiētikon tou pathous*] is white or sweet (192), because one may be disposed whitely even by something that is not-white or may be sweetened by something that is not-sweet" (=*SSR* IV A 213).

33. "(194) We must therefore say either that the affections are the *phainomena* or that the things productive of the affections are the *phainomena*. If we say that the affections are the *phainomena*, we will have to maintain that all *phainomena* are true and apprehensible. If, on the contrary, we say that the things productive of the affections are the *phainomena*, all *phainomena* will be false and not apprehensible. The affection occurring in us tells us nothing more than itself [*to gar peri hēmas sumbainon pathos heautou*

pleon ouden hēmin endeiknutai]. If one has to speak but the truth, the affection alone is therefore actually a *phainomenon* for us. What is external and productive of the affection [*to d'ektos kai tou pathous poiētikon*] perhaps is a being [*tacha men estin on*], but it is not a *phainomenon* for us. (195) We all are infallible as far as our own affection is concerned, but we all are in error about what is out there [*to ektos hupokeimenon*]" (=*SSR* IV A 213).

34. "No criterion is common to human beings, common names are assigned to objects [*onomata de koina tithesthai tois chrēmasin*]. (196) All in common in fact call something white or sweet [*leukon men gar ti kai gluku kalousi koinōs pantes*], but they do not have something common that is white or sweet [*koinon de ti leukon ē gluku ouk echousin*]. Each human being is aware of his own private affection [*hekastos gar tou idiou pathous antilambanetai*]. One cannot say, however, whether this affection occurs in oneself and in one's neighbour from a white object [*to de ei touto to pathos apo leukou enginetai autōi kai tōi pelas*], since one cannot grasp the affection of the neighbour, nor can his neighbour, since he cannot feel the affection of that other person. (197) And since no affection is common to us all, it is hasty to declare that what appears to me a certain way appears the same way to my neighbour as well. Perhaps I am constituted so as to be whitened by the external object when it comes into contact with my senses, while another person has the senses constructed so as to have been disposed differently. In any case, the *phainomenon* is absolutely not common to us all [*ou pantōs oun koinon esti to phainomenon hēmin*]. (198) That we really are not all affected in the same way because of different dispositions of our senses is clear from the cases of people who suffer from jaundice or ophthalmia and from those who are in a natural condition. Just as the first group of persons are affected yellowly, the second redly and the third whitely from the same thing, so it is also probable that those who are in a natural condition are not affected in the same way by the same things because of the different construction of their

senses, but rather that the person with grey eyes is affected in one way, the one with blue eyes in another, and the one with black eyes in another yet different way. It follows that the names we assign to things are common [*hōste koina men hēmas onomata tithenai tois pragmasin*], but that we have private affections [*pathē de ge echein idia*]" (=*SSR* IV A 213).

35. "What these philosophers [the Cyrenaics] hold about the criteria [of truth] seems to correspond to what they say about ends. For affections [*pathē*] do extend to ends too. Some of the affections are pleasant, others are painful and others are intermediate [*ta de metaxu*]. The painful ones are, they say, bad and their end is pain, whereas the pleasant ones are good, whose unmistakable end is pleasure. The intermediates are neither good nor bad, whose end is neither good nor bad, which is an affection in-between pleasure and pain (200)" (=*SSR* IV A 213).

From *Against the Mathematicians*, book VI

36. "Cyrenaic philosophers hold that affections alone exist [*mona huparchein ta pathē*] and nothing else. Since it is not an affection but rather it is something capable of producing an affection [*hothen kai tēn phōnēn mē ousan pathos, alla pathous poiētikēn*], sound is not one of the things that exist [*mē gignesthai tōn huparktōn*]. By denying the existence of every sensory object [*aisthēton*], the schools of Democritus and Plato deny the existence of sound as well, for sound is a sensory object" (VI 53=*SSR* IV A 219).

TIMON

37. "Such was the delicate nature of Aristippus, who groped error by touch [*trupherē phusis amphaphoōntos pseudē*]" (D.L. II 66=fr. 27 Di Marco).

NOTES

1. SCHOOLS AND SCHOLARSHIP

1. On Socrates' commitment to pleasure (and how such a commitment was understood and interpreted by the Socratic schools), see Tarrant (1994). Grote (1865: III, 555) identifies Aristippus' ethical theory with that of the Platonic Socrates in the *Protagoras*.
2. It is worth remembering here Gigon's (1946) interpretation of the influence Socrates exercised on the young: a young man meets Socrates who, through his words and actions, persuades him to abandon his way of life and devote himself to philosophy. This pattern has two variants: (i) the young man is at the lowest level and understands that only philosophy can bring him nobility; and (ii) the young man is self-confident but, through conversation with Socrates and by being in his company, he becomes aware of his inner nullity and, hence, devotes himself to philosophy. Aristippus, together with Alcibiades and Xenophon, belongs to the latter type, while Phaedo and Aeschines to the former (*ibid.*). On the Socratic origins of the Cynics and the Cyrenaics, see Tsouna (1994).
3. See Kerferd (1981b). The same term, "movement", is to be found in connection with the Socratic schools in Vander Waerdt (1994), which groups many useful articles on Socratic thinkers and schools.
4. The same caution I have invoked here in distinguishing arbitrarily between the "great" philosophical schools of Plato and Aristotle and the "minor" Socratic schools is shared by Döring (1988: 94) and Decleva-Caizzi (1981: 149).
5. On the evanescent figure of Arete, we still rely on Eccius (1776) and Chiappelli (1890).

197

6. Another positive account of Aristippus can be found in Thrige (1828: §94).
7. An English translation of a significant part of Giannantoni's *SSR* is being prepared by G. Boys-Stones and C. J. Rowe (Durham University).
8. Giannantoni (1958: 74–169; 1991: vol. IV, nn. 17, 18). It is clear that Giannantoni's argument may be interpreted the other way round: since there is no concrete evidence that in his dialogues Plato is actually referring either to Aristippus or to doctrines he may have elaborated, there is little point in attributing to Aristippus any foundation or the paternity of any serious philosophical view. I am not sure which implication Giannantoni likes most, since he seems to move freely from one to the other.
9. See Grilli (1959, 1960) and Giannantoni (1960). Wehrli (1959) is a review of Giannantoni (1958), advancing more than one criticism of Giannantoni's interpretations.
10. The literature of *Successions* is a Hellenistic genre aimed at providing historical as well as doctrinal sketches of ancient philosophical schools by describing the thought and life of the initial head of the school and of its successors. Diogenes Laertius' *Lives of Eminent Philosophers* is, for instance, from beginning to end structured along lines of successions. On the literature of the *Successions*, see Mansfeld (1999: 23–5).
11. For a brief account in English of Döring's views on the Cyrenaics, see Döring (2011).
12. Tsouna (1998: 124–37) discharges the Platonic testimony, at least as far as the *Theaetetus* is concerned.

2. ARISTIPPUS

1. "Every aspect and condition and thing suit to Aristippus, aiming at the best, yet capable to be happy for what he is presently having". See also Diogenes Laertius II 66.
2. Diogenes' account has been studied in depth by Mannebach (1961: 101–5). On the probable sources for Diogenes (mainly Aesichius), see Giannantoni (1991: vol. IV, n. 13, 135).
3. Even in the part of the account Diogenes devotes to the later Cyrenaics, there is a textual problem arising into a conceptual one. In the part that signals the transition from the Hegesians into the Annicerians (II 96), there is the following sentence: "the Annicerians agreed in other respects with them", leaving the reader uncertain about to whom "them" refers. Does the term refer, more narrowly, to the Hegesians, whose views are described in the preceding section (II 93–6), or does it

refer, more generally, to the proper Cyrenaics, whose views are reported at II 86–93? Noting lack of smoothness in the text in the passage from the section on the early Cyrenaics to the later ones (namely II 93), and in the one just indicated from the Hesegians to the Annicerians (II 96), Mannebach believes that there has been an inversion of order in the text, due to inaccuracy of a medieval hand. The correct textual order should be therefore restored as follows: the section on the Annicerians should precede, and not follow, the one on the Hegesians (Mannebach 1961: 44, 94). Giusta has made clear that the inversion in the text Mannebach proposes to adopt is highly improbable and, above all, does not make good sense of the text, where the points Diogenes suggests as peculiar of the Annicerians are in effect only those where there is an actual contrast with the Hegesians. I side fully with Giusta (1964: I, 136–7) in retaining the traditional order of the text.

4. Another source on Aristippus' life that may be worth consulting is the entry "Aristippus" in the lexicon *Suida*.
5. On the marvellous conditions in Cyrene, see Thrige (1828: 349–51). On Cyrene, see also Hdt. IV 157–8.
6. On other historical sources that may witness this meeting, see Xen. *An.* V 3, 9 and DL II 52.
7. Von Stein (1855: 64); Antoniades (1916: 17), where he argues that Aristippus left Athens and his successful teaching activities there to go to Syracuse.
8. In a letter to his daughter Arete (*SSR* IV A 226=*Socratic. Epist.* XXVII), it is said that Aristippus became ill on Lipari, a small island off the north coast of Sicily, on a stopover on the journey from Syracuse back to Cyrene. On the unreliability of this letter, see Grilli (1959: 344).
9. On Protagoras and mathematics, see Socrates' ironic remark about self-sufficiency in geometry at *Tht.* 169a. On the empiricist grounds Protagoras' relativism seems to endorse, see Zilioli (2007: 82–7).
10. In Zilioli (2007: 66–9), it is argued that *Tht.* 167b–168c may indeed reflect Protagoras' historical views.
11. On Aristippus' sayings, see also *SSR* IV A 101–39.
12. Christian authors often offer a too stigmatized characterization of Aristippus as an eager devotee of pleasure: see e.g. Lactantius, *Divinae Institutiones* III 8, 6=*SSR* IV A 193.
13. On pleasure as a smooth movement of the body, see also Sextus Empiricus, *Pyr.* I 215(=T 30) and *Math.* VII 199.
14. For Timon's chronology, see Di Marco (1989: 4–7).
15. See: "What about the Cyrenaics, by no means contemptible philosophers? They deny that anything can be perceived from the outside,

while they do say to perceive only those things they sense by means of an internal touch [*tactu intumo*], like, for instance, pain and pleasure; they say they cannot know whose sound or colour something is, but to sense only to be affected in a certain way" (Cic. *Acad. Pr.* II 24, 76=SSR IV A 209=T 11); "What about touch, of that touch philosophers call interior [*interiorem*], of either pleasure or pain, in which the Cyrenaics believe that only there is the criterion of truth [*iudicium*], because it is perceived by means of the senses?" (*Ac. Pr.* II 7, 20=SSR IV A 209= T 10). On internal touch, see Chapter 5, § "Internal touch".

16. Against the epistemological reading of Timon's fragment, see Di Marco (1989: 174–5).

17. Diogenes' text goes like this: "Some also maintain that he [Aristippus] wrote six Books of Essays; others, and among them Sosicrates of Rhodes, that he wrote none at all [book of essays, not absolutely]" (DL II 83). Mannebach (1961: 76–80) is on the right track when he observes that there is no need to emend Diogenes' text at I 16. Consequently, he rejects the view that Aristippus did not write anything. Mannebach is also correct when he points out that most of the apophthegms of Aristippus that Diogenes refers to in book II of the *Lives* are derived from Aristippus' actual books. Mannebach also adds that Aristippus' writings were lost in the third century BCE.

18. The concept of education that seems to be lurking behind Aristippus' apophthegms, namely that education mainly rests on the capacity of the mind to supervene on instincts, is curiously similar to the one Protagoras is made to propose in the section of the *Theaetetus* that has been termed the "Defence of Protagoras" (166a–168c). On this point, see Zilioli (2007: 59–66).

19. See Gigante's (1983: 481) note to DL II 86; Classen (1958).

20. "A rule of conduct [*agôgê*] is a choice of a way of life [*hairesis biou*], or of a particular action, adopted by one person, or many – by Diogenes [i.e. the Cynic], for instance, or the Laconians" (Sext. Emp. *Pyr.* I 145); "we oppose rule of conduct [*agôgê*] to rule of conduct, as when we oppose the rule of Diogenes [referring to the school derived from his way of life] to that of Aristippus" (150). It may be noted here that the translation of *agôgê* as "rule of conduct" is rather appropriate in the context, in so far as "rule of conduct" mixes up a reference to the practical way of life (conduct) with its philosophical connotation (rule).

21. For the testimonies on Arete and Aristippus the Younger, including Aristocles' fundamental one, see SSR IV B.

NOTES

3. THE *THEAETETUS*

1. More authoritatively, the idea that Plato can legitimately be interpreted as a source for the thought of his contemporaries has recently been defended by Irwin (2007: 46).
2. Plato's dialogues are quoted with the traditional Stephanus pagination, which can be found in the margins of current translations in modern languages.
3. Dümmler (1901: 64ff.) argues that the *Theaetetus* is the work where Plato actually contrasts Aristippus and Antisthenes on knowledge.
4. I accept Burnyeat's well-known view that there is an epistemological progression from the first to the third definition of knowledge, in so far as the latter is more comprehensive than the former and, hence, closer to truth (Burnyeat 1990: 2 and pt 3). Yet, all three definitions of knowledge in the *Theaetetus* are actually refuted by Socrates. The impasse with which the dialogue ends is, I take it, real: it is neither apparent nor preparatory for a better (and true) definition of knowledge, already there to be discovered by the perceptive reader, as Sedley (2004: 8–13, 30–37) believes.
5. "Peirastic" from *peirao*, which is used also for the kind of confrontation typical of agonistic races or war battles (*LSJ*).
6. Campbell (1883: 51) also believes that Aristippus the Elder is included among the subtler thinkers of the *Theaetetus*.
7. This may be a further reason for Plato not mentioning the Cyrenaics directly: they are the frontrunners of a perceptual theory based on indeterminacy that was shared, in its main lines, by other thinkers such as Protagoras.
8. For indeterminacy in the *Theaetetus*, see 152d6, 157a8, 166b7–8, 182b3–4; see also Chapter 4, § "Indeterminacy".
9. "What we say a given colour is will be neither the thing which collides, nor the thing it collides with, but something which has come into being between them; something peculiar to each one" (153e7–154a2).
10. On the Cyrenaics not questioning the existence (and persistence over time) of both objects and subjects (and, hence, as rejecting indeterminacy), see Tsouna (1998: 131–7).
11. For the passive and active elements in the theory of perception endorsed by the subtler thinkers, see *Theaetetus* 156a7, 157a3, 157a5, 157a6.
12. Greene (1938). See *Odyssey* IV, 271–89, where Menelaus magnifies the abilities of Odysseus by remembering the episode when, by imitating the voices of their wives, Helen calls by name all the men sitting inside

201

the wooden horse. Odysseus saves his fellows on that occasion by persuading them to remain silent.

13. See *Theaetetus* 156a–157c, in particular: "From their intercourse [of passive and active elements], and their friction against one another, there come to be offspring, unlimited in number but coming in pairs of twins, of which one is a perceived thing and the other a perception, which is *on every occasion generated and brought to birth together with the perceived thing*" (156a7–b2); see also 156b7–c3 and d4–5. In Aristocles' text, note the pair "man–stone", which also occurs at *Theaetetus* 157c1.

14. On the Platonic background for Aristocles' argument, in particular the *Theaetetus*, see Chiesara (2001: 139) and Grote (1865: 335). See also the section of Aristocles' *On Philosophy* devoted to discussing Metrodorus and Protagoras (F6 Chiesara), where, again, a derivation of Aristocles' argument from the ones Plato develops in the *Theaetetus* is openly recognizable.

4. INDETERMINACY

1. I refer to the Burnyeat–Fine debate on Cyrenaic subjectivity, which is illustrated in detail and assessed critically by Christopher Gill (2009: 391–407).

2. See, in particular, the remark of Theaetetus to Socrates: "I hesitate to tell you I've got nothing to say, Socrates, because when I said that just now you told me off for it. Still, I really wouldn't be able to object that people who are mad or dreaming don't make false judgements, when one lot of them imagine they're gods, and the others imagine they've got wings, and think of themselves, in their sleep, as flying" (*Tht.* 158a8–b4).

3. It is well known that Augustine was the first philosopher to elaborate an argument about the reality of the external world that was very close to the classical one of Descartes: I think therefore I am. See Augustine's argument: "*Si fallor, sum*" (*De civ. D.* II 26).

4. For the Cyrenaics as idealists, see Groarke (1990: 72–7); Tsouna (1998: 78–82); Kechagia (2011: 257–9).

5. Indeterminacy is widely discussed (also in connection with vagueness) in contemporary analytical philosophy of language and metaphysics. On metaphysical indeterminacy, for a start, see Bennett & Zimmerman (2011), which is a collection of many important papers on indeterminacy.

6. Readers interested in "bizarre" metaphysical theories denying the existence of ordinary objects may take profit in reading Merricks (2003) and Van Inwagen (1990).

7. On Protagoras' relativism and Plato's objection to it, see *Tht.* 151e–152d and 170a–171c. On a possible way out from the impasse caused by the self-refuation problem, see Zilioli (2007: ch. IV). Artosi (2012) insists on the ubiquity of the charge of self-refutation that can be levelled even against unsubjective theories of knowledge.

8. On correlativity as the fundamental element in Protagoras' theory of perception for Aristotle, see Gottlieb (1992).

9. On the impossibility of identification and re-identification of objects and persons in the context of the theory of the subtler thinkers, see *Theaetetus* 159a6–b6 and 159e7–160a2. Van Inwagen (1990: §13) speaks of a "history of maintenance" that we, as living organisms, can tell to make sense of virtual objects (as he calls them) devoid of stable essences. By contrast with virtual objects (that is, the commonsensical objects of our everyday life), human beings can be identified by means of the kind of life they lead (see §9).

10. While commenting on Protagoras' maxim that man is the measure of all things, the anonymous commentator also commits to indeterminacy the followers of Pyrrho when he remarks, "the Pyrrhonists say that everything is relative, inasmuch as nothing exists in its own right but everything is relative to other things. Neither shape nor sounds nor objects of taste and smell or touch nor any other object of perception has a character of its own" (col. LXIII, 3–11).

11. For the undoubtedly Cyrenaic background of Philodemus' text, see Indelli & Tsouna-McKirahan (1995: 118–26). Giannantoni (*SSR* IV H 30) and Winiarczyk (1981) include the whole passage in the *Testimonia* of Theodorus the Godless.

12. According to Aristotle, those who deny the principle of non-contradiction "seem … to be stating something indeterminate [*to aoriston*]" (Γ 5 1007b27–8); again, he says that those who believe that all appearances are true deny the principle of non-contradiction because "they believed that things-that-are are merely perceptibles; and in these things the nature of indeterminacy [*hē tou aoristou phusis*] is an important constituent" (Γ 5 1010a3–4).

13. Recently, Kechagia (2011: 257–61) has proposed a reading of Colotes' passage in Plutarch similar to my own here.

14. Another text that suggests a Cyrenaic commitment to indeterminacy is a long excerpt of Aristocles' *On Philosophy*. I discuss it in Chapter 5, § "Aristocles' criticism".

15. On logical faults in Aristotle's arguments against indeterminacy and in defence of the principle of non-contradiction, see Lukasiewicz (1910: chs 6–9).

16. For an alternative account of Pyrrho's philosophy and for a more conservative interpretation of Aristocles' passage, see Brunschwig (1994). Bett himself traces indeterminacy back to Plato's *Theaetetus* (Bett 2000: 132–40, 183–6). See also Thorsrud (2009: 20–22).
17. For ancient authors, see Cicero (*Acad. Pr.* II 46, 142=*SSR* IV A 209) and Eusebius (*Praep. evang.* 14.2.4=*SSR* IV A 216); for modern authors, see Mannebach (1961: 114–17); and Decleva-Caizzi (1981: 194–6).

5. PERSONS, OBJECTS AND KNOWLEDGE

1. On the problem, see Tsouna (1998: ch. I).
2. Diogenes too speaks of intermediate states: "they [the Cyrenaics] called intermediate states [*mesas te katastaseis*] the absence of pleasure and pain" (DL II 90).
3. Although the example of fire is rather common, there is no doubt – given the clear allusion in Aristocles to arguments employed and developed by Plato himself in the *Theaetetus* – that Aristocles is actually referring to the anonymous commentator (who could well have been almost a contemporary of Aristocles). On the point, see Chiesara (2001: 138).
4. That is the reason why I believe Döring misses the point when he condemns Aristocles' and Colotes' testimonies as careless (Döring 1988: 22ff.). The image of the torpor by which, in Aristocles' opinion, the Cyrenaics are oppressed is not only reminiscent of Colotes' image of the siege. Both images suggest a sense of detachment from the world that for Colotes and Aristocles is intrinsic to Cyrenaic philosophy.
5. Later Aristocles adds, "What discussion can there be with such men? It will be surprising if they do not know whether they are on earth or in the sky. And it will be even more astonishing if they do not know – while claiming to be philosophers – whether four are more than three and how many one and two make. For they cannot even say how many fingers they have on their hands, nor whether each of them is one or many" (*Praep. evang.* 14.19.6). The argument about the coexistence of the three factors of perceptual process we are now assessing is to be found also in Aristotle, *Metaphysics* Γ 5 1010b33–9.
6. Hume seems to have revised his view of persons and peronal identity in the Appendix to the *Treatise*. On this, see Strawson (2011).
7. Epicharmus' argument, which some say he took from Pythagoras, can be found in DL III 11; in the anonymous commentary col. LXXI 1–39 (commenting on *Tht.* 152e4–5) and in Plutarch, *De sera* 559a. A more technical version of Epicharmus' argument can be found in Plutarch *Comm. not.* 1083a–1084a.

8. For the claim that the Cyrenaics raised serious doubts about personal identity, see Irwin (1991: 66–70; 2007: 45). For the arguments against, see Tsouna (1998: 132).

9. For Parfit's views on persons and their identity, see Parfit (1984: pt III, 199–350, esp. 263, 281): "The truth is very different from what we are inclined to believe. Even if are not aware of this, most of us are Non-Reductionists [namely, refusing the all-or-nothing view about personal identity]. If we considered my imagined cases, we would be strongly inclined to believe that our continued existence is a deep further fact, distinct from physical and psychological continuity, and a fact that must be all-or-nothing. This is not true. Is the truth depressing? Some may find it so. But I find it liberating and consoling. When I believed that my existence was such a further fact, I seemed imprisoned in myself. My life seemed like a glass tunnel, through which I was moving faster every year, and at the end of which there was darkness. When I changed my view, the walls of my glass tunnel disappeared. I now live in the open air. There is still a difference between my life and the lives of other people. But the difference is less. Other people are closer. I am less concerned about the rest of my own life, and more concerned about the lives of others" (*ibid.*: 281).

10. See Van Inwagen (1990: §§13, 14). The other element of Van Inwagen's metaphysics, that is, living organisms such as human beings, have vague composition, identity and existence (§§17, 18, 19). I interpret Van Inwagen's idea of living organisms as something very similar to the concept of loose selves I have attributed to the Cyrenaics. In fact, Van Inwagen's overall metaphysics is, in its general lines, very close to the kind of Cyrenaic ontology of things and persons I have reconstructed in this book. For another interesting account where the proper existence of things and objects is denied for lack of causal powers, see Merricks (2003).

11. Because of the use of the verb *katalambanō* in the standard statement "*mona ta pathē katalepta*", Tsouna claims that the formulation of the standard Cyrenaic tenet that only affections are knowable was properly made in Hellenistic times, when the verb *katalambanō* was often used by the Stoics in their elaboration of the idea of *kataléptiké phantasia* (Tsouna 1998: 32–3). Döring (1988: 29), however, has pointed out that there is an occurrence of *katalambanō* in this technical sense in Plato's *Phaedrus* (250d1). This does not strictly rule out the possibility that the Cyrenaics may have originally used the term in the formulation of their epistemology.

12. Ancient sources often pair the Cyrenaics with the Epicureans, as far as

their epistemologies are concerned. Augustine (=T 9) says that both groups of philosophers defend a theory of knowledge based on senses. More importantly, Plutarch rebuts Colotes because he has not properly understood that the Cyrenaic epistemology and that of Epicurus come down to the same view (*Adv. Col.* 1120f–1121c). On Cyrenaics and Epicureans on knowledge, see Tsouna (1998: ch. 9) and Kechagia (2011: 268–82).

6. LANGUAGE AND MEANING

1. I refer to Tsouna (1998: 105–12) for the first sensitive appreciation of the Cyrenaic argument about language, although I find myself disagreeing with her about the overall interpretation of the argument.
2. I am aware that my presentation here of Aristotle's views is perhaps too brutally simplistic. What I wish to stress, however, is how the Cyrenaics substantially differ from mainstream positions of ancient semantics. Aristotle's own theory of meaning and reference, as well as the passage of *De Interpretatione* on which we focus, are open to alternative interpretations; see Charles (1994).
3. See also Brancacci (1990: 204–9). A reasoned account of the different interpretations of Gorgias' philosophy of language can be found in Mazzara (1999).
4. "When they (my elders) named some object, and accordingly, moved towards something, I saw this and I grasped that the thing was called by the sound they uttered when they meant to point it out. Their intention was shown by their bodily movements, as if it were the natural language of all peoples: the expression of the face, the play of the eyes, the movement of other parts of the body, and the tone of voice which expresses our state of mind in seeking, having, rejecting, or avoiding something. Thus, as I heard words repeatedly used in their proper places in various sentences, I gradually learnt to understand what objects they signified; and after that I had trained my mouth to form these signs, I used them to express my own desires" (1953: 1, quoting August. *Conf.* I 8).
5. To show this, Wittgenstein formulates the famous example of the diarist: "Let us imagine the following case. I want to keep a diary about the recurrence of a certain sensation. To this end I associate it with the sign 'S' and write this sign in a calendar for every day on which I have the sensation. – I will remark first of all that a definition of the sign cannot be formulated. – But still I can give myself a kind of ostensive definition. – How? Can I point to the sensation? Not in the ordinary sense. But I speak, or write the sign down, and at the same

time I concentrate my attention on the sensation – and so, as it were, point it inwardly. – But what is this ceremony for? For that is all it seems to be! A definition surely serves to establish the meaning of a sign. – Well, that is done precisely by the concentrating of my attention; for in this way I impress on myself the connexion between the sign and the sensation. – But 'I impress it on myself' can only mean: this process brings it about that I can remember the connexion *right* in the future. But in the present case I have no criterion of correctness. One would like to say: whatever is going to seem right to me is right. And that only means that here we can't talk about 'right'" (1953: 258).

7. PLEASURE AND HAPPINESS

1. See Annas (1993: 27–9). Irwin places the relevance of Cyrenaic ethics exactly in its rejection of eudaemonism and argues that "since the eudaemonist assumption may not seem as obviously correct to us as it seems to many Greek moralists, it is worth considering the views of those Greeks who dissent from it" (1991: 55). Contrary to the view that the Cyrenaics are really anti-eudaemonists, see Tsouna (2002).

2. Since Philebus does not even agree on this point, he is rapidly discharged as Socrates' interlocutor in that dialogue.

3. "They [the Cyrenaics] assert that some people fail to choose pleasure because their minds are perverted" (DL II 89).

4. The Cradle argument was often used in Hellenistic philosophy, especially by the Stoics and the Epicureans: see Brunschwig (1986). The standard source for Epicurus having formulated the Cradle argument is DL X 137.

5. See O'Keefe (2010: esp. 118–21) on the ethical debate between the Cyrenaics and Epicurus.

6. On this, see the view of the Annicerians: "The Annicerians maintained that there is no definite end of the whole of life, but claimed that there is a special end for each action – the pleasure resulting from the action. These Cyrenaics repudiate Epicurus' account of pleasure as the removal of pain, denouncing it as a condition of a corpse" (Clem. Al. *Strom.* II 21, 130.7–8=*SSR* IV F 4).

7. Following Mannebach (fr. 170) and Gigante (1983: 483), I retain the "*mē*" of some manuscripts, thus reading the whole sentence at II 90=T 25 in the following way: "there are things productive of certain pleasures that are often of painful nature and are the opposite of pleasure, so that the accumulation of pleasures that does not produce happiness is difficult". "Accumulation" (*hathroismos*), a rare term in

ancient Greek, recurs in Plato's *Theaetetus*, exactly at a crucial point of the subtler thinkers' theory, where subjects and objects, such as "man" or "stone", are best described as *hathroisma* (*Tht.* 157b9).

8. Although on different grounds, O'Keefe (2002) also argues for a presence in Cyrenaic ethics of both pleasure and happiness.
9. The places in the *Philebus* where Zeller detects a Cyrenaic heritage are 31d, 44e and, above all, 53c.
10. On the *Philebus* as a dialogue directed against Aristippus and Eudoxus, see also Bury (1897: X ff., 24, 122, 126, 163, 200).
11. On pleasure in the *Nicomachean Ethics*, see 7.1152b12–20; 10.1172b9–25 for (Eudoxus' views) and 1172b26–1174a12 (for Aristotle's counterarguments).
12. For the details of Giannantoni's argument, see Giannantoni (1958: 158–65).
13. See *Phlb.* 24c–d for perceptual qualities as unlimited items.
14. On the limited and unlimited in the *Philebus* as the two ways to classify reality see initially *Phlb.* 16c and 23b–31a, in particular 23b–27e.

8. CYRENAIC PHILOSOPHY AND ITS LATER EPIGONI

1. By relying on a substantial continuity between the Cyrenaics and the later sects of the school, in the course of the book I have in fact in some cases relied on views ascribed to the later sects in order to shed light on doctrinal commitments I take to be central to the whole Cyrenaic school.
2. On the epithet "death-persuader" for Hegesias, see DL II 86 and *SSR* IV F 2.
3. On a possible influence of Cynic ethics on Hegesias, see Long (1999: 638).
4. It is worth asking here whether the reference to the calculus of pleasure (*pros hēdonēs logos*) is alluding to the art of measurement (of pleasure) Socrates refers to in the *Protagoras* and whether the reference to the measure of pleasure (*pros hēdonēs metron*) is a possible echo of Protagoras' motto that one is the measure of one's affections. If it were so, a further conceptual linkage between Protagoras and the Cyrenaics, even the later sects of the Cyrenaic school such as the Hegesians, would be profitably established. At the same time, one may wonder whether the reference to something being "equally indifferent" to the measure of pleasure (*adiaphoron pros hēdonēs metron*) is an allusion to Pyrrho's idea that things are equally "indifferent [*adiaphora*], unstable and indeterminate" (fr. 53 Decleva-Caizzi=F4 Chiesara=Euseb. *Praep. evang.*

14.18.3). Again, if this were the case, a tighter connection between Pyrrho and the Cyrenaics could be suggested.
5. For a close parallelism between the idea of education the Hegesians seem to have endorsed on the basis of this brief passage of Diogenes and that of Protagoras, see Plato *Theaetetus* 166b-e.
6. On the Hegesians and the Epicureans, see Long (1999: 635-6).
7. Winiarczyk (1981) has collected and commented on all the sources on ancient atheists, such as Diagoras of Melos and Theodorus the Godless. Giannantoni has collected the sources on Theodorus in *SSR* IV H, and commented on them in Giannantoni (1991: n. 20). A useful, yet brief note on Theodorus can be found in Long (1999: 636-7).
8. On the possible relation between Pyrrho and Theodorus see also *SSR* IV H 2=Winiarczyk T 19, where Theodorus is said to have been taught by Pyrrho and to have based his own philosophy on imperturbability, one of the crucial concepts of Pyrrhonism.
9. See Winiarczyk (1981: T 66 and note); *SSR* IV H 30; Giannantoni (1991: 190). On the hypothesis that Philodemus' targets in cols II and III are the Hegesians, see Indelli & Tsouna-McKirahan (1995).
10. On Theodorus as a sophist, see also Winiarczyk (1981: T 57).
11. As evidence of Theodorus' critical confrontation with Anniceris one may think of Theodorus' disposal of friendship (DL II 98), which instead was highly valued by Anniceris and his followers.

FURTHER READING

Ancient sources are listed with reference to the numbering in the Appendix, "Cyrenaic Testimonies in Translation".

1. SCHOOLS AND SCHOLARSHIP

Ancient sources: 3, 4, 8

A good introductory survey on ancient philosophical schools, together with a useful chronology, can be found in Dorandi (1999a,b). Tsouna (1994; 1998: ch. 11) explains why the Cyrenaics are Socratic thinkers.

2. ARISTIPPUS

Ancient sources: 2, 3, 8, 12, 18

On Aristippus, the reader may consult Tim O'Keefe's entry in the *Internet Encyclopaedia of Philosophy*: www.iep.utm.edu/aristip/ (accessed May 2012) and Mann (1996). The reader may also profit from reading Tsouna (1994). A good source of information for Aristippus is Giannantoni (*SSR* IV, n. 13 [in Italian]).

3. THE *THEAETETUS*

Ancient sources: Plato's *Theaetetus* 156a2–157c3

To counterbalance my view that the subtler thinkers of the *Theaetetus* are best interpreted as the early Cyrenaics, the reader can profitably have a look at Tsouna (1998: ch. 10), where she argues for the opposite view. A similar case for denying the identification between the subtler thinkers and the early Cyrenaics has been attempted by Giannantoni (1958: 129–45 [in Italian]). Mondolfo (1953) has instead defended that identification on grounds different from the ones I relied on in this chapter.

4. INDETERMINACY

Ancient sources: 1, 5, 6, 16, 17, 29, 32, 33, 36

On indeterminacy in Greek philosophy, one may profitably read Bett (2000: ch. 1, and appendix 2). On the pervasiveness of indeterminacy in Greek metaphysics, the reader may wish to read Aristotle's *Metaphysics* Gamma, sections 4 to 6. Politis (2004: ch. 6) is helpful in locating indeterminacy as the view Aristotle sees as behind both relativism and subjectivism.

Those interested in the Cyrenaics as possible idealist philosophers could read Tsouna (1998: ch. 6), where she concludes that the Cyrenaics did not really put in question the existence of the external world.

5. PERSONS, OBJECTS AND KNOWLEDGE

Ancient sources: 1, 4, 5, 6, 7, 10, 11, 16, 17, 27, 32, 33, 34

For an interesting account of Cyrenaic epistemology, paralleled and contrasted with modern theories of knowledge such as sense-data theory, the reader may wish to read Tsouna (1998: ch. 4); in chapter 10 she shows how Cyrenaic epistemology and Protagoras' relativism amount to rather different theories of cognition.

Brunschwig (1999) locates Cyrenaic epistemology in the context of its philosophical background, as well as comparing it with scepticism.

O'Keefe (2011) draws a close parallel between the epistemology of the Cyrenaics and that of the Pyrrhonists and concludes that they differ significantly, despite their superficial affinities.

6. LANGUAGE AND MEANING

Ancient source: 34

Once again, Tsouna (1998: ch. 8) offers a good introduction to Cyrenaic philosophy of language, although she believes that it is less original than I suggest.

Alternatively, Mondolfo (1953: 127–35) argues that the Cyrenaics developed Gorgias' theory of meaning in an original and unexpected way.

7. PLEASURE AND HAPPINESS

Ancient sources: 2, 3, 4, 8, 12, 13, 15, 18, 19,
20, 21, 22, 23, 24, 25, 26, 30, 35

Irwin (1991) argues for the view that the Cyrenaics are a significant exception to Greek eudaemonism in so far as they do not make happiness the end of life. Irwin's article is significant because it openly recognizes in the Cyrenaics a very loose conception of person and personal identity (*ibid.*: 66–70). Irwin has also advanced such views more recently (2007: 44–58). Against Irwin's claim, the reader may profit from reading Tsouna (2002), where she interprets the Cyrenaics as not anti-eudaemonists. O'Keefe (2002) attempts to balance these opposite views by suggesting that the Cyrenaics are primarily concerned with pleasure but that they do not reject happiness.

8. CYRENAIC PHILOSOPHY AND ITS LATER EPIGONI

Ancient source: Diogenes Laertius II 93–104

On the later sects of the Cyrenaic school there is a brief note in Tim O'Keefe's entry on the Cyrenaics in the *Internet Encyclopaedia of Philosophy*: www.iep.utm.edu/cyren/ (accessed May 2012). One may profit from consulting Long (1999), where Cyrenaic hedonism as developed by the later sects of the school is compared with Epicurus' hedonism. Giannantoni (*SSR* vol. IV, nn. 19 and 20 [in Italian]) offers a succinct but detailed overview of the philosophical commitments of the later sects of the Cyrenaic school. Laks (1993) is an interesting contribution on the Annicerians.

BIBLIOGRAPHY

Algra, K., J. Barnes, J. Mansfeld & M. Schofield (eds) 1999. *The Cambridge History of Hellenistic Philosophy*. Cambridge: Cambridge University Press.

Ambrosius (Ambrogio Traversari) 1490. *Diogenes Laertius: De vita et moribus philosophorum*. Impensis nobilis viri Scoti.

Antoniades, E. 1916. *Aristipp und die Kyrenaiker*. Dissertation. Göttingen.

Annas, J. 1993. *The Morality of Happiness*. Oxford: Oxford University Press.

Annas, J. 1994. "Plato the Sceptic". See Vander Waerdt (1994), 309–40.

Artosi, A. 2012. "Miseria della Filosofia". *Diritto e Questione Pubbliche* 11: 12–45.

Barnes, J. (ed.) 1984. *The Complete Works of Aristotle*. Princeton, NJ: Princeton University Press.

Bastianini, F. & D. Sedley (eds) 1995. *Commentarium in Platonis Theaetetum*, Corpus dei Papiri Filosofici Greci e Latini. Florence: Olschki.

Bennett, K. & N. Zimmerman (eds) 2011. *Oxford Studies in Metaphysics*, vol. 6. Oxford: Oxford University Press.

Bett, R. 2000. *Pyrrho, his Antecedents and his Legacy*. Oxford: Oxford University Press.

Brancacci, A. 1982. "Teodoro l'Ateo e Bione di Boristene fra Pirrone e Arcesilao". *Elenchos* 3: 55–85.

Brancacci, A. 1990. *Oikeios Logos: La filosofia del linguaggio di Antistene*. Naples: Bibliopolis.

Broadie, S. & C. J. Rowe (eds) 2002. *Aristotle: Nicomachean Ethics*. Oxford: Oxford University Press.

Brunschwig, J. 1986. "The Cradle Argument in Epicureanism and Stoicism". In *The Norms of Nature*, M. Schofield & G. Striker (eds), 113–44. Cambridge: Cambridge University Press.

Brunschwig, J. 1994. *Papers in Hellenistic Philosophy*. Cambridge: Cambridge University Press.

Brunschwig, J. 1999. "Introduction: The Beginnings of Hellenistic Epistemology". See Algra *et al.* (1999), 229–59.

Burnyeat, M. 1982. "Idealism and Greek Philosophy: What Descartes Saw and Berkeley Missed". *Philosophical Review* 90: 3–40.

Burnyeat, M. F. 1990. *The Theaetetus of Plato*, M. J. Levett (trans.). Indianapolis, IN: Hackett.

Bury, R. 1897. *The Philebus of Plato*. Cambridge: Cambridge University Press.

Campbell, L. 1883. *The Theaetetus of Plato*, 2nd edn. Oxford: Clarendon.

Carlini, A. 1968. "Osservazioni sui tre *eidê tou logou* in Ps. Demetrio, *De eloc.* 296 sg". *Rivista di Storia e di Istruzione Classica* 96: 38–46.

Chappell, T. 2005. *Reading Plato's* Theaetetus. Indianapolis, IN: Hackett.

Charles, D. 1994. "Aristotle on Names and their Signification". In *Companions to Ancient Thought*, S. Everson (ed.), 37–73. Cambridge: Cambridge University Press.

Chiappelli, A. 1890. "Le donne alle scuole dei filosofi greci". *Nuova Antologia* 111: 613–41.

Chiesara, M. L. 2001. *Aristocles of Messene: Testimonies and Fragments*. Oxford: Oxford University Press.

Classen, C. J. 1958. "Aristippos". *Hermes* 86: 182–92.

Decleva-Caizzi 1981. *Pirrone. Testimonianze*. Naples: Bibliopolis.

Diels, H. & W. Kranz 1985. *Die Fragmente der Vorsokratiker*. Zurich: Weidmann [DK].

Diès, A. 1949. *Platon. Oeuvres Complètes: le Philèbe*. Paris: Belles Lettres.

Di Marco, M. 1989. *Timone di Fliunte: Silli*. Rome: Edizioni dell'Ateneo.

Dorandi, T. 1999a. "Chronology". See Algra *et al.* (1999), 31–54.

Dorandi, T. 1999b. "Organizations and Structure of the Philosophical Schools". See Algra *et al.* (1999), 55–64.

Döring, K. 1972. *Die Megariker: Kommentierte Sammlung der Testimonien*. Amsterdam: Gruner.

Döring, K. 1988. *Der Sokratesschüler Aristipp und die Kyrenaiker*. Mainz: Akademie der Wissenschaften und die Literatur.

Döring, K. 2011. "The Students of Socrates". In *The Cambridge Companion to Socrates*, D. Morrison (ed.), 24–47. Cambridge: Cambridge University Press.

Dümmler, F. 1901. *Kleine Schriften*, vol. I, 10–78 (=*Antisthenica*, Berlin 1882).

Dupré, J. 1993. *The Disorder of Things*. Cambridge, MA: Harvard University Press.

Eccius I. G. 1776. *De Arete philosopha disserit et lectiones suas indicit*. Leipzig.

Feyerabend, P. K. 1975. *Against Method*. London: Verso.

Giannantoni, G. 1958. *I Cirenaici: Raccolta delle fonti antiche, traduzione e studio introduttivo*. Florence: Sansoni.

Giannantoni, G. 1960. "Note Aristippee". *Rivista Critica di Storia della Filosofia* 15: 63–70.

Giannantoni, G. 1981. "Pirrone, la scuola scettica e il sistema delle successioni". In *Lo scetticismo antico*, 2 vols, G. Giannantoni (ed.), 13–34. Naples: Bibliopolis.

Giannantoni, G. 1991. *Socratis and Socraticorum Reliquiae: Collegit, disposuit, apparatibus notisque instruxit Gabriele Giannnatoni*, 4 vols. Naples: Bibliopolis.

Gigante, M. 1983. *Diogene Laerzio: Vite di Filosofi Illustri*. Turin: UTET.

Gigon, O. 1946. "Antike Erzählungen über die Berufung zur Philosophie". *Museum Helveticum* 3: 1–21.

Gill, C. 2009. *The Structured Self in Hellenistic and Roman Thought*. Oxford: Oxford University Press.

Giusta, M. 1964. *I dossografi di etica*. Turin: Giappichelli.

Glare, P. (ed.) 1995. *Oxford Latin Dictionary*. Oxford: Oxford University Press.

Gomperz, T. 1899. "Platonische Aufsätze, II". *Sitzungsberichte der kaiserlichen Akademie der Wissenschaft: Philosophisch-Historische Klasse* 144, 7.

Gottlieb, P. 1992. "The Principle of Non-Contradiction and Protagoras: The Strategy of Aristotle's *Metaphysics* IV 4". In *Proceedings of the Boston Area Colloquium in Ancient Philosophy, volume 8*, J. Cleary & W. C. Wians (eds), 183–98. Lanham, MD: University Press of America.

Gottschalk, H. B. 1972. "Notes on the Will of the Peripatetic Scholars". *Hermes* 100: 314–42.

Greene, N. (ed.) 1938. *Scholia Platonica*. Haverford, PA: Societas Philologica Americana.

Grilli, A. 1959. "Review of Giannantoni, *I Cirenaici*". *Rivista Critica di Storia della Filosofia* 14: 343–51.

Grilli, A. 1960. "Review of Giannantoni, *I Cirenaici*". *Rivista di Filologia e Istruzione Classica* 38: 412–23.

Groarke, L. 1990. *Greek Scepticism: Anti-Realist Trends in Ancient Thought*. Montreal: McGill-Queen's University Press.

Grote, G. 1865. *Plato and the Other Companions of Sokrates*. London: John Murray.

Hadot, P. 1995. *Philosophy as a Way of Life*. Oxford: Blackwell.

Hadot, P. 2004. *What is Ancient Philosophy*. Cambridge, MA: Harvard University Press.

Hartlich, P. 1888. "*De exhortationum a Graecis Romanisque scriptarum historia et indole*". *Leipziger Studien* IX: 207–336.

Heisenberg, W. 1926. "Über quantenmechanische Kinematik und Mechanik". *Mathematische Annalen* 95: 683–705.

Hume, D. 1888. *A Treatise of Human Nature*, L. A. Selby-Bigge (ed.). Oxford: Clarendon.

Indelli, G. & V. Tsouna-McKirahan (eds) 1995. *Philodemus: On Choices and Avoidances*. Naples: Bibliopolis.

Irwin, T. 1991. "Aristippus against Happiness". *The Monist* 74: 55–82.

Irwin, T. 2007. *The Development of Ethics: A Historical and Critical Study; Volume I: From Socrates to the Reformation*. Oxford: Oxford University Press.

Isnardi Parente, M. 1974. "Carattere e struttura dell'Accademia Antica". In *La Filosofia dei Greci nel suo sviluppo storico*, vol. III/2, E. Zeller & R. Mondolfo, 861–77. Florence: La Nuova Italia.

Isnardi Parente, M. 1986. "L'Accademia antica: interpretazioni recenti e problemi di metodo". *Rivista di Filologia e Istruzione Classica* 114: 350–78.

Joel, K. 1921. *Geschichte der antiken Philosophie*, vol. I. Tübingen: Mohr.

Kechagia, E. 2011. *Plutarch against Colotes: A Lesson in History of Philosophy*. Oxford: Oxford University Press.

Kerferd, G. 1981a. "The Interpetation of Gorgias' Treatise *On Nature or on what is not*". *Deukalion* 36: 319–27.

Kerferd, G. 1981b. *The Sophistic Movement*. Cambridge: Cambridge University Press.

Kerferd, G. 1984. "Meaning and Reference: Gorgias and the Relation between Language and Reality". In *The Sophistic Movement*, 215–22. First International Symposium on the Sophistic Movement, Greek Philosophical Society, Athens.

Laks, A. 1993. "Annicéris et les plaisirs psychiques: quelques préalabes doxographiques". In *Passions and Perception: Studies in Hellenistic Philosophy*, J. Brunschwig & M. Nussbaum (eds), 18–49. Cambridge: Cambridge University Press.

Liddell, H. G. & R. Scott 1996. *A Greek–English Lexicon*, 9th edn with revised supplement. Oxford: Oxford University Press.

Long, A. 1999. "The Socratic Legacy". See Algra *et al.* (1999), 632–8.

Lukasiewicz, J. 1910. *O zasadzie sprzecznosci u Arystotelesa*. Warsaw: PWN.

Mann, W. R. 1996. "The Life of Aristippus". *Archiv für Geschichte der Philosophie* 78: 97–119.

Mannebach, E. 1961. *Aristippi et Cyrenaicorum Fragmenta*. Leiden: Brill.

Mansfeld, J. 1999. "Sources". See Algra *et al.* (1999), 3–30.

Marcovich, M. (ed.) 1999. *Diogenis Laertii Vitae philosophorum*. Stuttgart: Teubner.

Mazzara, G. 1999. *Gorgia: La retorica del Verosimile*. Sankt Augustin: Akademia Verlag.

Merricks, T. 2003. *Persons and Objects*. Oxford: Oxford University Press.

Mondolfo, R. 1953. "I Cirenaici e i raffinati nel *Teeteto* platonico". *Rivista di Filosofia* 44: 127–35.

Mourelatos, A. P. D. 1987. "Gorgias on the Function of Language". *Philosophical Topics* 15: 135–70.

Natorp, P. 1890. "Aristipp in Platons Theätet". *Archiv für Geschichte der Philosophie* 3: 347–62.

Natorp, P. 1895. "Aristippos" (n.8). In *Realencyclopädie der Classischen Altertumswissenschaft*, F. P. Pauly & G. Wissowa (eds), vol. II 2, cols 902–6. Stuttgart: J. B. Metzler.

O'Keefe, T. 2002. "The Cyrenaics on Pleasure, Happiness, and Future-Concern". *Phronesis* 47: 395–41.

O'Keefe, T. 2010. *Epicureanism*. Durham: Acumen.

O'Keefe, T. 2011. "The Cyrenaics vs. the Pyrrhonists on Knowledge of Appearances". In *New Essays on Ancient Pyrrhonism*, D. Machuca (ed.), 27–40. Leiden: Brill.

Parfit, D. 1984. *Reasons and Persons*. Oxford: Oxford University Press.

Plato 1998. *Philebus*, D. Frede (trans.). Indianapolis, IN: Hackett.

Politis, V. 2004. *Aristotle and the Metaphysics*. London: Routledge.

Rowe, C. J. 2007. *Plato and the Art of Philosophical Writing*. Cambridge: Cambridge University Press.

Schleiermacher, F. 1804–28. *Platons Werke*. Berlin: G. Reimer.

Sedley, D. 1996. "Three Platonist Interpretations of the *Theaetetus*". In *Form and Argument in Late Plato*, C. Gill & M. M. McCabe (eds), 79–104. Oxford: Oxford University Press.

Sedley, D. 2004. *The Midwife of Platonism: Text and Subtext in Plato's Theaetetus*. Oxford: Oxford University Press.

Strawson, G. 2011. *The Evident Connexion*. Oxford: Oxford University Press.

Tarrant, H. 1994. "The Hippias Major and Socratic Theories of Pleasure". See Vander Waerdt (1994), 106–26.

Thorsrud, H. 2008. *Ancient Scepticism*. Durham: Acumen.

Thrige, J. P. 1828. *Res Cyrenensium, a primordiis inde civitatis usque ad aetatem, qua in provinciae formam a Romanis redacta*. Hafniae: Gyldendaliana.

Tsouna, V. 1994. "The Socratic Origins of the Cynics and the Cyrenaics". See Vander Waerdt (1994), 367–91.

Tsouna, V. 1998. *The Epistemology of the Cyrenaic School*. Cambridge: Cambridge University Press.

Tsouna, V. 2002. "Is There an Exception to Greek Eudaemonism?" In *Le style de la pensée*, P. Pellegrin & M. Canto (eds), 464–89. Paris: Les Belles Lettres.

Vander Waerdt, P. (ed.) 1994. *The Socratic Movement*. Ithaca, NY: Cornell University Press.

Van Inwagen, P. 1990. *Material Beings*. Ithaca, NY: Cornell University Press.

Von Stein, H. 1855. *De philosophia cyrenaica*. Göttingen.

Wehrli, F. 1959. "Review of Giannantoni, *I Cirenaici*". *Gnomon* 31: 412–15.

Wehrli, F. 1976. "Review of Lynch 1972 [J. P. Lynch, *Aristotle's School: A History of Greek Educational Institution* (Berkeley)]". *Gnomon* 48: 128–34.

Wilamowitz-Moellendorff, U. von 1881. *Antigonos von Karystos*. Berlin: Weidmannsche Buchhandlung.

Windelband, W. 1923. *Geschichte der abendländische Philosophie im Altertum*. Tubingen: Mohr.

Winiarczyk, M. (ed.) 1981. *Diagoras Melius, Theodorus Cyrenaeus*. Leipzig: Teubner.

Wittgenstein, L. 1953. *Philosophical Investigations*. Oxford: Oxford University Press.

Zeller, E. 1923. *Die Philosophie der Griechen in ihrer geschichtlichen Entwicklung: Sokrates und die Sokratiker. Plato und die alte Akademie*, II 1. Leipzig: Reisland.

Zilioli, U. 2007. *Protagoras and the Challenge of Relativism: Plato's Subtlest Enemy*. Aldershot: Ashgate.

INDEX

affection (*pathos*)
  as affective and representational
    104–7, 173
  and beyond 122–8, 147, 154,
    162
  as a crucial notion for Cyrenaic
    philosophy 101–3, 173
  and intermediate states 105–6
  and its main features 103
  and as restricted in time 107–8
  see also pleasure
anonymous commentary on the
  Theaetetus LXV, 19–35 60,
  91, 109–10
Anniceris and the Annicerians
  10, 16, 179–81, 198–9, 209
Aristotle
  De Interpretatione 16a4–8 135
  on meaning 135–6
  Metaphysics
    B 2 996a32–b1 21
    B 2 997b32–998a3 21
    Γ 5 1007a21–b1 98
    Γ 5 1007b27–8 203
    Γ 5 1010a3–4 203
    Γ 5 1010b33–9 204
  Nicomachean Ethics 168

on relativism and subjectivism
  122, 175
Aristippus
  as the founder of the Cyrenaic
    school 12, 14–15, 28, 177
  life 19–20
  on pleasure as the end 26–9
  sayings and way of life 23–5
  on the senses 30
  as a sophist 20–23
  writings 31–6
Aristippus the Younger 5, 10, 15,
  128–9, 182
  and the catalogue of affections
    26–7
Aristocles of Messene, Fr. 5
  Chiesara=T 3–7 27–8, 68,
  104, 109, 111
Augustine 142, 206
  De Civitate Dei III 11.26 81

Bett, R. 100, 204, 212
Brancacci, A. 181, 206
Brunschwig, J. 105, 207, 212
Burnyeat, M. 77

Campbell, L. 52

221

Kechagia, E. 203, 206

Laks, A. 181, 213
Long, A. 209

Mannebach, E. 15
 on the adjective 'Cyrenaic'
  37–40
 and Diogenes Laertius II 85 26
 meaning in Cyrenaic philosophy
  of language 132–4, 136–7,
  140–41
 and behaviourism 139–41, 175
 and conventionalism 134–5
 and Wittgenstein 143–4,
  146–7
Megarics 3–4, 51, 175
metaphysics of processes 55, 57
 and indeterminacy 112–13
Mondolfo, R. 140, 212

objects as aggregates of parts 54,
 59, 88, 90, 112, 117–18, 174
O'Keefe, T. 155, 157, 207–8,
 211–13

Parfit, D. 116–18, 205
perception as a uni-dimensional
 event 65–7
 as correlative 87–9
persons as aggregates of parts
 88, 90, 112, 114–17, 162, 174
Philodemus, *On Choices and
 Avoidances* 92–3, 182
philosophical schools in
 antiquity 6-10
Plato
 Philebus
  11b–c 150
  24c–d 208
  31a7–10 167

53c4–6 166, 169
Theaetetus
 152c5–6 54
 152d1–e1 169
 153a5–10 169
 153e7–154a2 201
 156a5–7 53
 156a7–b2 54, 87, 202
 156b2–5 54, 169
 156b4–6 62
 156c6–157a5 54, 169
 157a8–b1 54, 58, 90
 157c1–3 88
 157b9–c2 59, 115, 202, 208
 158a–e 80, 202
 160b5–c2 89
 166b2–4 66
 167b1–4 22
 179c2–4 66
 184d1–5 64
 185c9–10 64
 185e1–2 64
 186b12–c1 65
 186c1–10 64
 186d2–5 65
pleasure
 and beliefs 151–3
 bodily 150
 bodily and mental 151,
  154–5, 159–61, 162
 as the end 149
 and movement 158
 as restricted in time 155–6
 as a smooth movement 26,
  150
 see also Epicurus; happiness
Plutarch, *Against Colotes*
 1120d 69
 1120c–d 95–6
 1120e–f 95–6, 123
 problem of other minds 147